KNOWING THE SCORE

KNOWING
THE SCORE

*How Sport Teaches Us about Philosophy
(and Philosophy about Sport)*

DAVID PAPINEAU

Constable • London

CONSTABLE

First published in Great Britain in 2017 by Constable

1 3 5 7 9 10 8 6 4 2

A CIP catalogue record for this book
is available from the British Library.

ISBN: 978-1-47212-354-1 (trade paperback)

Typeset in Bembo Std by Hewer Text UK Ltd, Edinburgh
Printed and bound in Great Britain by Clays Ltd, St Ives plc

Papers used by Constable are from well-managed forests and other responsible sources.

MIX
Paper from
responsible sources
FSC® C104740

Constable
An imprint of
Little, Brown Book Group
Carmelite House
50 Victoria Embankment
London EC4Y 0DZ

An Hachette UK Company
www.hachette.co.uk

www.littlebrown.co.uk

For my family

CONTENTS

Part IV: TRIBES

Part V: VALUES

INTRODUCTION

Sometimes I wish I had been more of an athlete and less of a philosopher.

I have worked most of my adult life as an academic philosopher. I have written several books and many articles. A number of learned societies have elected me their president. And I am still employed as a professor, in two well-known philosophy departments, in London and New York.

My sporting career has been rather less distinguished. This hasn't been for lack of trying. I have competed at cricket, tennis, football, golf, rugby, squash, hockey and sailing. And that's not just at school – I have played organized versions of all these sports as an adult, not to mention recreational fishing, sailboarding and bodysurfing.

My enthusiasm, however, has always outstripped my success. It's not that I'm a duffer, but I have never risen above the lower echelons. I have scored centuries – but most were for teams of journalists playing village sides. In my time, I was a force to be reckoned with in the fourth division of the North Middlesex Tennis League. I am still competitive off my golf handicap of seventeen. You get the idea.

Perhaps I wouldn't have enjoyed life as a serious sportsman, even if my abilities had allowed it. One of the themes that will emerge in these pages is that top-level sport demands a peculiar mind-set, a blinkered focus on physical routine. It's not clear that it's a natural life for someone with philosophical inclinations. Still, this hasn't stopped me spending a large proportion of my waking hours playing, watching and thinking about sport, rather than working at my day job.

Until recently it never occurred to me to combine my two enthusiasms. There is an area of my subject that goes under the heading 'philosophy of sport'. But it has never excited me. Central topics are sport and politics, disability and enhancement, the ethics of drug use, the definition and value of sport, and so on. The normal strategy is to take some contentious topic that exercises sports practitioners or administrators, and then analyse the solutions implied by different philosophical theories. It is all a bit earnest, as if the writers want to counterbalance their frivolous subject matter with the sobriety of their prose. I have always kept away. I enjoy sport, and this seemed to make it dull.

Then a few years ago Anthony O'Hear, Director of the Royal Institute of Philosophy, asked me to contribute to a lecture series he was organizing on 'Philosophy and Sport'. It was the year of the London Olympics, and he thought it would be a good idea to devote the Institute's annual programme of lectures to the subject. I couldn't really refuse. I agreed it was a good idea, I was on the Council of the Institute, and I had an extensive knowledge of both philosophy and sport. If I wasn't going to say yes, who would?

So I set to work. I read some of the philosophy of sport literature, and started sketching out some thoughts about the definition and significance of sport. But nothing much happened. I couldn't get beyond the most obvious truisms, and was starting to have bad dreams about finding myself in front of the audience with nothing to say.

After struggling for a while, I made a decision. Instead of writing about one of the topics that philosophers of sport are supposed to write about, I resolved to write about something that interested me. If it didn't count as philosophy of sport, that would just be too bad.

The topic I chose was the peculiar mental demands of fast-response sports like tennis, baseball and cricket. When Rafael Nadal faces Roger Federer's serve, he has less than half a second to react. That's scarcely enough time to see the ball, let alone to think about how to hit it. Nadal can only be relying on automatic reflexes. Yet at the same time his shot selection will also depend on his consciously chosen strategy, on that day's plan for how best to play Federer in those conditions. This struck me as puzzling. How can unthinking reflexes be controlled by conscious thought?

I had great fun addressing this conundrum in my lecture. I didn't try to hide my enthusiasm as a sports fan, and I included as many anecdotes as seemed relevant. But I also ended up with a series of substantial philosophical conclusions. Even though I started with nothing but a few sporting incidents and some everyday questions, I was led to think hard about the connection between conscious decision-making and automatic behaviour, and the result was a series of ideas about the structure of action control that has opened up a new area of research for me. (If you want to read a written version of the lecture, you can find it as 'In the Zone', published in *Philosophy and Sport*, edited by Anthony O'Hear, Cambridge: Cambridge University Press, 2013.)

But that wasn't the end of it. Now that I had found a way of combining philosophy and sport, I was keen to do more of it. It struck me that there were a number of other sporting topics that could benefit from similar philosophical scrutiny, and that I was as well placed as anybody to supply it. I had recently built myself a website, and so I started posting a series of essays on sporting themes. Within a few months the subjects included the rationality of fandom, road cycle racing and altruism, national identity and sporting eligibility, and the moral standing of different sports.

This volume is the eventual upshot of those early efforts. It contains eighteen chapters on interlinked aspects of the sporting world. I think of them as telling us as much about philosophy as about sport. If there is a common form to the chapters, they start with some sporting point that is of philosophical significance. A first step is to show how philosophical thinking can cast light on the sporting topic. But in nearly all cases the spotlight of illumination is then reversed. The sporting example tells us something new about the philosophical issues, by highlighting ideas that are obscured in more familiar contexts.

The chapters fall into five sections: Focus, Rules, Teams, Tribes and Values.

Part I, Focus, is about the mental side of sport. The chapters in this section take off from my original interest in decision-making and fast sporting skills, and go on to an analysis of 'choking' and 'the yips', the twin perils that lie in wait for every unwary sports performer.

Part II, Rules, asks about the norms that govern healthy sporting competition. It distinguishes between the regulations in the rulebook, the varying conventions of fair play across different sports, 'gamesmanship' and downright immoral practices.

Part III, Teams, analyses the logic of fandom, the survival of teams over time, and the rationality of collective decision-making in team sports.

Part IV, Tribes, brings in a number of wider political and social issues, including citizenship, national identity, racism, and the debate about nurture versus nature.

Part V, Values, is about amateurism, the organization of professional sports and the importance of tradition. A final chapter then attempts to explain why sport is so important to so many people.

One problem facing anyone writing about sport is geography. Even in an age of increasing globalization, sports enthusiasts are fiercely protective of their local codes. They will insist that their own games are the pinnacle of sporting endeavour, while those played in other places are little better than children's pastimes.

Americans are mystified by cricket, while baseball is a closed book to the rest of the English-speaking world. Soccer is an obsession in Europe and Latin America, but in North America and the Antipodes it is regarded as an alien intruder. Sometimes these rifts are found even within countries. As I explain in a later chapter, 'football' refers to one game in Sydney, but a quite different one in Melbourne (and in neither place does it mean soccer).

This diversity creates a dilemma for any writer aiming to make general points about sport. If you illustrate your arguments with examples from particular sports, you are in danger of alienating many of your potential readers, as they will quickly lose patience with someone who takes silly games so seriously. But if you omit sporting illustrations altogether, you risk having no readers at all, for your arguments will become too abstract to hold anybody's attention.

I have aimed to steer a course between these two dangers. When a contract for this book was initially being discussed with my American publishers, Basic Books, we addressed the issue. 'We love your proposal,' said my prospective American editor, Lara Heimert, 'and we'd like to do it. But there's just one condition,' she added. 'No cricket!' In her view, any mention of the sport would make Americans put down the book straight away.

I assured Lara that I understood the problem, but pleaded for a little leeway. I told her that I was familiar with many sports from around the world, baseball as well as cricket, and all the many varieties of football, and that I would try to make sure that everybody had a look-in. I would do what I could to make sure that no readers felt alienated by my choice of illustrations.

I hope I have gauged this right, and that readers of this book will enjoy my range of references. I have used sporting examples to illustrate my arguments whenever I can, but aimed to avoid any bias in favour of particular traditions. Inevitably some readers will be introduced to games they don't know well. I can only ask them to be tolerant. Perhaps this book will make a small contribution to the harmony of nations. Sport plays a large part in many lives, and it will be better if it can unite people rather than divide them.

PART I

FOCUS

CHAPTER 1

HAVING YOUR MIND RIGHT

Great athletes are mentally as well as physically exceptional. They are capable of feats of concentration beyond the reach of ordinary people.

All sports fans will have their own examples. Muhammad Ali outwitting the fearsome George Foreman in the jungle. Steven Gerrard driving Liverpool back from 3–0 down to win the 2005 UEFA Champions League in the 'miracle of Istanbul'. Nick Faldo grinding out eighteen successive pars on his way to his first major on a windswept day at Muirfield.

My favourite is probably the sixteen-year-old Monica Seles beating Steffi Graf in the 1990 French Open. The previous year she had lost to Graf in the semis. But this time there was no stopping Seles. In the first set tie-break, she went 2–6 down but saved four set points, blasting the lines with her two-fisted ground shots. She went on to win her first grand-slam final in straight sets.

Seles knew why she had won the second time. As she explained at the press conference after the match, 'As a fifteen-year-old, I couldn't beat her mentally ... But today in the final, my strategy was to just play as well as I could ... and not be afraid of her.' It's understandable that a fifteen-year-old should be overawed by perhaps the greatest woman player in tennis history. But it takes a freakish sixteen-year-old to beat that same opponent by power of will.

Supreme athletes can fix on a goal and pursue it with every sinew, even in the most testing of circumstances. This kind of mental steadfastness is not to be taken for granted. It is one thing to formulate a plan, another to stick to it in the heat of competition. In the words of another great champion, Mike Tyson: 'Everybody has a plan, till they get punched in the mouth.'

Curiously, there are experts who downplay the mental side of sport, and hold that athletes perform best when their minds are empty. As these experts see it, elite athletes have honed their bodily skills in many thousands of hours of practice. Given this, they will do best simply to think about nothing and give their physical reactions free rein.

The Hall of Fame Yankees catcher Yogi Berra was very much of this opinion. Berra was notorious for swinging at bad pitches. According to one much-cited anecdote, his manager told him not to be so eager, but 'think, think, think'. On his next time at bat Berra struck out ignominiously. He stormed back into the dugout, complaining, 'How the hell can you hit and think at the same time?'

Berra has plenty of distinguished support. Hubert Dreyfus, professor of philosophy at Berkeley, has long argued that conscious thought is the enemy of physical expertise. Dreyfus appeals to the classic twentieth-century phenomenologists Martin Heidegger and Maurice Merleau-Ponty, who held that physical skills are guided directly by the physical environment without the intervention of conscious thought.

According to the phenomenologists, skilled performers like athletes and musicians do not think about what to do. Rather they respond directly to physical triggers. As Dreyfus puts it, 'Skillful coping does not require a mental representation of its goal. It can be purposive without the agent entertaining a purpose.'

Dreyfus quotes Merleau-Ponty: 'To move one's body is to aim at things through it; it is to allow oneself to respond to their call, which is made upon it independently of any representation.' From the phenomenological perspective, conscious thought only interferes with immediate reactions. 'Just do it.' The Nike slogan perfectly encapsulates the phenomenologists' message.

Dreyfus supports his case by citing the unfortunately named 'Chuck' Knoblauch, one-time second baseman for the New York Yankees, who after years of exceptionally reliable fielding started spraying around his throws to first base. He had to be moved to left field and his career tailed off.

According to Dreyfus, Knoblauch's decline was due to a destructive self-consciousness about his performance. Once Knoblauch started thinking about what he was doing, he couldn't do it any more. What he needed was to empty his mind and go with the flow.

In her book *Choke: What the Secrets of the Brain Reveal about Getting It Right When You Have To*, the psychologist Sian Beilock investigates how pressure can undermine performance across a variety of fields. She argues that in sporting contexts this typically involves what she calls 'paralysis by analysis'. Athletes underperform because the stress of competition makes them start thinking about what they are doing. Beilock cites a range of studies showing that athletes perform better when they are distracted from their own actions by some irrelevant task like counting backwards or singing a song.

I'm going to call Berra, Dreyfus and Beilock's view the 'Yoga' theory. In their view, athletes will do best to emulate the disciplines of meditation practised by eastern religions, and clear the mind of any intruding thoughts.*

Not all theorists are persuaded by the Yoga theory. An opposing school of thought insists that skilled athletic performance relies crucially on mental control. In her book *Thought in Action*, Barbara Montero, my colleague at the City University of New York Graduate Center, emphasizes the role of the conscious mind in skilled action. As Montero sees it, athletic skill is a matter of intelligent agency, not brute reflex. 'Just do it' is a myth.

A significant number of contemporary philosophers side with Montero on the need for intelligent control of sporting reactions. As they see it, a mindless athlete is a poor athlete – you can't simply leave it to unthinking reflexes to decide which shot to play, but must actively control your performance.

In my view, both sides of this debate are right, and both wrong. There are some things that athletes must think about,

---

* As it happens, Berra gained his nickname 'Yogi' because a childhood friend thought he sat like an Indian mystic when waiting to bat. The cartoon Yogi Bear, if you are wondering, didn't appear until 1958, long after Yogi Berra was a household name, and was no doubt named after him – although the animation studio Hanna-Barbera denied this when challenged legally.

and others that they must keep their minds away from. If you think about too much, you will become disabled, just as the Yoga theorists insist. But at the same time, if you think about too little, you won't perform to the best of your ability, in line with Montero's view.

Let me start with the danger of thinking too little. This hazard will be familiar to anybody who has competed at any sporting level. It really isn't a good idea to empty your mind completely and just go with the flow, whatever the phenomenologists and other Yoga theorists may say. You will only end up doing the wrong thing. We don't need iconic triumphs like those of Ali, Gerrard or Seles to make the point. Even at the most mundane sporting level, you need to get your mind right if you want to win.

When I play tennis, it is competitive even if not hugely accomplished. We knock up first. It can be very pleasant in England in the summer. I sometimes think how enjoyable it is to be knocking the ball back and forth with my friend. Then we start playing a match – and suddenly, to my dismay, I notice that I am three games down.

I have forgotten to start concentrating. Instead of stroking the ball cooperatively back in roughly my friend's direction, I must now hit it as hard as I can to where I know he doesn't want it hit. This doesn't happen automatically. I need to keep my game plan in the front of my mind. If I start daydreaming about what's for dinner, or worrying about tomorrow's lecture, I will stop playing properly and start throwing away points.

Examples like this show that the Yoga theory is wrong to hold that athletes must empty their minds completely. But at the same time it also contains an element of truth. There are aspects of athletic performance that it doesn't pay to think about.

To properly sort out what is right and wrong in the Yoga theory, we need to introduce a theoretical distinction. Philosophers differentiate *skills* from their *components*. A skill is something that you know how to do, without having to think about how you do it. Its components are the more specific movements that you perform when you are exercising that skill.

Walking is a skill. If you decide to walk down the road, you don't then have to consider how to do it. You just walk down the road.

The components of this skill are the more specific movements involved in walking. You raise one foot, move it forward, put it down, raise the other one, move it, put it down, and repeat until you're there.

Athletes must not let their minds wander from the skills they are aiming to exercise at any given time. If they lose this focus, their bodies are likely to betray them. This is where the Yoga theory falls down, and its opponents have things right. Athletic performance calls for precise focus, not an empty mind. That's the reason why serious athletes need to be mentally exceptional. They need to devote their minds entirely to the skills they are exercising, often for sustained periods.

But, at the same time, athletes must not think about the *components* of their skills. Any concern with these components will hamper their performance. To the extent that this is their message, the Yoga theorists have it right. Thinking about the details of your technique is incompatible with sporting success.

Not all skills are developed automatically, like knowing how to walk. Most of them are deliberately learned. We need to practise them explicitly before they become automatic. For example, when we are young, we learn to tie our shoelaces. We lay the two ends of the lace one over the other, form a loop in one, and so on.

After a while this sequence becomes automatic. Once we have learned to tie our shoelaces, we don't need to think about the sequence of components any more. We simply decide to tie our shoelaces, and then do it – no more thinking is needed.

When you become expert in some sport, you acquire a new repertoire of skills. This is what distinguishes top-level athletes from novices. Accomplished golfers can hit a power fade at will, tennis players can play a forehand slice, gymnasts can perform a backflip, and so on. These are skills for the sporting performers, but not for most people.

Sporting skills, like shoelace tying, also derive from practice. You have to learn how to hit a forehand slice, just as you had to learn how to tie your shoelaces. And when you are learning to hit a forehand slice, you will need to think about its behavioural components. You must cock your wrist, open the racket face, and hit down on the ball. The learner will be instructed to perform each movement deliberately and in sequence.

But after a while – after hitting hundreds or thousands of balls – the sequence becomes automatic, and you no longer have to think about what movements to make. It is enough simply to form the intention to 'hit a forehand slice'.

No doubt, even after such skills have been learned, performers will still be able to perform the component movements separately. Learning to hit a forehand slice doesn't stop you being able to cock your wrist as such, or deliberately to hit down on the ball. Still, once you have learned to hit a slice, its execution will proceed quite differently – more automatically – from performing its components in sequence as separate actions.

In effect, there are two very different options here for a trained athlete: you can simply execute the skill that you have learned – hit the slice; or you can perform the components in sequence in the way you did when you first started learning the slice – cock your wrist, open the face, hit down on the ball.

It would not be a good idea, however, for expert tennis players to choose this latter option while competing. This would throw away all the benefit gained from those hours of practice. It would reduce them to the level of the novice who has not yet learned how to hit a slice and still has to do it by numbers. That is the whole point of practising – to take a physical process that is slow, halting and imprecise, and render it fast, automatic and reliable.

Andre Agassi's father understood the principle well. In his autobiography, *Open*, Agassi described his childhood practice regime: 'My father says that if I hit 2,500 balls each day, I'll hit

17,500 balls each week, and at the end of one year I'll have hit nearly one million balls. He believes in math. Numbers, he says, don't lie. A child who hits one million balls each year will be unbeatable.'

Not only must experts not revert to rehearsing the components of their skills, in the manner of a learner, they mustn't even *think* about those components. To be aware of the angle of your wrist, or the plane of your backswing, when you are playing a forehand slice, is to tempt your conscious mind to start trying to control these components directly.

This is the rationale for Beilock's idea of 'paralysis by analysis'. If you start analysing the exercise of your skills, it will have a paralysing effect on your actions and reduce you to the level of a beginner. To perform well, you need to forget what you did as a learner, and allow the unconscious mechanisms honed by those hours of practice to take over.

Yet the Yoga theory is quite wrong to say that *any* kind of thinking will undermine your performance. It is crucial that you do think about *what* you are trying to do, as opposed to *how* you do it. You need more guidance than 'Just do it'. You need to form a plan, to have a clear idea about which skills you are going to deploy. Are you going to try slicing low to your opponent's backhand, or will you stick to the topspin?

What is more, you need to hold your plan firmly in mind, for reasons that will become clear over the next two chapters. You can't start daydreaming or the contest will get away from you, as happens all too often in my park tennis games.

Where exactly is the line between the skilful plan that you must think about and the components that you mustn't think about? This is an important issue for high-level athletes and coaches. Attention needs to be directed at fruitful plans, but not at destructive details. But there is no hard and fast rule about where the difference lies. It will depend on the specifics of exactly what skills have been learned, and this will vary from sport to sport and even from individual to individual.

If there is a pattern here, it is perhaps that expert athletes will think of their skills in terms of the results they are aiming to achieve, rather than the bodily movements involved. When I hit a forehand slice, my focus is on the anticipated trajectory of the ball, not on the arc of my arm or racket. What I have learned is how to slide the ball low over the net with back-spin, and in order to do this well I have to aim to do just that – without thinking about how I do it.

When asked how she could vary between fading her drives from the left and drawing them from the right, the three-time golf major winner Nancy Lopez is reputed to have answered, 'I just think *fade*, or I think *draw*.' Lopez simply needed to visualize the ball trajectory she was aiming for, and the unconscious techniques instilled by her training would take over. (Nancy Lopez is also supposed to have said, 'To me every putt inside four feet is straight.' She just rammed them all into the back of the hole. I can't say it worked for me. When I tried to follow her advice, all I got was lots of long return putts.)

Can athletes really leave all the details of their techniques to automatic control? What if they need to attune the components of their skills to the specific conditions of the game? A tennis player notices that the ball is holding up on this court and lengthens the backswing accordingly. The golfer notes that the greens are fast, and reduces the club speed on putts. Don't examples like these show that competitors need to be consciously aware of the detailed movements they are making? How else can they modulate their techniques, except by consciously figuring out how to deal with the conditions?

But this isn't how it works. Perhaps explicit instructions played a role when the skills were being learned. 'You need to lengthen your backswing on these courts,' your coach tells you. Or, 'Slow down the putter head, but make sure you still follow through.' Still, with training these adjustments too become automatic. The unconscious systems that manage your sporting techniques learn to take the conditions into account, and to adjust your shots to suit.

So, for example, it would be fatal for golfers to start thinking consciously about the speed of their putters when addressing putts. Sure, they need to make sure that information about the green speed is made available to the automatic systems that control their putting. Some time on the practice green will help; it will be even better if one of your playing partners hits a similar putt just before you.

But once this information has been absorbed by the unconscious processes that execute the stroke, the golfer must simply focus, as always, on hitting the ball into the middle of the hole at a moderate pace. Opting for some specific component of technique – slower club speed – in the context of a fast green is something that can be – must be – left to the automatic procedures that have been shaped in previous practice.

What if there is some flaw in your technique? You aren't playing the forehand slice well. Your doubles partner suggests that the problem is that your grip is too far forward. Won't you do better to rotate your grip backwards, in the hope that this will enable you to execute the slice more effectively?

Almost certainly not, if you start doing it in the middle of a match. All that will happen is that you will lose control of the shot and start making unforced errors. Your current execution of the shot is geared to your faulty grip position, so simply altering that without changing the rest of your technique will only foul things up.

What you need is practice. You need to try out the new grip against a hitting partner, or a machine, or a tennis wall, exploring the further adjustments that it demands, and then repeating your new shot until it becomes automatic. When you next play a match with your adjusted grip, you want to be thinking about where the ball is going, not how you are holding your racket.

In the early 1980s Nick Faldo was the leading British golfer. In 1983 he won five tournaments and led the European order of merit. He came to feel, however, that his rhythmic-looking swing concealed too many flaws to stand up to the stress of a major championship. He was in contention going into the last round of both the 1983 Open and 1984 Masters, but faded away badly both times.

In 1985 he approached the coach David Leadbetter and asked him to rebuild his swing from the ground up. Leadbetter flattened it out and made a number of other adjustments, designed to render Faldo's routine impervious to even the highest levels of pressure.

For the next two years Faldo hit over 500 balls a day, working to make his new technique automatic. He continued to compete in tournaments, but his form collapsed. He was an embarrassment in the 1985 Ryder Cup, and failed to win a tournament for three years.

Eventually, though, the pain paid off. Faldo won the Spanish Open in the summer of 1987, and began to regain his confidence. In the Open at Muirfield he started the last round one shot behind Paul Azinger. The conditions were tough, with a high wind and misty rain, but Faldo didn't falter.

He crafted eighteen pars in succession, while Azinger dropped four shots on the back nine. I don't know what was going through Azinger's mind, but I am sure that Faldo wasn't thinking about the mechanics of his swing. He was able to focus on putting the ball where he wanted to, secure in the knowledge that two years of mind-numbing practice had given him a routine he could trust.

Faldo went on to win five more majors. It is striking that, apart from one runaway victory at St Andrews, he owed all these triumphs to mental collapses by his opponents, rather than any exceptional brilliance on his own part.

Everybody remembers Greg Norman's sad meltdown in the final round of the 1996 Masters. But Faldo similarly benefited from Scott Hoch's stuttering eighteen-inch miss in the 1989 Masters's play-off, followed by Raymond Floyd's feeble pull into the water in the play-off the following year. And then there was John Cook in the 1992 Open, missing a two-footer on the seventeenth and bogeying the eighteenth to hand Faldo victory by one stroke.

As I said, the true champions are mentally exceptional. They can stick to their goals even in the most trying of conditions. It is easy to find ways to lose. The hard thing is to keep your mind fixed on winning, even when the pressure is at its most intense.

CHAPTER 2

IN THE BLINK OF AN EYE

When Roger Federer serves to Rafael Nadal, he hits the ball at around 135 mph from about 78 feet away. That means less than half a second for the ball to reach Nadal. (Around 400 milliseconds, to be specific – a millisecond is 1,000th of a second.) That is very quick indeed. It is about as long as it takes you to blink.

The figures are very similar in other fast-reaction sports. In major league baseball, the pitchers average over 90 mph from 60.5 feet away. In cricket the batsmen are less than 66 feet distant and the top bowlers can reach 100 mph. The proportions work out similarly in squash and table tennis. Well under half a second every time. It is surprising that athletes in these sports manage to see the ball at all, let alone craft their responses to its trajectory.

These numbers might appear to support the Yoga theory of sports psychology. There simply doesn't seem enough time for deliberate thought to influence your performance in fast-reaction games. So surely the best strategy will be to rely on your automatic reactions. If you try to control your behaviour consciously, you will only interfere with the instantaneous reflexes you have built up in thousands of hours of practice.

But this is a fallacy. Even in the fastest sports, it is crucial for performers to fix on a strategy consciously and make sure they keep it firmly in mind. The points made in the last chapter continue to apply. While fast-reaction athletes mustn't think about the details of their movements, they must still think about which skills they are aiming to deploy. If they await the oncoming ball with minds cleared of all thought, they can well end up doing the wrong thing.

Still, how *can* the athletes' conscious mind-set possibly make any difference, in sports where the ball arrives in the blink of an eye? Won't the time for thought have passed, once the moment for action arrives? To understand fully why conscious focus does matter, even in fast-reaction sports, we first need to appreciate how the athletes cope with their extreme temporal constraints. Understanding the mechanics of fast-reaction sports will deepen our understanding of where the Yoga theory works and where it goes wrong.

Over the past two or three decades, sports scientists have learned much about the special techniques athletes use to intercept fast-approaching balls. This is a fascinating topic in its own right, and this chapter will explore many of these findings.

An initial question is how the athletes manage to hit the ball in the first place. A reaction time of 400 milliseconds seems to take us beyond the limits of possibility. Once we are counting in milliseconds, our brains and bodies take time to get things done. Even the simplest response to a straightfor-ward stimulus eats up time.

Take a sprinter's reaction to the starter's gun. Modern

technology can tell us exactly how long after the report the runner starts pressing on the blocks. When Usain Bolt set his world record of 9.58 seconds for the 100 metres in 2009, his reaction time was 0.146 seconds. That wasn't outstanding – some sprinters can get down to 120 milliseconds – but it was good enough for a world record that still stands at the time of writing. (Any reaction time under 100 milliseconds will get the runner disqualified, on the grounds that it's not physically feasible to respond so fast.)

Sprinters aren't doing anything complicated when they start. They only have to push off once they hear a bang. But, even so, Bolt's reaction time of 146 milliseconds constitutes a good proportion of the 400 milliseconds available for Nadal to respond to Federer's serve.

So, let's analyse the more complex business of intercepting a fast-moving ball with a bat or racket. Once the receiver has selected which shot to play, it takes about 25 milliseconds for the nerve messages to travel from the motor cortex to the arms and legs. And then it takes about another 150 milliseconds actually to swing the bat or racket and, with luck, make contact with the ball.

That's 175 milliseconds, nearly half the time available, to make contact with the ball once the athletes have committed themselves to which shot to play. But before their shot-selection, of course, they first need to see where the ball is going.

Now the story gets puzzling. It is generally agreed by vision scientists that it takes at least half a second, from the time light rays hit our eyes, for the nerve messages to reach the higher levels of the visual cortex and form a clearly focused picture of the objects in our environment.

These numbers don't add up. If it takes 500 milliseconds for the ball to come into clear focus, and another nearly 175 milliseconds to execute the shot, that's a lot more than the 400 milliseconds it takes for the ball to whiz past you.

The solution to this conundrum is that the athletes don't wait until they see the ball clearly before making their move. Instead they use initial clues and fragments of visual information to direct their movements, long before the ball has come into full focus.

The sports scientists now know a lot about the way fast-reaction athletes manage to start moving so quickly. One finding is that athletes who hit moving balls do not keep their eyes on the ball throughout its flight. Instead they follow its path for about 100 to 200 milliseconds after it is projected towards them, and then 'saccade' their eyes – that is, shoot them forward – to an anticipated later point in the ball's path.

In games where the ball typically bounces before it is hit, like tennis and cricket, the athlete's eyes will jump ahead to its predicted landing point. In baseball, the batter's eyes similarly saccade to the latter part of the ball's trajectory. The more skilled the players, the sooner their eyes will leave the ball's initial path, and jump forward to its predicted later position.

To anybody who has played fast-reaction games, this may seem surprising, not to say incredible. The first thing youngsters are taught is to 'keep your eye on the ball'. And certainly, when you are actually playing, your conscious awareness is of a ball moving continuously through the air. Ted Williams, the last man to average over .400 in a baseball season, was reputedly able to watch the stitching on the baseball as it came towards him.

In 2010, a distinguished Australian test batsman was in the audience at a Cricket Australia talk about the research into eye movements. 'I don't believe a word of it,' he expostulated, when the speaker explained about the saccading eyes. The cricketer was sure that he never took his eye off the ball when batting, and was conscious of it throughout its trajectory.

Perhaps the distinguished Australian was more surprised than he should have been. It is familiar knowledge in vision science that, when humans are surveying a scene, their eyes are constantly skipping around in order to bring different items into central focus.

For example, as you are reading these words right now, your eyes are unconsciously making a series of jerky movements to help you see different areas of the page with high resolution. Still, your conscious experience when you view the page is not of a series of jerky visual fragments. Rather your brain mechanisms build up a representation of a stable display of words, and that is what you consciously experience.

In the same way, fast-reacting athletes will start with fragmentary information gleaned from their saccading eyes, and construct an overall representation of the ball moving continuously through the air – even complete with stitches in some cases. But this construction takes time, much longer than it takes the ball to arrive, and is no use to the athletes in selecting their shot. Instead, their bodies respond directly to the initial jerky information delivered by their eyes, long before consciousness can focus it into a clear picture of the ball.

Somewhat surprisingly, there is evidence that the very top athletes are distinguished from other professionals, not just by the speed with which their eyes leave the ball after release, but by continuing their eye saccades right up to the impact with the ball. One Australian study showed that two elite international cricketers watched the ball right on to the bat, whereas two journeymen professionals followed it only to the bounce.

Another study compared action photographs of Roger Federer and Rafael Nadal with those of a number of lesser professionals. It turned out that Federer and Nadal, but not the others, also turned their heads and eyes to focus on the point of contact between racket and ball. It's the same in baseball. Ted Williams is sadly beyond the reach of modern sports science, but pictures of him and other top hitters show them watching the ball right onto the bat.

What's surprising about these findings is that watching the ball as it makes impact can't possibly make any difference to the execution of the shot. Even if the brain is taking shortcuts, reacting to visual clues before they contribute to any focused awareness, there's just no time. Remember that it takes Usain Bolt 140-plus milliseconds just to push off his blocks in response to a loud bang. Any visual information gathered from the last few feet of the ball's flight will arrive far too late to help the shot.

It seems that the elite athletes benefit from watching the point of contact, not because it gives them any extra information, but because it makes them keep their head still. Hitting is essentially a matter of balance and timing, and it doesn't help if your head is waggling around.

When Roger Federer and Rafael Nadal play their shots, they continue to fix their gaze on the point of contact for some while even *after* the ball has been dispatched. These geniuses have the ability to get themselves into the perfect position to hit their shot, and they make absolutely sure they don't lose it too soon.

Keeping your head still is the key to success in many sports. Golf is the antithesis of a fast-reaction game, but while we are on the topic I can't resist repeating this advice from the golf writer Peter Dobereiner: 'Golf instruction books can be immensely valuable to the novice. What you do is balance it on top of your head and then swing the club as hard as you can. Once you have mastered the art of taking a full vicious swing without dislodging the book, you can play golf.'

Of course, saccading eyes and head positions are no part of what the athletes think about when they execute their shots. These physical techniques all operate below the level of consciousness. It could scarcely be otherwise. There's just no time to think about what you're doing when you hit a ball within 400 milliseconds.

A recent study by the Australian sports psychologist David Mann provides further confirmation for the unconscious nature of fast sporting skills. It is well known that the human visual brain analyses information via two distinct pathways – a fast dorsal (or 'where') stream, which is largely unconscious and guides immediate physical movements like reaching and grasping, and a slower ventral (or 'what') stream, which allows us consciously to recognize objects and classify them.

Given the timing involved, fast-reaction sporting skills must come under the control of the unconscious dorsal stream. Rafa Nadal's first imperative is to ascertain where the ball is going and intercept it with his racket, not to classify it consciously. But this leads to a surprising prediction. Since the fast dorsal stream has only limited visual acuity, bad eyesight shouldn't make much difference to hitting a fast-approaching ball.

Mann decided to test this prediction for cricket. He used contact lenses to reduce the visual acuity of expert batsmen from 20/20 vision to 20/60, 20/120 and 20/180 (20/20 is normal; 20/180 means that things 20 feet away look as blurred to you as they do to most people at 180 feet).

Mann discovered that for bowling of up to 70 mph batting was hampered only by the highest degree of 20/180 blurring. That's legal blindness. Anything short of that left batting performance unimpaired.

Even for bowling of up to 80 mph – a respectable pace even at international level – the 20/60 lenses did nothing to affect performance. Most countries won't give you a driving licence if you have 20/60 vision. But it seems that this is no handicap if you want to hit fast-medium bowlers.

The significance of good vision for fast-reaction sports performance is not well understood. As a group, major league baseball players have unusually good eyesight: surveys suggest that contemporary players average as high as 20/12. This might seem inconsistent with Mann's findings that blurry vision does not affect batting performance. But it is not to be taken for granted that the reason elite baseballers have unusually sharp eyesight is that this helps them to hit major league pitchers.

One possibility is that their visual acuity – seeing things in sharp focus – is not itself a cause of strong batting performance, but is correlated with other things that are. The 20/12 vision of the baseball players does mean that on average they have exceptional optical mechanisms. But these might matter in other ways than bringing balls into sharp focus – for instance, by ensuring that their dorsal 'where' visual streams work faster.

Another possibility is that selection for sharp focus happened much earlier, when the athletes initially learned to play baseball. When kids first start hitting, they begin by swinging very deliberately at slow practice balls that they are consciously keeping in sight. Those with sharp eyesight would inevitably have developed much faster that their more optically limited peers.

I favour a yet further hypothesis. I suspect that sharp eyesight is important because it helps you to *anticipate* what pitch is coming. Anticipation is a crucial factor across a large number of sports. The very best players are often said to 'have a lot of time'.

Roger Federer is balanced and ready, pretty much whatever shot is hit at him. The most elegant cricket batsmen – David Gower, Brian Lara, Mark Waugh – never seem to be hurried as they play their shots. I haven't watched much ice hockey, but I do remember once seeing Wayne Gretzky play. It was easy to pick out The Great One, even among the padding and helmets. He was the one playing in slow motion.

You might think that these gifted athletes are distinguished by their exceptional reactions, that their eye–limb coordination is superior to the average. But that isn't how it works. In simple reaction tests – pressing a button as soon as a bell rings, for example – elite athletes typically score little better than the average person. What marks them out from the crowd isn't that they move faster once their opponents have launched the ball, but rather that they know well beforehand where the ball is going to go.

Where the top athletes really stand out is in tests that check their reactions *before* they see the trajectory of the ball. In a typical such test, the athletes will wear special glasses that can be occluded by a switch operated by the experimenter. They watch opponents readying themselves to deliver the ball, but their vision is blocked at the moment the ball is projected. For example, a tennis player might observe an opponent preparing to serve, but the glasses will be occluded as the server's racket hits the ball.

Elite athletes far outscore lesser performers on these tests – they have a pretty good idea where the ball is going before it starts on its path. Research shows a consistent pattern across tennis, squash, soccer, baseball and cricket. The best players anticipate the ball's trajectory from the posture and other bodily features of their opponents.

Perhaps this is where very good eyesight makes a difference. Some of the visual information used by the athletes is fairly coarse-grained, concerning chest position, flexing of legs, and so on. But they also use finer detail, especially in baseball and cricket, about the way the ball is gripped and the angle of their opponent's wrist. Getting these details right at a distance of 60 feet calls for sharp eyes.

The role of anticipation in elite sport was highlighted a few years ago when the USA Olympics softball star Jennie Finch had a chance to pitch at some major league batters in a 2004 celebrity softball game. You'd think that her stuff would have been easy for them. Her pitches came at up to 70 mph from 43 feet away, which gives about the normal 400 milliseconds until arrival, but in addition a softball is about a full third bigger than a baseball in diameter. Even so, the major league stars couldn't lay a bat on her. Albert Pujols and Mike Piazza whiffed repeatedly at her underarm pitches.

Their trouble was that they couldn't read her in the same way as normal baseball pitchers. Pujols and Piazza had spent years facing every species of big-league hurler, and knew how to glean all kinds of information from the way they set themselves to throw the ball. But this didn't help them with Finch.

They had no stored knowledge about the variations in her action, and so performed no better than softball novices. Finch's normal female opponents did much better, because they know how to read the clues implicit in her whirling underarm deliveries. But the big-time major leaguers had no idea what to look for.

As before, reading your opponents' intentions from bodily postures and hand angles is an entirely unconscious skill. Until the sports scientists came along, nobody had any idea that this was how it worked, least of all the athletes themselves. This provides yet further confirmation that hitting balls in fast-reaction sports operates below the level of conscious awareness. The athletes start moving prior to the ball's release, their eyes jag around, they swing before the ball is in focus, it all happens in the blink of an eye.

Let us return to the Yoga theory of athletic performance. At first pass, the reflex speeds involved in fast-reaction sports might seem to support the Yoga theory that athletes will do best to empty their minds completely and let their unconscious reactions take over. If their shot selection operates below the level of consciousness, how can it help for them to think about what they are doing? Won't this simply interfere with the smooth operation of their automatic routines?

Not at all. The Yoga theory is still ignoring a crucial mental dimension of performance, even in the context of fast-reaction sports. Sure, there are plenty of sports where there's no time to think about what to do in the heat of the action. But even then the athletes must keep their plan firmly in mind. If they don't, they will end up doing the wrong thing.

Take an example from baseball. Suppose you are the third baseman, with a single runner on third, and the ball comes at you. What is your play? Well, it depends on how many outs there are. If there are two outs, you must immediately throw hard to first to make sure you get the batter out. But if there is zero or one outs, you must first pause momentarily and hold the runner on third, to stop him making a dash for home, before you throw to first.

These are fast, trained reactions. Once you've fielded the ball, there's no time to think about what to do, you just do it.

Still, you need to know how many outs there are in order to respond correctly. It is no good emptying your mind and letting your physical environment tell you what to do. The physical set-up on the field can be exactly the same whether there are one or two outs. To react correctly, you must hold the score in mind, and respond accordingly. After all, it is not uncommon, even at the highest levels, for a fielder to start daydreaming, or become agitated, or otherwise lose concentration, and make the wrong play as a result of forgetting the score.

It is pretty clear, once you think about it, that even the fastest sporting reactions are often controlled by the conscious mind. Baseball batting provides another obvious illustration. Any halfway competent batter will set himself to swing more readily on some counts than others.

Maybe Yogi Berra really couldn't do this – he is widely regarded as the most eager bad-ball hitter in baseball history – but I rather doubt it. Even he must have known that it's not a good idea to swing at a bad pitch on a 3–0 count with the bases loaded and one run to win in the last innings.

It's the same in tennis. You might decide that your opponent's backhand is weak and resolve to play on it whenever possible. On another occasion, you might opt to concentrate on slicing to your opponent's forehand. While you are in the middle of a rally, you will be on autopilot, responding directly to the ball's trajectory. But how you respond will depend on your earlier tactical resolutions.

Batsmen in cricket need to suit their mode of batting to the circumstances, batting defensively or attackingly as the situation of the game demands. Sometimes they will cut out particular shots, avoiding the hook or leaving wide balls outside off stump, or alternatively look to play specific attacking shots against specific bowlers.

In the end, nobody can seriously doubt that conscious decisions often make a difference to how athletes respond to fast-approaching balls. Even so, there remains something very puzzling here. How *can* conscious decisions make a difference to fast automatic reactions?

Note that we are not talking about dumb premeditation. Good batters or tennis players don't generally commit themselves to some particular response before they've seen what's coming at them. Their shot selection still depends on the ball's delivery and approaching trajectory. But on different occasions they will consciously adopt differently strategies, so that a ball that previously produced one response will now call forth a different one.

It seems almost paradoxical. We're talking about eye-blink-fast unconscious reactions, mediated by neural channels that must necessarily bypass anything like conscious decision-making. Yet which shot is prompted in that flash of time is also somehow influenced by the athlete's earlier conscious thinking.

To resolve this conundrum, we need to go back to the distinction between skills and their components. To repeat, skills are things you know how to do without thinking about how you do them. Their components are the constituent movements that compose those skills.

In the last chapter I stressed how athletes need to hold in mind which skills they are aiming to perform. But they mustn't let themselves think about the components of those skills, lest they reduce themselves to the level of a learner.

What the focus on fast-reaction sports has now highlighted is that athletic skills are often complex, involving a range of different responses to different possible stimuli. Sports performers don't just learn isolated skills like how to hit a forehand slice, or fade the golf ball, or throw a slider. They also acquire complex capacities like how to field at third base when there is one out, or how to play to the backhand when they get the opportunity, or how to bat defensively at cricket.

Philosophers call such complex skills 'multi-track dispositions'. Tennis players who have set themselves to play to the backhand won't hit it there every time. Their shot will still depend on how the ball comes at them, the position of their opponent, and so on. Their consciously chosen strategy will involve a profile of different responses, each appropriate to a different situation on the court. But it will differ in its profile from a 'slice to the forehand' strategy, or a 'chip and charge' strategy. The ball will be returned to the backhand more than on these other strategies, even though not every time.

Many sporting skills have a similar structure. Third basemen know how to field when there is one out. This won't commit them to any particular play, prior to seeing how the ball is coming at them, but their reactions will be different from when there are two outs. Cricket batsmen who are playing defensively react differently from when they are attacking, but they will still tailor their shots to the bowler's delivery.

These complex skills are acquired in practice. The athletes train themselves, over many hours on the practice ground, to react automatically to oncoming balls in the requisite ways. It's a bit like installing different computer programs. Once each program has been installed, all you need to do is open it, and it will run automatically.

That's how conscious decisions make a difference to the fast reactions of athletes. It's not that the athletes consciously decide what to do once they see how the ball is coming at them. There's no time for that, indeed no time to see the ball properly.

Rather the conscious decision is made beforehand. It is a decision about which complex skill to deploy, about which program to open. It activates one set of automatic neural reflexes rather than another. You turn on the 'one batter out' instead of the 'two batters out' program, and then you leave it to your automatic neural reflexes to do the right thing.

CHAPTER 3

CHOKING AND THE YIPS

When I used to bat at cricket, I would go into a mental cocoon. 'Watch the ball, watch the ball,' I would tell myself, repeating the mantra between balls, and not talking to anybody as long as my innings lasted – which could take as long as three hours, though unfortunately it was often rather shorter.

I was just a club cricketer, but it's the same at every level of sport. Players talk about being 'in the bubble'. They screen out all distractions – the crowd, the umpires, the prize money, their personal life – and focus exclusively on the task at hand.

Not all sports performers put themselves into a trance for the whole duration of the contest. Some will talk and joke between balls, or when changing ends at tennis, or while waiting on the tee. Golfing legend Lee Trevino was a great one for wisecracks between shots. This didn't always suit his opponents. On one occasion when Tony Jacklin was paired with Trevino, he told Trevino, 'Lee, I don't want to talk today.' Trevino replied, 'I don't want you to talk. I just want you to listen.'

Still, even Trevino needed to turn on his concentration when it was time to play his shots. No doubt it is less tiring to tune in and out, taking mental breaks in the gaps in the action, if you can manage it. But no serious competitor can afford to let their mind wander when they are actually playing.

Still, *why* is it so important to maintain focus in this way? I have stressed how competitors often need to select a strategy to cope with their current opponent, or weather conditions, or playing surface. But once they have fixed on their plan, why do they need to maintain continual focus? Why isn't it enough consciously to form an intention beforehand, or as the changing circumstances of the game demand, and thereafter simply leave it to their trained abilities to execute it?

The answer is that it is not always enough to form an intention. You also need to carry it out. And this is by no means guaranteed, especially if you are thinking of something else when the time for action arrives.

I decide to post a letter on the way to the bus stop, and even put it in my pocket, yet fail to do so when I pass the pillar box because I am thinking about the mind–body problem. Similarly, a tennis player may decide to cut out the drop shot against a speedy opponent, but find themselves playing it anyway in the heat of a rally because they have been distracted by a bad line call on the previous point.

To appreciate fully what goes wrong in such cases, we need to understand the structure of action control in human beings. In particular, we need to distinguish two levels in this structure.

First, there are the behavioural systems that we share with other animals, in which initially innate or haphazard movements are shaped by experience of success or failure. These are the automatic systems that govern unthinking actions, as when a rat scurries down a familiar drain, or a bird catches some insect prey, or you tie your shoelaces.

This is also the level at which the components of sporting skills are managed. Repetitive training will have instilled in your automatic behavioural systems the ability to hit a forehand slice at tennis, or bat defensively at cricket, or field at third base with one out. The automatic systems will note the speed and trajectory of the ball, the wind conditions, the movements of your opponent, and so on, and automatically direct your limbs to execute the responses to these stimuli that are appropriate to your chosen strategy.

Recent psychological research with rats, monkeys, crows and other animals has shown that these automatic control systems can be remarkably sophisticated. They involve nested neural circuits whose interactions can end up producing novel responses to new circumstances.

The tricks that Lionel Messi pulls as he accelerates into the penalty area will often be a surprise to himself as well as to the defenders, a combination of moves that he's never executed in just that order before. But this isn't because he is consciously thinking things out as he dodges and weaves. Rather, he has an unparalleled wealth of behavioural dispositions which, once acquired, can combine to produce results that have no precedent in his past training.

Still, despite the complexity that allows them to generate such novel responses, the automatic systems we share with other animals are also limited in other ways. In particular, they are constitutionally short-term. The triggers that prompt them to respond are all here-and-now, a matter of which desires are currently active and which opportunities are perceptually salient. This leaves little scope for sustained long-term plans. You can always deflect a monkey from its current task by offering it a banana.

This is where the second level of action control comes in. We humans can do better than other animals, courtesy of an extra system that enables us to form long-term *intentions* and stick to them. As the Stanford philosopher Michael Bratman has argued for some decades, this extra intention-formation system gives human behaviour a structure that can't be explained by the simpler control mechanisms we share with other animals.

We humans pause, we deliberate about what to do, and then we commit ourselves to a certain plan of action. This intention-formation system then directs the automatic control systems accordingly, telling them to carry out the intended steps in the plan, rather than simply responding to the imperatives of the present moment.

The advantages are obvious. Our choices can be informed by the wealth of information that our culture provides, and not just by our personal experience. And we can make sure that we are acting in our long-term interests, and not just in pursuit of some passing temptation.

This is the level where athletes formulate their game plans. They think about the playing conditions, the stage of the match, and so on, and work out how best to use their acquired skills to maximize their chances of victory. Having formed their plan, they then hand it over to the automatic control systems to execute the required components.

Except this isn't always sure-fire, either within sports or without. The problem is that the long-term intention system isn't always foolproof in controlling the automatic behavioural systems. It can send instructions, but they aren't always obeyed. In particular, whenever there is a time gap between the formation of an intention and its execution, the more primitive systems can all too easily be deflected from the chosen plan. You decide to post the letter later, but forget to slip it in the post-box as you go past. You have resolved to cut out the drop shot, but then find yourself playing it in the heat of the moment.

There is a topic in psychology devoted to this issue, called 'prospective memory'. How do we remember to carry out the plans we have made earlier? It can't be said that the psychologists' findings are clear-cut, but they do suggest various tricks to make sure you stick to your intentions.

The most effective is the simplest. Once you have formed an intention, keep it in the front of your mind, and don't allow your thinking to be distracted. This will ensure that the primitive control systems are continually receiving the relevant instruction, and will stop them wandering off on their own accord.

So now we can see why athletes have to concentrate. They need to make sure that their bodies stick to the game plan. They need to keep reminding their basic control systems what to do. It can be hard to keep concentrating for extended periods of time. That is why the ability to maintain focus is as important a component of sporting success as physical prowess.

What about sports where performers always do the same thing? Maybe you need to concentrate when you've opted for one among a range of alternative strategies in tennis or baseball, but what about the gymnasts, sprinters and others who have simply perfected one routine that they perform over and over again? What does it matter what they think about? Can't they just leave it to their repetitively trained habits?

But this forgets the difference between active competition and practice routines. Active competition is different, calling for extra precision, timing and effort. You can't achieve that level of perfection every time you practise your routine. So even the gymnasts and the sprinters need to focus on producing the extra elements when they are seriously competing. If they allow their minds to wander, and open themselves to distractions, they will risk reverting to practice mode, and end up underperforming.

So, across the board, you must Have Your Mind Right to succeed in a sporting contest. It is no good daydreaming or getting into a temper. This will turn your mind away from your chosen plan, and leave you at the mercy of whatever haphazard habits are waiting to commandeer your body.

There are many mental traps lying in wait for the competitive athlete. The road to sporting success is beset with potential diversions. Two of the most insidious pitfalls are 'choking' and 'the yips'.

'Choking' refers to a deterioration in an athlete's performance in the face of competitive pressure. Often a competitor will be doing well, perhaps nearing victory, but will be distracted by the importance of the contest, and as a result fail to do themselves justice. (The term is associated with the unkind gesture commonly used to suggest that someone is crumbling under pressure: a hand to the throat, accompanied by strangled coughs.)

'The yips' are the result of an excessive self-consciousness about technique. Concern about your movements becomes compulsive, and constantly undermines your skill. Instead of thinking about your game plan, you can't stop yourself thinking about the angle of your wrist, or the speed of your racket head, or one of the many other things that you should be leaving to ingrained habit rather than conscious control.

No good can come from yippish self-consciousness about your technique. It is the enemy of performance. By turning your mind away from your adopted plan and towards the components of your skills, you reduce yourself to the level of the beginner who is trying to play by numbers. 'Paralysis by analysis', as Sian Beilock calls it. You end up desperately stitching together movements, rather than exercising the smooth skills your hours of practice have instilled in you.

The yips can become a kind of mental compulsion, and it is never easy to get rid of them. They are the sporting equivalent of a cancer that cannot be cured, but only placed in remission. Even if you regain your health temporarily, the danger remains.

Choking and the yips need to be distinguished from each other. Many sports commentators talk as if they are pretty much the same thing. But this is a mistake. While they are often found together, they can also dissociate in both directions, as we philosophers say. You can have choking that doesn't involve the yips, and the yips in the absence of choking. After all, chokers are perfectly capable of being distracted by other aspects of competitive pressure, even when they aren't worrying about their techniques. And sometimes a yippish concern with technique is so ingrained that it doesn't need any competitive stress to bring it out.

The term 'yips' comes from golf, and was originally coined to describe the involuntary twitching and jerking that can afflict the putting stroke of even the most accomplished golfer. Many of the greatest players have suffered. Some cure themselves by changing their grip, but others never recover. The list of those whose careers were ended by the yips is long and distinguished: Tommy Armour, Ben Hogan, Sam Snead, Johnny Miller, David Duval.

It is a nasty business. Hitting a ball into a hole from a few feet away is not athletically demanding. Your granny could do it. But once the yips get into your head, putting can become an ordeal. You are no longer in control of your hands. They slow down at the last moment, they jerk forward, they turn the clubface away from the hole. Sam Snead's putting in his later years was said to be 'painful to watch'.

The word may come from golf, but the phenomenon is far more general. In pool and snooker, the ailment is known as cueitis. In darts, it is dartitis. Tennis players can be overcome when tossing the ball up to serve, and in basketball it can afflict free throws. In baseball, fielders and pitchers can suffer, and in cricket there is a sad tradition of bowlers who have succumbed.

Still, the poison does not extend to all sporting activities. Sports writers sometimes attribute the poor form of batters in baseball or cricket to 'the yips'. This doesn't make any sense. You can't get the yips while batting in these sports. Nor can you get it while playing soccer, or gridiron football, or when you are road cycling, or boxing, or running the marathon.

This is because the yips are restricted to a quite specific range of sporting activities. They afflict only those actions that are triggered by the players themselves, as opposed to those that are responses to someone else. It is specifically when you need to initiate a sporting action that you are in danger of thinking about the movements you must perform. When somebody else is in control of the timing and direction of an approaching ball, or some other trigger to your movement, you can't start thinking about your technique – you can only react.

That is why batters can't get the yips. As we have seen, in both cricket and baseball there is typically no more than half a second between the release of the ball and the completion of the batter's response. This leaves no time to think about making the right movements, indeed no time to think of anything. You can only rely on your reflexes. The same applies in any sport where you must respond immediately to some externally generated stimulus.

Perhaps the purest form of the yips is 'dartitis'. Darts players don't need to do anything except project their darts at a board just under 8 feet away. Somewhat strangely, there is no time limit on how long you can take for your turn of three throws. Dartitis occurs when competitors start thinking too much about what they are about to do. This leads to an inability to release the dart or to other throwing-action problems. The career of Eric Bristow, 'The Crafty Cockney', five-times world champion, went into a terminal decline in 1987 after he started having trouble letting go of the darts.

Snooker and pool players can suffer similarly. The fine Irish player Patsy Fagan, UK snooker champion in 1977, had a particular problem with the cue rest. He would move his cue back and forth dozens of times on the rest, to the extent that he became unable to make himself hit the ball. 'Oh dear, he's going to need the rest for this next shot,' the television commentators would whisper, anticipating the imminent agonies. Fagan's affliction eventually led to his premature retirement from professional snooker.

In baseball and cricket, while the batters are immune, the yips can afflict those who throw or bowl, particularly when they do so in their own time. Baseball pitchers are particularly vulnerable, given the way they stand on the mound and pick their moment to throw.

Steve Blass was a star pitcher with the Pittsburgh Pirates, with a 103–76 win–loss record in the 1960s and early 1970s. He won two games in the 1971 World Series against the Orioles, sealing the Pirates's triumph with a victory in the seventh game, and the next year he made the National League All-Star team. However, he is best known, not for his successes, but for 'Steve Blass Disease'. In 1973 he completely lost control of his pitches, walking a batter every inning and ending up with an embarrassing ERA (earned run average) of 9.85. He retired soon afterwards.

Overthinking your throwing action is an occupational hazard for pitchers. Many have succumbed over the years, and few recover. Rick Ankiel of the St Louis Cardinals managed to stay in baseball only by converting to an outfielder. He was *Sporting News* Rookie Pitcher of the Year in 2000, but in the post-season he started to spray wild pitches around and never featured as a major league starter again. Happily, after seven long years in the minors, he re-emerged as an outfielder for the Cardinals, and enjoyed a number of successful seasons with the bat.

Where baseball pitchers throw from a standing start, in cricket the bowlers run in to bowl. In consequence, it is the slow bowlers who are most at risk of the yips. Fast bowlers are running at full speed when they let the ball go, and so their bowling action is part of an extended automatic routine. But the slower bowlers don't really run in, but simply project the ball after a few slow steps, and with them the yips are not uncommon.

For some mysterious reason, the disease targets slow left-arm bowlers far more than right-armers. Phil Edmonds went through a series of bad patches when in the England side, and the Surrey all-rounder Keith Medlycott had to retire at twenty-six because he became unable to let the ball go when bowling. Most recently, poor Simon Kerrigan had a nightmare in his first test at the Oval in 2013, scarcely able to land the ball on the pitch, and it seems unlikely that he will be picked for England again.

In general, it seems to be the more cerebral athletes who are most at risk. Unreflective players who never pause to analyse their technique need not fear the yips. At most danger are the thinkers and tinkerers, those who are curious about the nature of their skills. It is noteworthy that Tommy Armour, Patsy Fagan and Keith Medlycott all became renowned coaches after their problems forced them into premature retirement.

Now for choking. As I said, commentators sometimes muddle this up with the yips. But they aren't the same. Choking is when you fold mentally under pressure. This needn't involve any yippish focus on your movements.

Of course, in some cases the two can coincide. Some athletes have a tendency to start fretting about their techniques specifically in clutch situations. While they are normally able to focus on the right things, and keep their minds away from their movements, they lose confidence in their physical abilities just when it really matters, and start trying to play by numbers.

Those are cases where choking and the yips overlap. The pressure of the competitive situation makes you start worrying about the components of your skills. But not all cases of choking are like that.

Consider perhaps the most famous case of choking in sporting history. In the Wimbledon ladies' singles final of

1993, Jana Novotná was playing a blinder against the great Steffi Graf and closing in on victory, serving at 40–30 to reach 5–1 in the final set – at which stage she double-faulted and scarcely won another point. She collapsed in tears after the match and had to be consoled by the Duchess of Kent when she was presenting the prizes. (To Novotná's eternal credit, she eventually gained her sole grand slam title by winning the same tournament five years later.)

There is no doubt that Novotná was overwhelmed by the occasion. She choked because she could not stop herself thinking about the fact that she was about to win her first grand slam final – or then that she was about to throw it away – and this stopped her thinking about what she was supposed to be thinking about, namely her game plan of getting to the net and volleying it away whenever possible.

But there is no reason at all to suppose that Novotná's discomposure had anything to do with her focusing inappropriately on the components of her basic actions. She had no history of a yippish tendency to worry unhelpfully about her technique. Indeed, she had no particular history of choking. She was a hardened competitor who had closed out many important matches. But winning her first grand slam final at Wimbledon against Steffi Graf was not something she had experienced before, and the occasion simply proved too much for her concentration.

The conflation of choking with the yips is common among those who subscribe to the Yoga theory of sporting mentality. After all, from their point of view there is no need to concentrate on strategy. You need only empty your mind and rely on your acquired skills. So, as they see it, there is just the one mental danger facing the athlete – that of thinking yippishly about technique and regressing to the level of a novice.

When the phenomenologist Herbert Dreyfus cites second baseman Chuck Knoblauch's throwing difficulties, he refers to Knoblauch's ailment as 'choking'. From his analysis, however, it is clear that Dreyfus has in mind what I am calling the yips. Dreyfus thinks that Knoblauch's problems were brought on by an excessive concern about his throwing movements, not by a failure of concentration due to competitive pressure.

In her book *Choke*, Sian Beilock, another Yoga theorist, presents some evidence to support the view that choking in sport always involves the yips ('explicit self-monitoring' in her terminology). She cites a series of studies by herself and her associates that purport to show that expert sporting performance is adversely affected by self-monitoring, but not by other things that might be expected to disrupt concentration.

For example, in one typical study Beilock and her team compared two groups of experienced golfers, one told to think about their hand movements while putting, and the other asked to putt while performing a distracting task like listening for a series of tones. The golfers were adversely affected by the self-monitoring, but not by the distracting task.

On the face of it, this does suggest that experienced athletes will do fine as long as they keep their minds off their movements, and that it doesn't matter if they are distracted in other ways. Still, Beilock's data are scarcely conclusive in showing that yippish self-monitoring is the only route by which pressure can affect sporting performance.

For one thing, it is not clear that the golf putters in her studies were mentally in competitive rather than practice mode. As we saw earlier, practice mode does not always demand focused precision, and so need not be affected by distractions. Moreover, we shouldn't assume that concentration requires an active conscious rehearsing of your intended strategy; it might be enough simply to prevent certain kinds of disrupting thoughts from intruding; and for this it may be helpful to occupy your mind with music, say, or a meaningless mantra, or indeed attention to a sequence of tones.

So, all in all, I see no reason to accept the Yoga theory that competitive pressure only adversely affects athletes when it makes them think yippishly about their movements. Sometimes it also undoes them in other ways, by making them think about the importance of the result, or the money that hinges on it, or how much they dislike this opponent, and so not about the skills they are intending to deploy.

If we can have choking without the yips, what about the yips without choking? Can someone's sporting focus be undermined by a concern with the components of their actions, even though this is not precipitated by the pressure of the competitive situation?

Yes, there can be cases like this too. Even though it is often specifically extra competitive pressure that makes athletes start worrying about their techniques, sometimes the yips are so compulsive that they intrude even when competition is not an issue. Many suffering golfers struggle with their putting even when on a practice round.

Perhaps the most famous pure case of the yips was that of Mackey Sasser, a successful catcher for the New York Mets in the 1980s and 1990s. He started having trouble flipping the ball back to the pitcher between plays. There's nothing stressful about returning the ball to the pitcher. There is no competition involved. It is not even part of the game.

Still, it is an interesting skill, if you think about it. There's the speed of your arm, and the point of release, and then there's the extra impetus imparted by your wrist, and the angle of the ball's departure, all of which can vary from throw to throw as long as the ball is projected towards the target appropriately. Many of us have learned to adjust and compensate all these independent factors in real time, without knowing how we do it, so that we can reliably lob a ball 20 yards. But, of course, this skill will begin to unravel if you start to worry about how the trick is done.

That's what happened to Mackey Sasser. Even though there was no pressure involved at all, he became so obsessed with the mechanics of throwing that he lost the ability to lob the ball to the pitcher, and had to retire from the professional game. (Interestingly, and in line with my analysis, he had no trouble firing the ball to second on a steal, when he had no time to think about what he was doing.)

Athletes need to Have Their Mind Right when competing. They must focus on their intended plans, and clear their minds of everything else. Choking and the yips are two dangers that they must circumvent to achieve this. But these are not the only ways of failing to Have Your Mind Right. You can always be distracted by matters that have nothing to do with competitive pressure or paralysis by analysis.

I was a spectator at the Oval cricket test between England and South Africa in 2012. In England's first innings, Ravi Bopara was dismissed for a duck. He started to hook at a short ball from Dale Steyn, but then tried to pull out of the shot, as if realizing halfway that it was the wrong choice early in a test innings, with the result that he merely feathered the ball and was caught behind.

After the match, he asked to be stood down from the team, citing 'problems at home'. It certainly looked as if Bopara was distracted while batting. His personal issues made it hard for him to focus on the specific demands of test cricket, with the result that he half-reverted to the habits of the one-day batsman.

There is no reason to suppose that Bopara's distraction was caused by the pressure of the situation. He was an experienced test batsman with three centuries to his name. Nor is there any reason to suppose that his distraction was mediated by any worries about his batting technique. Rather his inability to focus was simply a result of his personal turmoil. He was unable to clear his head of his private anxieties and focus instead on the task in hand. He could Not Get His Mind Right, even though he was neither choking nor a victim of the yips.

Here is a little diagram illustrating the relationships between different ways of Not Having Your Mind Right.

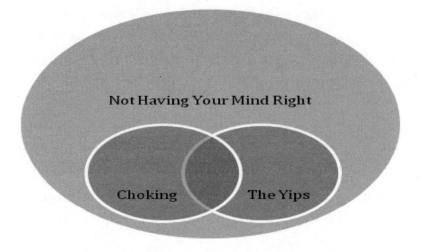

Choking and the yips are two species of the larger genus. Sometimes they occur together, but both can occur in the absence of the other. And then there are the many cases where athletes fail to Have Their Mind Right for other reasons. Troubled personal relationships can make it hard for them to concentrate – or other issues, nothing to do with the sport in question, disturb their minds. After all, nothing says that competitive athletes can never worry about anything except sporting technique and competitive pressure.

The bottom line is that sporting achievement depends on sustained mental effort. Concentration is of the essence. The Yoga theory offers precisely the wrong advice when it tells you simply to go with the flow. On the contrary, you need to place your intended game plan at the front of your mind and keep it there. It won't do to let your thoughts wander. If you start thinking about your backswing, or the importance of the match, or indeed anything else, you will soon be undone. Distraction in any form is the enemy of sporting success.

PART II

RULES

CHAPTER 4

PROFESSIONAL FOULS AND POLITICAL OBLIGATION

Some philosophers say you can't win a sporting contest by cheating. Their idea is that games wouldn't exist apart from the rules that govern them, and so someone who ignores those rules isn't even competing, let alone winning.

This is the kind of thing that gives philosophy a bad name. Tell it to the Irish soccer team, after they failed to qualify for the 2010 World Cup because of Thierry Henry's blatant handball. 'It's all right, boys. We're going to South Africa after all. France didn't beat us, because you can't win a game of football by transgressing the rules that define the game.'

You might think that there's a distinction to be made here between being credited with a win, as France was, and really winning. A student who steals the answers beforehand might be deemed to have 'passed' the exam, and have a certificate to prove it, but the student hasn't really passed. In the same spirit, perhaps we can deny that Henry's handball resulted in a genuine victory, even though France's name went down as the winner.

But it's not a good analogy. Of course, France really won. Indeed, they did so as a direct result of Henry's cheating. That's why they and not Ireland went to South Africa.

It's different from the exam case. If it were discovered afterwards that the student had stolen the answers, the exam result would be quashed and the certificate reclaimed. But there was no question of revising the football score once Henry's handball became public. After all, the foul was as public as could be from the start, to everybody but the referee.*

So you can break the rules and still be competing, whatever the philosophers say. Still, there remains a good question here. What exactly does it take to be playing a game? Maybe you can break some rules, but there are limits. You can't win a football match by shooting the referee and carrying the ball over the goal line.

To sort this out, we need to distinguish between the rules of the game, the code of fair play, and the authority of the officials. And once we have done that, it will turn out that there are some interesting analogies between playing a game and being a citizen of a state. We'll see that fair play is often consistent with breaking a game's rules, and this will then suggest, against philosophical orthodoxy, that there is no general moral requirement for good citizens to conform to the law of the land.

Let's start with the difference between the official rules of a game and the code of fair play. By the code of fair play, I mean

---

* Curiously, anti-corruption investigators have since exposed a 5-million-euro payment made by FIFA to the Irish Football Association after that match. The Irish now say this was to block legal action contesting the handball decision, while FIFA say it was to help build a new stadium. If you ask me, however, there was never going to be a legal action, nor were stadium costs the issue – this looks like just one more of the dodgy payments with which Sepp Blatter and other FIFA officials sought to maintain the support of their member associations.

the expectations that the athletes have of each other, their sense of what is and is not acceptable behaviour. Such unwritten codes of fair play can diverge from the official rules in both directions. There are rule violations that count as fair, and unfair strategies that don't break the rules.

Basketball offers a good example of the first kind of divergence, where breaking the rules is in line with accepted standards of fair play. If you are one point down and your opponents gain the ball with twenty seconds to play, you are downright *supposed* to foul them. It's the only way you can prevent them keeping the ball until the final whistle. So you foul them, stop the clock, and hope that you can beat their score once you get the ball back after their free throws. It's an accepted part of the game. Everybody expects you to do it, the referee's whistle is pretty much a formality, and nobody thinks of it as bad practice at all.

Then there are the converse cases, where you can violate an unwritten sporting code even though you aren't breaking the rules. In 1981 New Zealand needed a six off the last ball to win a one-day cricket match against Australia. The Australian captain Greg Chappell instructed his brother Trevor to roll the ball underarm at the batsman, making it physically impossible to hit a six. While this was fully allowed by the laws of cricket, it was universally condemned as against the spirit of the game. (The Kiwi prime minister at the time, Robert 'Piggy' Muldoon, didn't hold back: 'the most disgusting incident I can recall in the history of cricket ... an act of true cowardice and I consider it appropriate that the Australian team were wearing yellow.')

It is interesting to compare notions of fair play across different sports. Simon Barnes, for many years the chief sports writer on the *Times*, once described a friend of his saying, 'I would die rather than cheat at golf. In cricket, I cheat sometimes . . . And when I played football I cheated all the time.'

Barnes's point wasn't that his friend was an honest citizen on the golf course, but turned into a moral leper on the soccer field. He was just the same character in all these sporting contexts. Rather, Barnes was making the point that different sports impose different requirements on their participants. Some look askance at any deviation from the rules, while others regard it as quite proper to break them and take any consequent penalties.

Golf is at one end of the spectrum. It's easy to tee up your ball in the rough when no one is watching. But improving your lie like this is quite beyond the pale, even in the most insignificant competition. Someone caught out surreptitiously fiddling with their ball won't just be penalized the two strokes required by the rules. They will be ostracized in the bar and very likely expelled from the club.

In soccer, by contrast, all kinds of technical infractions are an accepted part of the game. You steal as many yards as you can at throw-ins, you tug and pull at your opponent as the corner comes over, you give away a free kick rather than let the attacker beat you.

Still, this doesn't mean that there aren't clear standards of fair play in soccer. It might be all right to take a red card for a foul that stops an opponent scoring, but it's not all right to take one for a two-footed tackle that might break a leg.

Play-acting in order to get an opponent sent off is widely frowned upon, at least in northern countries. When one side kicks the ball out because a player is injured, everybody respects the obligation to give it back at the throw-in.

And so it goes. In rugby union, punching and even stamping are regarded as in the spirit of the thing. (When the saintly Northern Irishman Willie John McBride captained the 1974 Lions tour of South Africa, his dressing-room instruction before the first test was, 'Let's get our retaliation in first.') On the other hand, disagreeing with the referee is a decided no-no. (In 2013, the French coach voluntarily dropped his star forward Louis Picamoles for mildly mocking a referee's decision.)

Ice hockey similarly allows, indeed encourages, its players to vent their frustration in honest fisticuffs, with a standard penalty of five minutes off the ice. But it's strictly arms and fists that are tolerated. Any player who uses his stick as a weapon will be suspended for a number of games.

In cricket, it has now become acceptable to 'sledge' the batsman between balls, trying to distract him with some verbal dig. But no fielder would dream of talking once the bowler begins his run. That wouldn't be cricket.

I could go on. All sports have their own quirky codes, unwritten rules of behaviour handed down from generation to generation. But let's get back to our original question. What does it take to be playing a game?

If conformity to the formal rules isn't the right answer, perhaps it's that you must stick to the unwritten code of fair play. But that doesn't seem right either. Take Thierry Henry and Ireland again. I'd say his handball overstepped the bounds of fair play, even by the standards of professional football. But this didn't somehow invalidate the result. There were no serious grounds for appeal. The referee's decision, as they say, was final.

Perhaps there is room for dispute about this specific case. Did professional footballers really consider Henry's handball beyond the pale? It's debatable. I doubt that any of them thought that Henry should have confessed to the referee after the goal was given. But I for one was disappointed that he handballed in the first place. Bobby Charlton wouldn't have done it, nor would Gary Lineker.

Still, let's not get bogged down in one example. The general point is clear enough. If a less controversial case is needed, just consider the Trevor Chappell underarm ball again. Even though everybody thought it a terrible violation of the spirit of cricket, the umpires had no option but to call it a legal delivery, and Australia won the match. Maybe they won by sharp practice, but they certainly won. That's precisely what was so galling to the Kiwis.

Sports performers can behave very badly indeed while still competing in every sense. Take the 'Bountygate' scandal that engulfed the NFL's New Orleans Saints in 2011. Their coaching staff had been running a 'bounty' system, rewarding players financially if they succeeded in injuring targeted members of the opposition. The practice was greeted with universal incredulity and revulsion once it was exposed, and heavy suspensions and fines followed. But none of the Saints wins was overturned.

A not dissimilar episode shamed the English rugby union side Harlequins in 2009. The rules of rugby make special provision for substitutions of players with blood injuries. To take tactical advantage of these 'blood replacements', the Harlequins management started cutting lips, issuing players with blood capsules, and otherwise spilling fake blood. When the story came out, the rugby union fraternity was shocked, and the club coach, doctor and physiotherapist were banned. But, once more, nobody suggested that Harlequins hadn't really been playing rugby matches and that their results should therefore be nullified.

Still, as I said, there are clearly some limits beyond which you aren't playing any more. To my mind, the crucial issue is whether you continue to accept the authority of the referee or other officials. However badly you behave, you're still playing if you defer to the decisions of the on-field authority. Once you refuse to do what the referee says, though, you've abandoned the game. You can have a game of football with innumerable and immoral fouls – we need only think of Holland's 'tactics' in the 2010 World Cup final against Spain – but you can't have one where the players don't listen when the referee blows his whistle.

I think that there is a moral for political philosophy here. A central issue – *the* central issue – for political philosophers is 'political obligation'. Why are we under any moral obligation to respect the state? After all, newly naturalized citizens apart, none of us had any choice about being ruled by our institutions of government. Nobody asked us whether we wanted to be subject to the police, the courts, and the tax system. These authorities simply imposed themselves on us. So why exactly do we have to obey them?

Nearly all political philosophers pose this issue in terms of respect for the law. The first sentence in the entry on political obligation in the authoritative *Stanford Encyclopedia of Philosophy* states: 'To have a political obligation is to have a moral duty to obey the laws of one's country or state.' Philosophers debate the precise basis for this duty, but they nearly all take it as given that we do have a duty to obey the law. Their dispute is only about why this is so.

Of course, philosophers also recognize that even legitimate democratic states can sometimes have immoral laws, such as laws prohibiting homosexuality, say, or enforcing racial segregation. But they don't regard these as invalidating the moral standing of the law, so much as generating moral *conflicts* – on the one hand we have the general moral duty to obey the law, and on the other the more specific moral duty not to discriminate unjustly – so somehow we need to resolve the two, perhaps by campaigning to get the unjust law changed.

I wonder if the political philosophers aren't missing a trick here. The sporting analogy suggests an interesting option. Perhaps citizens have a moral duty to respect the authority of the state, but no further moral duty to obey the law as such – just as participants in a game must defer to the authority of the officials, yet beyond that are under no compulsion to conform to the rules.

I don't think that there is much doubt that we all benefit from the protection of the state. As Thomas Hobbes observed in his *Leviathan* over 350 years ago, life would be 'nasty, brutish, and short' without a central authority that success-fully claims a moral monopoly on the use of force. When states fail, basic public services disappear and life quickly degenerates into lawless looting.

Even a bad state is much better than none at all. When the hated regimes of Eastern Europe and South Africa collapsed at the end of the last century, their populations had the good sense to carry on recognizing the existing police, courts and other state institutions until new constitutional arrangements could be made. By contrast, the misguided disbanding of the defeated Iraqi army and police by the US authorities in 2003 created a vacuum for mob rule, and is viewed by many commentators as the main source of the subsequent chaos in the Middle East.

Still, even if the threat of anarchy creates a moral imperative to recognize the authority of the state, I don't see that this carries with it any further moral duty to obey its laws. As we've seen, playing a game depends on ceding authority to the officials, but not on adhering to the rules – it can be quite proper to break a rule and take the penalty. So too with civil society, I say. As a good citizen, I must respect the state, but not necessarily its laws.

What if someone murders his wife and accepts the prison term that follows, figuring that a few years behind bars is a small price to be rid of her? Would that be all right then? Absolutely not. But that's because murder is wrong, not because there is a law against it.

Just as in sport, we need to distinguish between breaking the formal rules and genuinely unacceptable behaviour.

Sometimes breaking the formal rules also oversteps the standards of fair play, like two-footed soccer tackles. But that's not just because it's breaking a rule, but because it's nasty. Think of all the cases where it's quite appropriate to break a rule, such as fouling in the last seconds of a basketball game.

As I see it, then, while we should certainly respect the state's authority, we only have a duty to obey the law when it would be moral to do so anyway. You might wonder whether this holds good in all cases. What about the law requiring you to drive on the left in Britain? Surely that wasn't a moral requirement until Parliament said it was. It's not as if there is some universal and eternal moral principle saying you must drive on the left, independently of what Parliament decrees.

This is an interesting case, but it doesn't suffice to show that Parliament can create duties *ex nihilo* without any prior moral backing. As it happens, the convention of driving on the left arose independently of Parliament. This by itself was enough to create a moral requirement to conform, simply because you would endanger others if you didn't. Later on, Parliament specified penalties for those who violated the convention. But that only made Parliament the enforcer of the moral requirement, not its original basis.

I'd say something similar even if parliamentary intervention had in fact been the sole source of the rule about driving on the left. Parliament would then have been helping people to settle into a useful agreement, which they would then have a moral duty to observe. But this moral requirement wouldn't have derived from some general principle that you must obey

Parliament, because it is Parliament, whatever it says, but simply from the principle, as before, that you shouldn't endanger others needlessly.

We can apply this idea more widely. It is in everybody's interest, independently of any legal system, that we share the burden of paying for roads, police, defence, and so on. However, it will always be a bit arbitrary exactly how this burden is shared, just as it is arbitrary which side of the road we drive on. So one sensible solution is to set up some body that will figure out some reasonable rules about taxation, which we will then all have a moral duty to follow.

As it happens, elected governments are the bodies that we use for this purpose, and so we all have a moral duty, within reason, to pay the taxes they require of us. But, again, this isn't because we must blindly obey the decrees of governments as such, but because they are asking us to do something that is independently moral.

The point is that the state sometimes plays a coordinating role in setting up moral arrangements, as with taxes, the highway code, and so on.

Most moral requirements, however, are not like this. We don't need the state to tell us that it's wrong to murder, assault, rob or kidnap. These things are morally wrong, whatever the state says.

At most, the state's role with murder, robbery and similar immoral crimes is to specify the punishments that are due to offenders. But that's a different thing. That's not what makes murder wrong. It's just a matter of coordinating our social responses to those who transgress.

So I say that when we have a moral duty to obey the law, that's not because it's the law, but because breaking it would be wrong anyway. You shouldn't commit murder even if there weren't a law against it.

Conversely, sometimes states get it wrong. They say that certain acts, like homosexuality, racial intermarriage or drinking, are immoral, when in fact they aren't. In cases like these, I don't see that I have any moral duty to obey the law. I certainly don't want to get rid of the state, for that way lies chaos. But when it prohibits me from doing things that aren't wrong, I will happily ignore its requirements, even while respecting its authority to penalize me if I am caught.

So the analogy between games and politics turns out to be remarkably close. In both cases, we need a central authority that wields power, otherwise we will have nothing but a brutish mess. But beyond that there is no moral requirement to obey the authority's regulations. We can reasonably take our own view on whether it is right to transgress and risk official punishment.

This freedom does not mean a world without morality in which everything is permitted. Just as most competing athletes will have a clear sense of which sporting infractions are and aren't acceptable, so will most citizens recognize that many actions aren't just illegal but downright immoral. These are the codes that really matter. We need officials to make sure things don't get out of hand, and for this reason I'm the last person to question their authority. But, when my sense of fair play allows it, I'm quite ready to break the rules.

CHAPTER 5

MORALITY, CONVENTION AND FOOTBALL FAKERY

When a baseball outfielder traps the ball as it bounces – or picks it up on the half-volley, as non-Americans would say – he will generally leap up as if he has caught it cleanly, hoping to persuade the umpires that the batter is out. This is by no means considered bad behaviour in professional baseball. It's what good fielders do. You'd be letting your side down if you didn't try your hardest to take advantage of the umpires' uncertainty.

The contrast with cricket is striking. Fielders in cricket are supposed to say whether or not they have caught the ball. Traditionally the batsman and indeed the umpires have accepted the fielder's word on whether a catch was fairly made, even at the highest levels of the game.

The modern Television Review System is complicating the situation, with its tendency to make fair catches look foul, but the principle still runs deep in cricket. It's not just embarrassing to be found out pretending to have made a catch you know you didn't make – it's downright shameful. Your team-mates won't want anything to do with you, let alone the opposition. You will have been exposed as someone lacking in moral fibre.

No doubt many cricket fans will take this comparison to be yet more evidence of the inferiority, not to say degeneracy, of the American summer game. But I think that this is quite the wrong reaction. I love cricket above all other sports, but baseball is also a fine game, with many virtues of its own. What is more, it has a great deal of pride in its traditions, and a strong concern, bordering on obsession, with propriety and good behaviour.

In truth, the two games place different moral demands on their players. While it would be disgraceful for a cricketer to claim a catch he hasn't made, this is morally quite acceptable in a baseball player.

This might seem puzzling. How can one and the same action be immoral in one sport, yet moral in another? We seem to be getting dangerously close to the idea that all morality is relative – that there is no real difference between right and wrong, just different ideas of what is socially acceptable. But this does not follow at all. I believe in absolute moral standards as much as the next philosopher. It is just that this absolute morality manifests itself differently in cricket and baseball.

To understand cases like these, we first need to distinguish between morality and convention, and then to understand their relationship.

From an early age, all humans recognize that there is a difference between morality and convention. They understand that morality is universal, independent of authority, and to do with genuine welfare, while convention varies across societies, depends on decree, and governs matters of no intrinsic importance.

This distinction has been much studied by social psychologists, following the influential work of the Berkeley psychologist Elliot Turiel in the 1980s. In *The Development of Social Knowledge: Morality and Convention,* Turiel showed that children discriminate naturally between moral principles, which they view as unalterable, and rules instituted by parochial authorities, which they assume can easily be changed. Turiel's work has since been confirmed by a wide range of studies covering subjects of different ages and religious and cultural backgrounds.

In one of Turiel's original studies, children were asked whether the teacher's permission would make it all right (a) to speak without raising your hand first, and (b) to steal. The children all agreed that talking without hand-raising would be legitimated by the teacher's say-so, but they felt differently about stealing. No, it would not be all right to steal, insisted one thoughtful eight-year-old in Turiel's original study. 'People wouldn't like to have things stolen.'

At first pass, the difference between cricket and baseball is clearly a matter of convention, not morality. No issues of human welfare hinge on whether catches are self-policed or left to umpires; both games could easily enough decree that things be done differently; and the example itself shows that nothing universal is at issue. Whether or not you own up to trapping a catch is a conventional matter, like raising your hand before speaking, not a moral issue like stealing.

As I explained in the last chapter, every sport has an agreed code of fair play, a set of conventions that governs the players' behaviour. These don't always line up with the formal rules – sometimes the players' conventions license rule contraventions, and sometimes they prohibit actions that don't break the rules. The conventions are a set of expectations the players bring to the game and that define their sense of sportsmanship. When youngsters are introduced to a sport, they are taught how to behave, which tricks are acceptable and which not, and in time they will teach these traditions to the next generation.

Our puzzle was: how can one and the same action – claiming a catch you know you haven't made – be morally shameful in cricket but acceptable in baseball? In response, I have drawn attention to the difference between morality and convention, and observed that different sports have different conventions about acceptable behaviour.

You might be wondering whether this takes us any closer to a solution. True, we can now see that the cricketer who falsely claims a catch is departing from the conventions of the sport in a way that his baseball counterpart isn't. Still, the issue wasn't just that the cricketer was being unconventional, but that he was being *immoral*. Yet deviating from social conventions is by no means always a moral transgression. Somebody who holds their knife in the wrong hand, or who addresses a duke as 'my lord' rather than 'your grace', may be committing an embarrassing faux pas, but it would be silly to condemn them as morally inferior simply because of their social incompetence.

Not all conventions, however, are as morally insignificant as rules about holding knives and addressing dukes. In other cases, conventions substantially alter the moral landscape. Conventions are not themselves the same as moral principles, as Turiel's work makes clear. But, even so, the particular conventions adopted by a social group often make a difference to what morality requires of its members.

The most obvious examples involve physical coordination. Take driving on the left rather than the right once more. In itself this certainly isn't a moral issue. There's nothing morally amiss with countries that do it differently. But if you are in a country where everybody else is driving on the left, it would be downright immoral, and not just eccentric, to insist on driving on the right. The point is that we have an absolute moral duty, applicable across all societies, not to endanger the lives of others recklessly, and this imposes a moral requirement on us to conform to the local highway code, whatever that might be.

The same logic applies to codes of manners. It is a matter of arbitrary convention that shaking hands is the normal manner of greeting in England, while bowing is expected in Japan. But at the same time, it is a universal moral rule that we should respect our fellow human beings and not insult them wantonly – from which it follows that we all have a moral obligation to hail our fellow citizens politely, by shaking hands in England, or bowing in Japan, or in general by adopting whatever form of greeting is expected locally.*

* The moral status of manners was the subject of an interaction between unlikely adversaries a couple of decades ago. When the eminent Oxford philosopher Philippa Foot contrasted moral principles with the 'silly rules' of etiquette in her influential paper 'Morality as a System of Hypothetical Imperatives', she aroused the attention of the novelist Judith Martin, probably better known as the author of the widely syndicated 'Miss Manners' etiquette

As well as ensuring road safety and enabling expressions of respect, socially variable conventions also play a role in deciding what counts as an agreement or promise. In America, someone hailing a taxi is implicitly promising to tip the driver above the set fare, but this doesn't apply in Australia. Because of the underlying universal moral principle that you should not renege on your commitments, conventions like these also make a difference to the moral landscape. If you scoot off without tipping the cab driver, you are acting immorally in the States, but not in Australia.

These are the conventions that matter in sporting contexts. Anybody taking part in a cricket match has effectively agreed to abide by the cricketers' code of practice, and in particular not to claim catches they haven't made. So someone who does pretend that they've made a catch, when they haven't, is like someone who enjoys an evening in the bar with friends but then sneaks off when it's their round. They are reneging on an implicit agreement in order to gain an unfair advantage.

That is why the cricketer is immoral where the baseball player is not. The deal made by baseball players when they sign up to a game is different. They aren't counting on each other to self-police catches. Instead, they have agreed to leave

---

advice column. In a long and carefully reasoned article in the *American Scholar*, Martin pointed out that the particular forms of etiquette adopted in different times and places might be arbitrary, but in general they function to uphold the universal and by no means silly requirements of communal harmony and respect for others. In my judgement, Miss Manners had far the better of this argument.

it to the umpires. And so they are not breaking ranks and taking advantage of the others if they try to get away with a phoney 'catch'.

The point generalizes. The various understandings of fair play observed by different sports are like contracts that you enter into when you start a match. This is why players who violate the spirit of the game aren't just choosing to be unconventional. They are transgressing the universal moral principle that you shouldn't gain advantage over others by breaking your promises.

Sports fans are very quick to complain about standards. Their favourite targets are games other than their own and the depravity of the present day. Cricket fans are sniffy about baseball players, rugby fans are shocked by footballers, golf fans look down on tennis players, and all of them agree that contemporary sports performers can't hold a moral candle to those of past generations.

If you ask me, these Jeremiahs are nearly all mistaking conventional differences for moral failings. The different standards upheld by different sports are at first pass just alternative contractual arrangements, different sets of expectations about what the players owe each other. Given these arrangements, the players of any given sport have a moral responsibility to adhere to their agreed code. But it doesn't at all follow that the sports with less restrictive codes are morally inferior.

Of course, sporting codes change over time, just as social rules of etiquette do. There is now more shirt-pulling in soccer than when I was young, cricketing tail-enders are no longer spared the short stuff from the fast bowlers, it is now standard practice to 'ice' the kicker in American football, rugby spectators no longer fall silent for place kicks, and so on. But I see no reason to view these changes as moral deterioration, as opposed to a shift from one set of workable social expectations to another.

To look down on other games just for being different is the sporting equivalent of despising all foreigners for their uncouth ways. The true sports fan will recognize that there are many equally good ways of arranging games – and that there's therefore nothing morally wrong with baseball players claiming catches they haven't made.

Still, having said this, I don't want to insist that all sporting codes are equally admirable. Some sports do end up encouraging genuinely immoral behaviour.

In one of the early group matches in the 2014 soccer World Cup, the Portuguese defender Pepe held off a challenge from Germany's Thomas Müller with an arm that brushed Müller's chin. The latter's reaction was to throw himself to the ground clutching his head. This so infuriated Pepe that he promptly head-butted Müller and got himself sent off.

I was watching (in a bar in Paris, after a philosophy workshop) and I was shocked. Not by Pepe's head-butt – that was just dumb, and not particularly surprising from a player well known for his volatility. Rather it was Müller's play-acting that dismayed me. Germans don't fake injuries to get other players into trouble. It was like seeing Mary Poppins steal a purse.

This got me thinking. Why wasn't this just another case of one set of conventions replacing another? Historically, professional soccer players didn't use to play-act to engineer penalties for the opposition. But it has increasingly become common practice. So why was I so shocked? Why didn't I view this as just another change in sporting customs? Müller was simply behaving in a way that had become normal among his fellow professionals. He would arguably have been a fool not to. Given that everybody else was using this trick, he would have been letting down his side by not doing so too.

But on reflection I realized I didn't see it like that. I admired the Germans for holding to the old ways, and was distressed precisely because I was observing a falling-off in standards. It is morally better if footballers don't lie to gain an advantage over their opponents. I felt it was a pity if the Germans had joined those teams that did this.*

The comparison with social conventions is again instructive. As a general rule of thumb, it is not a bad idea to observe existing social customs. However, the principle 'when in Rome, do as the Romans do' only takes us so far. Not all social mores are harmless variations of protocol.

Many traditions demean women, others reinforce prejudice and some are downright abhorrent. Female foot-binding in China, racial segregation in the American south and the subjugation of Jews were all once regarded as acceptable,

---

* Incidentally, it is a matter of some dispute in my household whether Müller really was faking, as opposed to reacting instinctively to a genuinely painful blow. I would be pleased to learn that he wasn't, but I remain unconvinced. In any case, it doesn't matter to my substantive point, which is that it *would* represent a moral falling-off if Müller *were* faking. (You can judge for yourself: https://www.youtube.com/watch?v=P6nf4hdSwMg.)

indeed essential, components of historical societies. With codes like these, it is more honourable to breach than observe them. We can be thankful that they are all now regarded as occasions for shame rather than pride.

Some sporting codes are similarly reprehensible. They invite athletes to behave in ways that are morally indefensible. I have already discussed how some soccer players feign head injuries hoping to get opponents sent off. It is not hard to think of other clear-cut examples.

The rugby culture of punching opponents tends to spill over into biting, eye-gouging and even sticking your finger up your opponent's bottom (though it should be said that this last practice is frowned upon even by front-row forwards). Until recently competitive road cyclists fed themselves a battery of performance-enhancing drugs, and this self-abuse was compounded by the corrosive hypocrisy of repeated public denials.

I would say that these practices are the sporting equivalent of Chinese foot-binding. They take us beyond local customs and into the realm of objective immorality. Even if the sporting communities in question condone them, this doesn't make them all right.

Are there any general rules specifying when sporting codes overstep the limits of acceptability and become objectively immoral? As it happens, it is surprisingly difficult to draw any principled boundary between valid sporting conventions and morally repugnant practices.

A first thought might be that a code is bad to the extent that it authorizes violations of the rules. Isn't that just cheating, and so automatically contemptible? As we have seen, however, this doesn't hold up at all. It is often perfectly proper to break a sporting rule and take the penalty. I have already mentioned the example of basketball players fouling in the last seconds to stop the clock and give themselves a chance to win. Nobody thinks of this ploy as immoral sharp practice. It's a perfectly normal move in the game.

Stopping the clock in basketball is by no means an isolated case. There are plenty of other examples of morally acceptable rule-breaking. In soccer, a forward will happily risk an offside penalty in the hope of catching the defence napping. In rugby, it is illegal to hang on to the ball when you are on the ground after a tackle, but you'll be letting your side down if you don't do this to prevent an imminent try. Snooker players are penalized four points if they 'miss' – that is, end up playing a foul shot to avoid leaving their opponent an easy pot – yet it often makes sense for them to do this many times in succession. Penalties for these technical infractions are simply part of the game, like paying rent when you land on someone's square in Monopoly.

All right, but what about codes that actively encourage players to deceive the officials? Surely that at least is beyond the moral pale. Openly taking one for the team in full view of the referee still preserves a kind of honesty. But trying to get away with an infraction without being detected looks like a paradigm of immoral behaviour.

Yet this doesn't work either. In baseball, young catchers are taught to 'frame the pitch' – to choreograph their catching movements in such a way as to make it seem as if they took the ball in the strike zone. The aim is precisely to deceive the home-plate umpire into calling balls as strikes. Far from being regarded as a dirty underhand trick, this skill is widely admired throughout the game.

Buster Posey of the San Francisco Giants is regarded as a supreme practitioner of this art. As Major League Baseball's own website explains, Posey's 'ability to frame pitches ... requires a catcher to employ deft hands, remain limber physically and exercise sound judgment. A successfully framed delivery typically travels on the fringes of the strike zone. It's the catcher's duty to receive the ball in a way that erases any doubt the pitch is a strike.'

Cricket offers a similar example of benign deception. Batsmen who have feathered a catch to the wicketkeeper will often feign insouciance in the hope of persuading the umpire that they didn't touch the ball. In first-class cricket, or even serious league cricket, this is perfectly proper, even required on behalf of the team.

Cricket fans sometime argue that the modern practice of leaving it to the umpire represents a moral falling-off from the time when batsmen 'walked' without waiting for the umpire's decision if they knew they'd touched the ball. But it is something of a myth that there ever was such a time. In serious games with proper umpires, batsmen have nearly always waited for the umpire's decision. (True, a decade ago the great Australian wicketkeeper-batsman Adam Gilchrist was an egregiously quixotic walker. But this was by no means popular with his teammates, many of whom felt that Gilchrist was fostering his image at the expense of the team.)

If there ever was a tradition of walking, it was restricted to a few English gentlemen-amateurs who affected this theatrical means of showing their social superiority for a couple of decades after the Second World War. And even then, they weren't always consistent. Colin Cowdrey, the last in the great line of English amateur captains, had a reputation for walking for obvious decisions, but not for the harder ones, in the hope that his reputation as a walker would influence the umpire in his favour.

Perhaps we shouldn't be surprised that there are no simple rules that tell us when sporting practices overstep the boundaries of morality. According to an influential school in contemporary moral theory, this is just a special case of a difficulty that arises with all moral judgements.

The defining feature of the moral doctrine known as 'particularism' is its distrust of general moral principles. Particularists maintain that there are always exceptions to rules like 'thou shalt not kill', or 'always tell the truth', or even 'do unto others as you would have them do unto you'. In their view, real life is far too messy for any such all-purpose prescriptions.

As particularists see it, difficult choices involve genuine moral complexity. You can't always satisfy the demands of both kindness and honesty, friends and family, non-violence and justice. No set of mechanical principles can tell you how to balance these issues across the board. Instead, in any concrete situation, you must rely on your moral intuition to tell you the right thing to do.

I am not myself convinced that there are no general principles to be found in the moral realm. Still, there's no doubt that sporting practices provide a good case for particularists. There really doesn't seem to be any mechanical formula for morally grading codes of accepted sporting behaviour. The relations between the scoring systems, the rules and the officials are too complex and varied to allow any easy generalizations. In the end, perhaps all we can do is appeal to our inbuilt ethical sense to tell us when sporting customs have moved beyond local practices and become downright immoral.

In most cases, the divergent customs of different sports are simply alternative conventions, akin to the divergent customs observed in different societies. If you think that there's something morally wrong about baseball players claiming catches they haven't made, then you are just making a mistake. But in other cases all should recognize that sporting customs cross the moral line. Even if most football players faked injuries, or most cyclists surreptitiously took drugs, that wouldn't morally legitimate these practices.

The distinction may be difficult to analyse, but it is one worth drawing. It is only by marking the difference between legitimate conventions and corrupt practices that we can hope to keep the latter out of sport.

CHAPTER 6

CADS OF THE MOST UNSCRUPULOUS KIDNEY

'Kokkinakis banged your girlfriend. Sorry to tell you that, mate.' Thus spoke the Australian tennis player Nick Kyrgios to his opponent Stan Wawrinka during a Masters match in Montreal in 2015. Kyrgios was referring to his Davis Cup teammate Thanasi Kokkinakis, who had partnered Wawrinka's girlfriend, the young Croatian star Donna Vekić, in the mixed doubles in the Australian Open the year before. Kyrgios was one set down at the time, but after this remark Wawrinka not surprisingly lost concentration, dropped the second set, and then retired with a 'back problem' at 0–4 in the third.

Is it always unacceptable for athletes to try to unsettle their opponents mentally? Not necessarily. Conduct like Kyrgios's clearly breaks the boundaries of the tolerable. It would be bad behaviour in a bar, let alone on a tennis court. The Association of Tennis Professionals had no hesitation in slapping him with a $10,000 fine.

But other ways of trying to disconcert your opponents are part of normal sport. You don't need to be Kyrgios to take a toilet break when your tennis adversary is running away with a series of points, or to give your golf opponent time to think about missing a putt.

The 1947 US Open went to an eighteen-hole play-off between golfers Sam Snead and Lew Worsham. On the final hole, with their scores level, Worsham had a two-footer left for par. Snead missed his birdie putt from 15 feet and left himself a marginally longer one. By this stage of his career, Snead was known to be yippish on the short putts. He was about to play when Worsham called for a tape measure to check that Snead was really further away and so due to putt next.

By the time it had been confirmed that it was indeed his turn, Snead was flustered. He pushed his tiddler to the right, leaving Worsham to hole out for the championship. It wasn't exactly generous of Worsham. Still, all he did was create time for his opponent's mental frailty to manifest itself.

Another of my favourite examples is cricketer Mark Ramprakash's second-innings dismissal in the third Ashes test in 2001. He'd been batting steadily and had reached 26, when for no apparent reason he charged down the wicket to Shane Warne and was stumped by miles.

The cricket writers were not sympathetic. As Jack Bannister saw it, 'The red mist descended and he charged down the pitch . . . his attempted slog . . . would have been unacceptable in village cricket.' David Gower was perplexed: 'Nobody but Ramps can imagine what was going through his mind when he decided to play that shot at such a crucial time.'

In fact, we later found out exactly what was going through Ramprakash's mind. Apparently, Shane Warne had been goading him for some overs. 'Come on Ramps, you know you want to.' Warne was a great psychologist as well as a great spinner, and he knew his man. Once he had inserted the tempting vision of a lofted drive into Ramprakash's thoughts, the batsman's commitment to a steady test innings was soon undone.

You might think that ploys like this have no place in sport, and that healthy competition should be based on generosity and openness, rather than psychological trickery. But this strikes me as unrealistically idealistic. Manoeuvres designed to gain a mental edge have always played a central part in top-level sport, and always will.

As we saw in Part I, competitive sport is as much a trial of mental powers as physical ones. Success demands that you maintain focus on your game plan, often for sustained periods of time, and do not allow yourself to succumb to performance-undermining distractions. Given this, any serious competitor will look for ways to nudge the opposition out of their comfort zone, to make them start thinking about things they shouldn't be thinking about. If you can befuddle your opponent, the match is half won.

You might worry that sporting codes that license mind games will inevitably degenerate into outright nastiness. Once the needling starts, what is to stop it escalating to personal attacks like Kyrgios's, or worse? But that isn't how it seems to work.

For a start, there are the players' own understandings of where the limits lie. As the last two chapters showed, each sport has its own sense of fair play, and this restricts the moves that most players are prepared to make. Someone who makes a habit of Kyrgios-like personal taunts will soon be ostracized by his peers, and few athletes are happy to pay this price.

Still, this is only part of the story. Conventions evolve, in sport as elsewhere, not least under the internal pressure of players pushing the boundaries to gain an extra advantage. By their nature, unwritten codes of fair play are flexible and open-ended, and leave ample room for enterprising athletes to interpret them in new ways.

In the course of this chapter we shall look at a number of ways in which athletes have sought to steal a march by doing things differently. Innovative mind games are not the only way of stretching the limits of conventional practice. Athletes are also constantly searching for new physical techniques, new tactics, new interpretations of the rules – anything that will give them an extra edge.

Sometimes these innovations threaten to cross the last chapter's division between acceptable conventions and object-ively immoral behaviour. When the sporting authorities judge that this line has been crossed, they will normally aim to stamp out the corruption. However, sports administrators are less than infallible in their assessment of novelty. As a species, they tend towards conservatism, and are prone to regard any change as moral degeneration. Sporting bodies are at best a crude arbiter of the distinction between benign custom and immoral practice.

Mental mind games pose a particular challenge to the authorities. It is not easy to police what competitors murmur as they explore new ways of unsettling their opponents.

Fortunately, a number of moderating mechanisms keep innovative psychological ploys under control.

One is the threat of retaliation. A player who oversteps the line will be marked down as fair game for future abuse. This applies especially in high-level professional leagues, where the players are likely to meet each other many times in the future, and perhaps even be traded to the same team.

The impact of needling remarks – 'trash talk' in America and 'sledging' elsewhere – is also typically moderated by humour. 'Why are you so fat, Eddo?' an Australian fast bowler asked the Zimbabwean Eddo Brandes, frustrated at his failure to dismiss the plump tail-ender. 'Because every time I screw your wife she gives me a biscuit,' replied Brandes.

In the end, the most important brake on bad behaviour is probably the need to keep your own mind on an even keel. Players who get caught up in slanging matches will disconcert themselves as well as their opponents. Losing your temper is the enemy of concentration. Many top athletes find it easier to lock themselves into their own world, and not to worry too much about what their opponents are thinking.

The word 'gamesmanship' has negative connotations nowadays. But it wasn't always so. The term was coined by the British humourist Stephen Potter in his runaway 1947 bestseller *The Theory and Practice of Gamesmanship*. The book was subtitled *The Art of Winning Games without Actually Cheating* and describes a range of ploys designed to put your opponent on the mental back foot.

Potter's account of his first introduction to gamesmanship is worth quoting at some length:

In those days I used to play lawn tennis for a small but progressive London College – Birkbeck, where I lectured. It happened that my partner at that time was C. Joad, the celebrated gamesman, who in his own sphere is known as a metaphysician and educationist ...

In one match we found ourselves opposite a couple of particularly tall and athletic young men from University College. We will call them Smith and Brown ... fifteen-love ... thirty-love ... Now Smith was serving again to Joad – who this time, as the ball came straight towards him, was able, by grasping the racket firmly with both hands, to receive the ball on the strings, whereupon the ball shot back to the other side and volleyed into the stop-netting near the ground behind Brown's feet.

Now here comes the moment on which not only this match, but so much of the future of British sport was to turn ... Joad called across the net, in an even tone: 'Kindly say clearly, please, whether the ball was in or out.'

Crude to our ears, perhaps. A Stone-Age implement. But beautifully accurate gamesmanship for 1931 ... These two young men were both in the highest degree charming, well-mannered young men, perfect in their sportsmanship and behaviour. Smith stopped dead.

SMITH: I'm so sorry – I thought it was out. (*The ball had hit the back netting twelve feet behind him before touching the ground.*) But what did you think, Brown?
BROWN: I thought it was out – but do let's have it again.

JOAD: No, I don't want to have it again. I only want you to say clearly, if you will, whether the ball is in or out.

There is nothing more putting off to young university players than a slight suggestion that their etiquette or sportsmanship is in question. How well we know this fact, yet how often we forget to make use of it. Smith sent a double fault to me, and another double fault to Joad. He did not get in another ace service till halfway through the third set of a match which incidentally we won.

Most of the gambits proposed by Potter are similarly innocuous. For example, he suggests standing in the line of your opponent's putt at golf, but then jumping out of the way with profuse apologies just as your opponent is about to ask you to move. As Potter explains, this is particularly effective when reiterated through the course of a round. ('A simple but good gambit. And remember, to make it effective, repeat it again and again and again.')

Another trick is to make your opponents feel as if they have taken unfair advantage. It is hard for them to press hard if you quietly let slip that your old injury is playing up. In a similar vein, I find that it is normally worth at least a point or two to insist on giving the opposition any close line calls in tennis.

On the Sunday morning in the 2015 Solheim Cup between the European and US professional women golfers, the final fourball match, carried over from Saturday, had Suzann Pettersen and Charley Hull all square with two holes to play against the Americans Brittany Lincicome and Alison Lee. On the seventeenth Lee missed her birdie putt and it ran eighteen inches past the hole. Under the impression that her opponents had given her this short tap-in, she picked it up for the half, and started off for the eighteenth tee, together with her partner and Hull.

Pettersen stood fast, however, and insisted that the putt had not been conceded, leaving the match referee no choice but to award the hole to Europe. The Americans were aghast, and Pettersen was asked whether she wanted to reconsider, to no avail. When the last hole was halved, that put Europe 10–6 up and needing only four points from the remaining twelve singles matches to retain the cup.

I was watching and promptly went online and made a bet on the USA to win at 4–1 against. It was a big deficit for them to make up, but I knew the Europeans would be in mental disarray. They wouldn't be able to maintain their intensity, knowing that they had gained a point by sharp practice.

As Mel Reid, one of the European team, explained afterwards: 'It was difficult because we were in a lose–lose situation then. If we'd have won the cup we'd have had bad press and if we lose it we've still got bad press.' In the event, the European team collapsed and lost the cup by a point.

This particular wound was self-inflicted. It was Pettersen who was responsible for the Europeans gaining an undeserved point. But the story illustrates Potter's idea. If you can arrange for your opponents to feel that they have gained an unfair advantage, they will be hard put to keep trying.

Incidentally, the 'C. Joad' whom Potter credits with the origin of gamesmanship was a small, spiky philosopher, who, apart from being Head of the Department of Philosophy at Birkbeck College London (where I later lectured for a year), became a national celebrity during and after the Second World War for his appearances on the radio panel show *The Brains Trust*, where he invariably began his contributions with the words 'It all depends what you mean by . . .'

He came to a sad end, though, impaled by his own sharpness. In 1948 he was caught travelling by train from London to Exeter without having troubled himself to buy a ticket. His fame meant public humiliation and dismissal by the British Broadcasting Corporation. He died a couple of years later.

As I said, the term 'gamesmanship' has acquired a negative connotation since Potter introduced it. But I think that this does Potter a disservice. He may have had his tongue in his cheek, but in my view his book liberated a generation of athletes from outmoded attitudes. I like to think of Potter as exposing a body of secret lore that had previously only been available to a privileged few.

Potter was writing soon after the sweeping 1945 general election victory of the Labour Party had marked the end of aristocratic domination of British life. The novelist Kingsley Amis and the poet Philip Larkin, both from lower middle-class backgrounds, were leaving Oxford and embarking on their mission of 'stamping their taste on the age', as Larkin later put it. Amis's anti-hero Jim Dixon in *Lucky Jim* (1954) was unrelenting in his crusade against upper-class phoneys and phoniness, not unlike his transatlantic counterpart Holden Caulfield in *The Catcher in the Rye*.

I don't think it's too fanciful to view Potter's *The Theory and Practice of Gamesmanship* as part of this movement. Potter too was from an emphatically middle-class background (as indeed was his friend Joad). The whole thrust of Potter's book was to puncture the myth of the gentleman-amateur who owed his sporting victories to nothing except his effortless superiority.

The ideal peddled to schoolboys at the time was of sportsmen who tried hard but were never less than fair. Playing the game honourably was more important than the result. As Potter himself portrayed the character, he was the kind of chap who purported not to 'care a damn whether he wins or loses, as long as he has a good match'.

Perhaps C. B. Fry (1872–1956) was the most perfect example of the species. Educated at Repton and Oxford, he played cricket and soccer for England and equalled the world record for the long jump. A successful writer and diplomat, he was offered the throne of Albania when the country found itself in need of a new king during the interwar years.

Fry ceded to no one in his advocacy of the gentleman's code. When the penalty rule was adopted by soccer in the 1890s, he professed to be outraged at the suggestion that footballers might deliberately cheat. In his view, 'It is a standing insult to sportsmen to have to play under a rule which assumes that players intend to trip, hack and push their opponents, and behave like cads of the most unscrupulous kidney.'

But somehow, despite their insistence that results didn't matter, the gentlemen-amateurs always seemed to win. Fry played for the Corinthians, a soccer club founded towards the end of the nineteenth century to uphold amateurism. They refused to play in the normal professional competitions, but on occasion they played charity matches against the winners. They beat the 1884 FA Cup champions Blackburn Rovers 8–1, and in 1903 they defeated the winners Bury 6–0. The following year they thrashed Manchester United 11–3 – still United's biggest defeat.

The Corinthians must have been a formidable side to achieve these victories. But I bet that their air of patrician unconcern gave them an added advantage – not just because of the extra confidence that comes with class superiority, but because their professed attitudes would inevitably have dulled their opponents' competitiveness. It's not easy to exert yourself against a side that says they are only playing for fun. (When I returned to England in the late 1960s after ten years as a teenager in South Africa, I didn't realize that all those languid public schoolboys were really trying their hardest, both on and off the sports field. It took me a while to learn to watch out for people who say that results don't matter.)

Edward Charles Bambridge ('Charlie Bam') was one of the Corinthians' greatest players, scoring eleven goals in his eighteen games for England. There's a well-known story about an important match that he was in danger of missing because of a broken leg. On the day, he arrived in a dog-cart, with a shin pad ostentatiously strapped outside his stockings on one leg, and played through to the end, scoring the winning goal.

As the story is normally told, Bambridge put the pad on his good leg, in order to direct his opponents' attention away from his injury. But, even apart from that, the whole story strikes me as something straight out of Stephen Potter. Imagine the other side's reactions, on seeing their star opponent turn up hobbled and apparently unable even to walk to the pitch. They would have been hard put to stop themselves relaxing, at least a little bit.

In any event, we have Potter to thank for bringing these issues into the open. None of us need have the sporting wool pulled over our eyes any more. By giving us the concept of gamesmanship, Potter has improved our understanding of the psychological side of sport. Nowadays, all serious competitors know that they need to be on guard against mental trickery, and have their own defences ready.

Getting inside your opponents' heads isn't the only way of 'winning games without actually cheating'. Athletes are constantly looking for new ways of getting ahead of the opposition. They stretch the limits of technique and explore the boundaries of the rules. Sometimes this leads them to ways of playing that simply weren't envisaged by their predecessors. They find unconventional ploys that expand the range of skills and tactics demanded by the game.

The natural conservatism of the sporting authorities tends to resist such novelties. If you ask me, any such innovations should be evaluated on their merits. I am certainly not against those who want to preserve the character and traditions of their sport. As I shall argue later, sports are defined by their history. Without a past of famous contests and iconic figures to celebrate, they would be little more than idle pastimes. Still, we can respect tradition without resisting change in any form. All institutions must evolve, and there is plenty of room to allow sporting novelty without rejecting the past. New ways of playing will often add to the attractions of a game, building on the old traditions to create something yet better. In some cases, the sports administrators are sensible enough to recognize this. But as often their traditionalism makes them dig in their heels, and mistake healthy innovation for a degeneration of standards.

In 2008 Kevin Pietersen introduced the 'switch-hit' to cricket, turning himself into a left-hander in mid-delivery to slog-sweep the ball over the cover boundary. This put some pressure on the existing rules, as they take account of which stance the batsman adopts. In this case, to their credit, the Marylebone Cricket Club took the view that the novelty only added to the excitement of cricket, and declared it legitimate.

In a similar spirit, the athletics authorities raised no difficulties when Dick Fosbury started 'flopping' over the high-jump bar in the 1960s. As it happens, it wouldn't have been crazy for them to decide against Fosbury. High-jump rules have always been pretty arbitrary. For example, two-footed take-offs, tumbler-style, have never been allowed, even though they would probably add a couple of feet to the world record. Still, I think the rule-makers were right about the flop. There was something very pedestrian about the 'scissors', 'straddles' and 'Western rolls' that preceded Fosbury.

Golf is probably the most conservative of all sports. In 2016, it outlawed 'belly putting', in which a long putter is anchored against the player's stomach or chest. I never saw the problem. If belly putting suits some players, then why not? You might as well outlaw unusual grips, or marked pauses at the top of the backswing, just because they're different.

The joint statement by the US Golf Association and the Royal and Ancient Club of St Andrews justifying their new rule was revealing. In a document of some thirty-two pages, they nowhere raised the issue of whether golf would be a *better* game if belly putting were allowed. Their objection was solely that it would be different. As they saw it, the trouble with belly putting was that it did not preserve 'the essence of the traditional method of golf stroke'. I suppose it's not surprising to find the golf authorities winning the prize for mindless conservatism. They'd probably prefer a world without electricity too.

And then there are the guardians of gridiron football. In the 2015 play-offs, the New England Patriots found a way of using the NFL's complex regulations about pass-receiving 'eligibility' to so bemuse the Baltimore Ravens defence that Tom Brady was able to complete a 16-yard pass to a wide-open tight end, and then to repeat the gambit a few plays later. The NFL owners' response was to promptly change the rules. No doubt they were fearful that ingenuity might become a permanent feature of football.

There is one particular species of gamesmanship that sometimes gets people very worked up. In many multi-stage tournaments, a group competition is followed by a knockout stage, with the match-ups in the knockout determined by positions in the groups. (The winner of group A plays the runner-up in group B, and so on.) If the organizers aren't careful, this can create opportunities for clever competitors to manoeuvre themselves an easy path through the tournament by being economical with their talents.

In the 2012 Olympics, the women's badminton doubles featured a groups-followed-by-knockout format for the first time. The trouble started when one of the top Chinese pairs failed to win their group. This meant that the top two teams in the adjacent group, already assured of progress to the knockout stage, both had an incentive to lose their final group match and so sidestep the strong Chinese pair in the next round.

Just the same situation arose in the other half of the draw. The upshot was that spectators at the Wembley Arena for the final group games were treated to two 'looking-glass' matches, in which both sides tried their hardest to lose. The players repeatedly served out of court, put the shuttlecock in the net, or missed it completely, prompting jeers and boos from the crowd.

The organizers' response was to disqualify all four pairs, for 'not using their best efforts to win a match' and 'conducting themselves in a manner that is clearly abusive or detrimental to the sport' – with the result that the gold eventually went to the Chinese pair that had initially failed to top their group (a placing that in retrospect itself came to look suspect).

Most commentators sided with the organizers, lamenting a deterioration of standards, shameful manipulation, letting down the Olympic spirit, and so forth. I had the opposite reaction. I thought it was outrageous that the players should have their Olympic hopes shattered, just for doing their best to win the tournament. What did the organizers expect, if they didn't have the gumption to organize a competition properly? The hazards of group–knockout competitions are well-known. If anybody betrayed the Olympic spirit, it was the incompetent badminton authorities, not the players.

The 'disgrace of Dijon' was a 1982 football World Cup match between West Germany and Austria. Algeria had upset West Germany in the group's opening match, which meant that Algeria would go through at West Germany's expense if the latter failed to beat Austria, and at Austria's expense if West Germany won by more than two goals. The only result that would eliminate Algeria was a one- or two-goal win for West Germany.

In the event, West Germany scored inside ten minutes, after which both sides played out an implicit agreement not to threaten the other's progress to the next round, each taking turns to pass the ball around in their own half. It was a miserable spectacle, but only to be expected. Neither side had any incentive to risk elimination by contesting the match. The Algerians at least kept their dignity. In the words of their full-back Chaâbane Merzekane, 'To see two big powers debasing themselves in order to eliminate us was a tribute to Algeria. They progressed with dishonour, we went out with our heads held high.'

Soccer has learned its lesson. In subsequent World Cups, the last two matches in each group have always been played simultaneously, which pretty much eliminates the possibility of a team deliberately engineering a sub-optimal result in order to improve its knockout chances. The UEFA Champions League adds an extra safeguard to thwart this kind of game-playing, leaving it to a partly random draw to decide who plays whom after the group stages.

It is hard to believe that the Olympic badminton organizers weren't aware of the dangers of their ill-designed format. What did they expect the players to do? Fight tooth and nail to ensure that they would be knocked out in the next round? Perhaps the organizers were counting on the players to be better actors and disguise their determination to lose. If you ask me, the public should be grateful that the incompetence of the authorities was so clearly exposed. They're the ones who should have been banned, not the players.*

Not all glitches in tournament design, however, are foreseeable. In the 1994 soccer Caribbean Cup, the organizers decided that all matches should have a winner: if the scores were tied after ninety minutes, the games would go to a 'sudden-death' extra time, to be decided by the first goal, which would count double for goal-difference purposes if necessary.

In the final game of their qualifying group, Barbados needed to beat Grenada by two goals to top them on goal difference and advance to the finals in Trinidad. At first everything went well for Barbados. They scored the two goals they needed, and kept Grenada at bay for most of the second half.

Then in the eighty-third minute Grenada got one back. Barbados desperately tried to restore their two-goal lead. But,

---

* In a partial admission of guilt, the Badminton World Federation changed the rule for the 2016 Olympics, adopting a version of the UEFA system in which a partly random draw determines the knockout matches.

as the clock ticked down, some of their players realized there was another way. If Grenada were only to score again, then that would mean 2–2, extra time, and Barbados would then have unlimited time to score the deciding goal, which would then count double and give them their needed goal difference.

So, with three minutes to go, the Barbados defenders calmly passed the ball into their own goal to tie up the scores. At which point both sides needed to think quickly. Another goal *for* Grenada would make them clear winners, but another goal *against* them would also leave Barbados without the two-goal lead they needed. This meant Grenada would go through with a goal at *either* end. So, for the last three minutes of normal time, the spectators watched Grenada scrambling to put the ball in either goal, with Barbados staunchly defending at both ends. (Barbados succeeded in denying Grenada, and then scored the 'golden goal' they needed in extra time.)

I bet that there were some mean-spirited pundits at the time who felt that the two sides had betrayed the spirit of the game, 'not using their best efforts to win a match', and should both have been disqualified. I couldn't disagree more. I would have loved to have been there. I'm always interested when athletes find new ways of winning without actually cheating.

We need to recognize that gamesmanship, in all its forms, is an integral part of competitive sport. All serious athletes are constantly striving to avoid defeat and ensure victory. If they can find some new angle to help them, they would be perverse not to go for it. An athlete who ignores an open avenue to victory is an athlete who is not competing seriously.

Of course, there are plenty who hide their competitiveness behind a veil of affability, in the style of the old Corinthians. But this can itself be just another form of gamesmanship, as Stephen Potter so helpfully demonstrated. The most dangerous competitors are those who lull you into a false sense of ease.

Sometimes innovations threaten to degrade the game. They can shift tactics in a destructive direction or stretch the conventions of fair play into the realm of immorality. In cases like these, it is right for the authorities to impose sanctions. But, as often, novel ways of playing enrich the game. Unthinking resistance to change can impede progress in sport, as elsewhere.

PART III

TEAMS

CHAPTER 7

THE LOGIC OF FANDOM

A while ago I signed up to teach at the City University of New York for a semester each year. When I announced this new appointment on Facebook, I added that it probably meant I'd become a Yankees fan.

This prompted an animated email from my philosophical acquaintance Alva Noë:

> There is something you need to know. All decent, true, right-thinking, generous, progressive, beautiful people from New York are Mets fans. We repudiate the Yankees and everything they stand for. I can understand how, from afar, this might not be clear. But the Yankees are to New York as the Republican Party is to America – Loud, Rich, All-Too-Victorious, and Very Very Bad.
>
> As a fellow philosopher, as a born-and-bred New Yorker, I invite you, I urge you, I implore you, do not turn toward the New York Dark Side up there in the Bronx, but open yourself to the Light in Queens, the hapless, loveable, New York Mets. Supporting the Mets, following the Mets, will enrich your life, and heart, and soul.

Well, I thanked Alva for the information, and expressed sympathy with his sentiments. But his email didn't do the trick. Not that I disbelieved what he said. But it didn't turn me into a Mets fan, or even rule out becoming a Yankees one.

This set me wondering. What makes someone a fan, beyond appreciating the objective merits of a team? On reflection, the answer is obvious enough. Fans are partisan. They attach more importance to the success of their team than is warranted by their real virtues – or lack thereof, if Alva is right about the Yankees.

Put this way, you might wonder whether supporting a team is fully rational. How can fans sensibly suppose that it is important for their side to win, even when there is no objective basis for their favouritism? Sometimes, fans pray for their team's victory. What can they be thinking? Why should an all-wise God, who presumably dispenses reward in proportion to desert, attach any weight to their partisan enthusiasms?

This is a question about value and the perception of value. Arsenal fans attach great value to their team beating Spurs, while the Spurs fans see it just the other way around. It looks as if at least one faction has lost touch with reality, or at least with any reality that might carry any weight with God.

Is there really a problem here? Don't the two sets of supporters simply have different sets of desires, just as I desire chocolate ice cream while you desire strawberry? And doesn't that in turn show why their appeals to God make sense after all? Won't God agree that it is objectively good, other things being equal, that human desires be satisfied? The different fans are simply reminding God that satisfying their respective wishes will add to the stock of human good.

Plausible as it is, this account of fandom does not hold water. It's just not true that satisfying desires is always a good thing. Imagine a woman who finds herself with a strange compulsion to eat a plate of mud. When asked about this, she can't explain how it would benefit her. It's not going to taste nice, she won't feel good after eating it, she's not going to win a bet, there's nothing uncomfortable about leaving the urge unsatisfied. It's just that somehow she feels pulled towards the mud. In this case, the mere fact that the woman desires the mud doesn't make it good that she gets it. The world will be just as good a place if she doesn't. Even from her own point of view, there is nothing at all worthwhile in the outcome.

In fact, there are real-life cases that aren't far off this. Consider people with an eighty-a-day cigarette habit. As soon as they have finished one fag, they have a yen for another. But they may well know that they won't enjoy it at all when they get it (it will turn to ashes in their mouth). They themselves can see that they will get nothing valuable from the next smoke. They are just compelled to have it.

These examples show that explaining value in terms of desire-satisfaction has things back to front. A healthy person will desire what they take to be valuable, not take it to be valuable because they desire it. If you do find yourself desiring something that you don't take to be valuable, as with the plate-of-mud woman or the cigarette addict, then you can see that you are in a bit of a mess. We want our desires to aim at what's independently worthwhile, not to be floating in thin air.

That's how it is with the Arsenal and Spurs supporters. They don't think that they are in a mess. They think that what they desire is really worthwhile, namely the Gunners thrashing Spurs, or vice versa, as the case may be. And when they pray to God, they aren't just petitioning for a general increase in the level of human desire satisfaction – for after all that could be achieved just as well by satisfying their opponents' desires – but to foster what is objectively important, their own side winning, and their unworthy opponents losing.

But this now looks close to incoherent again. How can a grown-up person seriously think that it is objectively valuable that their side win, when the opposing fans have just as good a claim?

Still, before we condemn fandom to the dustbin of irrationality, it's worth noting that this kind of partisanship runs deep through human life. I am devoted to the welfare of my two wonderful children, but I am not so blind as to think that in the greater scheme of things they are more deserving than everybody else's offspring. I am ready to do things for my friends that I wouldn't dream of doing for equally worthy strangers. I am delighted when my philosophy departments trounce others in the rankings tables, for no other reason than that I am in them. And so on.

Still, even if partisanship is rife, there remains something puzzling about it. If everyone's children are equally valuable, then how can it be right to think that your own are more important? More generally, how can certain outcomes be valuable from some perspectives, but not from others? Many philosophers are deeply suspicious of such 'agent-relative values'. They feel that they are inconsistent with the idea that healthy desires ought to aim at what is objectively worthwhile, not just at partisan fancies.

Some theorists argue that the only way out of this tangle is to stop thinking about *outcomes* and start thinking about *duties*. In philosophy, it is normal to distinguish between 'teleological' and 'deontological' theories of moral correctness. Where teleological theories assess actions in terms of *outcomes*, deontological theories focus on *rules*, on what's required and what's allowed.

The difference between the two theories is not always obvious, but there are cases that bring it out. Imagine that you see an advertisement for a job supervising slaves in some foreign country. You can't do anything to stop the country practising slavery. You are unemployed and need a job to support your family. If you don't take it, there are plenty of others who will, most of whom will undoubtedly treat the slaves much worse that you would.

As far as outcomes go, this looks like a no-brainer. Your family's poverty is alleviated, and the slaves are better off. Where's the bad bit? Go for it, say the teleologists.

But deontologists will hold that complicity in slavery is always wrong, whatever the consequences. Even if the world would be a better place overall, it still wouldn't be right for you to take the job. The wrongness of supervising slaves isn't washed out by the benefits. Deontologists think that there are basic principles about right and wrong actions, quite independently of whether they lead to good results. The end does not always justify the means.

Whatever you think about this general issue, deontology certainly seems to have an advantage over teleology when it comes to partisanship. The reason I should care about my children more than yours, say the deontologists, is not that this leads to better net outcomes all round – after all, my children are no more important than yours – but simply that we all have a duty to look after *our own* children.

More generally, once you start thinking in terms of *right* rather than *good*, say the deontologists, the problem of partisanship simply goes away. Of course, humans owe special duties to their nearest and dearest, just because they are near and dear, and not because they are otherwise special.

Well, this may work fine for children, and friends, and maybe even for university departments. But it seems to fall down for sports fans. Duty doesn't seem to come into it. Not even the most enthusiastic deontologist would say that Arsenal fans have a *duty* to support their team. Even if you grew up in an Arsenal household, you just might not find football interesting. Or your enthusiasm for your team might fade away. We look askance at parents who neglect their children, or at people who drop their friends, but there seems nothing wrong with losing interest in a football team.

Fandom can only be understood in terms of outcomes, not duties. So it only makes sense if we acknowledge the legitimacy of agent-relative values, recognizing that some outcomes can be genuinely valuable from one perspective but not others. Supporting a team isn't a matter of duty, but of viewing importance through partisan spectacles. A Gunners victory is valuable from the standpoint of the Arsenal supporter, but not of course from the Spurs angle. To appreciate the logic of fandom, we have to accept that the worth of some things is irreducibly parochial.

If fandom were an isolated case, then perhaps the right conclusion would be that it really doesn't make sense to be a sports fan. But in truth there are many other personal values that similarly can't be explained in terms of duties. I value, in ways you might not, the environment in the Dengie peninsula of Essex, the music of New Orleans and the Mississippi Delta, the niceties of English grammar, the fate of the European Ryder Cup team, and so on. It's not that I think everybody has a duty to foster and appreciate these things. But for me they are part of what makes life worthwhile.

I would say that such things are valuable for me because they form part of my identity. I have taken them on, made them part of my life's projects. This involves more than just desiring them. As we saw earlier, you can desire something without viewing it as in any way valuable. But here I do regard these things as valuable. I have signed up to the mission.

We humans give meaning to our lives by adopting projects and working to achieve them. We care about our villages, schools, reputations, careers, houses, gardens and hobbies. Some of these are individual commitments, while others are collective. But what they have in common is that they create agent-relative values. Once you have embraced a project, it comes to have a special importance for you, but not for those who lack it, in a way it didn't before. So it is with supporting a team. Once you become a fan, the success of the team becomes one of your projects.

Does it have to be such a big deal? How much of a project is it to check your team's scores on the Sunday sports pages? But it is not hard to discern ambitions and plans in ordinary fandom. Once you support a team, you take on a kind of responsibility for its welfare.

For a couple of years my son Louis and I had tickets at the Emirates. I am no Arsenal supporter (I remember 'boring Arsenal' from the 1970s), but Louis and his friends very much are. In the pub before the game, the conversation went like this. 'How do you think we'll do today?' 'I hope we're not playing Chamakh.' 'Yeah, we badly need another striker.' My silence was awkward, but I couldn't bring myself to say 'we'. Once I tried to join in and started by saying, 'Arsenal will . . .' The whole pub turned to look at me.

Louis and his friends are typical sports fans. They aspire to shape the destiny of their teams. They think about strategy and team selection, and they do what they can to make their views known. They debate with other fans, contribute to websites and phone-ins, and scream encouragement and advice during games – even if they are only watching on television. They may have no real influence, of course, but that doesn't stop them feeling involved.

Can't you root for a team or player even if you haven't adopted them as a project? Certainly. You can want them to win because they deserve to, not because you follow them. I had no axe to grind when Muhammad Ali recaptured his stolen title in the jungle, or when Usain Bolt joyfully ran away from the field in the 2008 Olympics 100 metres. I was delighted simply because excellence had prevailed. Any right-thinking person would have felt the same.

I am not saying that it is terribly difficult to start supporting a team. It's just that it demands more than an impartial approval of the team's merits. You need to sign up. You need to add a new commitment to the other projects that define you. I'm not sure that there is any logic to how we acquire the projects that add extra value to our lives. Many of them come with growing up. Later in life we may lose old ones and find new ones. It depends on what interests and attracts us, on where and how we live, on whom we hang out with.

The contingency of sporting affiliations is illustrated by a story I was told by a friend, the psychologist Tony Marcel: 'My cousin and I were at my mother's bedside when she was in a seemingly terminal coma shortly before her death. We fell to discussing when we had become Arsenal supporters. I remembered a photo of me at about three in an Arsenal strip, and wondered if it was a present from a family member. Suddenly, without opening her eyes, my mother said, "No, your uncle's friend Peter gave it to you to spite us. We were all Spurs supporters." Apart from amazement at my mother's capacity, this has caused a continuing identity crisis for me.'

Some of our sporting attachments may be haphazardly acquired, like Tony's, but this doesn't stop them from adding meaning to our lives. Along with other agent-relative values, they are products of the projects and commitments we use to define ourselves. Without affiliations of these kinds, the world would be a thinner place. We would be constrained by the duties we share with other moral agents, but we would have no basis for the particular enthusiasms that animate us. Agent-relative values add a kaleidoscope of varying passions to the black-and-white uniformity of duty.

Postscript

When I arrived in New York in the spring of 2015, I tried out both the Yankees and the Mets.

Alva was right. Yankee Stadium was a big disappointment. I'd been to watch the Yankees before – back in 1975, when I'd seen Catfish Hunter pitching and the late Thurman Munson catching (I still have a Yankees T-shirt with Munson's retired number 15) – and I'd had a great time. But that was a different era.

The new modern stadium, opened in 2009, was just as Alva said – noisy, brash and all-round unpleasant. We were drowned in a flood of raucous music, sponsors' jingles and novelty events. I'd gone with a friend, but conversation was impossible. The only time the cacophony stopped was during actual play – which was the one time we wanted to watch, not talk.

The Mets's Citi Field Stadium was better. There were still big screens and sponsors' promotions, but it was much quieter, suburban, almost rural. I liked it a lot, and quickly warmed to the hapless Mets, riding out to Citi Field whenever I could.

Except that year they weren't hapless at all. They went from strength to strength as the season unfolded, and their roster of young pitchers took them all the way to the World Series, brushing aside the Dodgers and the Cubs in the play-offs.

But it wasn't to be. The Kansas City Royals, steeled by their experience as losing finalists the year before, hustled the Mets out of it. I was back in England by then, but I watched every game on television.

The final game of the World Series summed it up. The Mets were up 2–0 going into the top of the ninth, but then Eric Hosmer drove in a Royals run with a double, and then advanced to third with one out. The next man up hit a weak ground ball to third baseman David Wright. Now, in this situation, as we saw in Chapter 2, you must first pause moment-arily to hold the runner on third before you throw to first. And Wright did exactly that. But Hosmer must not have read the manual, or maybe he just fancied his chances, for as soon as Wright let it go he took off for home, and tied up the score when Lucas Duda's throw to the plate from first went a few feet wide.

So it goes. That was pretty much it. The Royals took the World Series when they ran up five runs in the twelfth inning. I was gutted. Still, it was fun while it lasted. There'll be more seasons. I'm glad I'm a Mets fan.

CHAPTER 8

SPORTING TEAMS, SPACETIME WORMS & ISRAELI SOCCER

For many years, I played for a travelling cricket team called the Old Talbotians. Every weekend during the summer months we matched ourselves against village sides, or teams from London newspapers like the *Times* or the *Guardian*, or simply against other sides like ourselves. There was no league, but matches were intensely competitive, and the Old Talbotians were considered one of the tougher fixtures on the circuit.

Our name sounds as if we were an old boys' side from some minor public school. But in fact it was a joke. The team had originally been started by the journalists at *Now!* magazine, the short-lived attempt at a British version of *Time* founded by the financier James Goldsmith in 1979. For some reason, long since forgotten, the satirical magazine *Private Eye*, which was constantly at loggerheads with Goldsmith, always referred to his magazine as *Talbot!*

Now! magazine folded within two years. But the cricket team was more successful, and so the journalists kept it going, defiantly incorporating *Private Eye*'s slight into their club name. Over time, however, the links with *Now!* faded. When I first joined the team around 1989, there were still a few players left who had worked on the magazine. But age takes its toll, in cricket as elsewhere, and by the time I gracefully retired, some fifteen years later, all the old *Now!* hands had gone.

Were we still the same team that the journalists had founded a quarter-century earlier? We still had the same name, but that was about it. The team had been replenished by friends of friends, younger acquaintances whose only qualification was that they knew what to do with a bat or ball. They included lawyers, salesmen, actors and a baker. Scarcely any of them had ever heard of *Now!* magazine.

Team identity may seem a funny thing to worry about, but it is an issue that matters a great deal to sports enthusiasts. Players and fans form intense attachments to particular teams, and they maintain these attachments over time. They bask in past glories, look forward to future successes, engage in long-standing rivalries, and remember injustices from decades ago.

Still, do such continued attachments make any sense? Sports teams change significantly over time, as did my Old Talbotians. Often this involves more than just turnover of personnel. Teams can move location – the Los Angeles Dodgers were once the much-loved boys of Brooklyn. They can divide into two – Hapoel Katamon Jerusalem and Hapoel Jerusalem, both in the second tier of Israeli soccer, are fierce rivals who have claimed the same ancestry since they split a decade ago. And teams can even merge – when I lived in Sydney, I was a fan of the proud Balmain Tigers, one of the founders of the Australian Rugby League, but in 1999 they were sadly amalgamated with Western Suburbs to form 'Wests Tigers'.

How much change can a team tolerate and still remain itself? Philosophers have long asked this kind of question about other entities. The ancient Greeks started it when they asked if Theseus's ship would remain the same ship even if all its planks had been replaced over years of repairs.

This might seem an easy one. Isn't it obvious that it would still be the same ship? You don't destroy a ship just by replacing planks. But what if some smart Athenian had hung on to the discarded planks, tidied them up, and put them together again to make another ship? Wouldn't that have a better claim to be Theseus's original ship? After all, it wouldn't just look the same, but be made of exactly the same planks. Still, if this reassembled ship is the original ship, then the one with the replacement planks can't also be Theseus's ship – two different ships can't both be the same ship.

Philosophers ask similar questions about people. If I suffer an advanced case of Alzheimer's disease, and my memories and character fade away, am I still there? Again, a first reaction might be that of course I am, even though in a sadly depleted state. But what if some future technology allows my memories and dispositions to be copied into some specially created healthy body before they fade away? Wouldn't this imprinted being have as a good a claim to be David Papineau instead? Still, as before, both answers can't be right. The depleted body and the imprinted one can't both be me, since they're clearly two different people.

Even though philosophers have been asking such questions for centuries, it can't be said that they have agreed on any answers. In the case just raised, for example, some experts take the depleted body to be David Papineau, some the imprinted one, some say that both the depleted and imprinted being were present in embryonic form in the young David Papineau's body, some say that the original David Papineau ceases to exist once the two candidate successors come into being, some say that ... well, take my word for it, the list of options is long and exotic.

Part of the trouble here is that many philosophers try to resolve these issues by appealing to intuitions rather than analysis. They check their theories against our gut reactions to ingenious hypothetical cases. What would we say if the *Star Trek* beam-me-upper malfunctioned, and sent a Captain Kirk up to the *Enterprise* without eliminating the Captain Kirk on the planet below? What would we say if my brain was split in two and transplanted into two different host bodies? And so on.

People differ in their reactions to these scenarios, however, and even a single person's reactions are not guaranteed to be consistent. It is scarcely surprising, then, that the method of intuition leaves us undecided between a range of incompatible theories. Instead of appealing to intuitions, we will do better to step back, and ask about the underlying purpose of distinguishing parts of reality as *persisting objects*, like stones, trees, cats, ships and people – or indeed sporting teams.

A good way to focus this issue is to compare persisting objects with *events*, like battles, storms, lectures, political demonstrations or football matches. In some ways, persisting objects and events are similar. At any time, both occupy a limited region of space, and this region can move about as time progresses. The demonstration starts in Hyde Park and makes its way to Trafalgar Square; similarly, I have breakfast at home and then go to my office.

For the mathematically minded, both events and persisting objects can be represented as 'spacetime worms' in a space-time coordinate system: the cross-section of the worm at any time T represents the spatial extent of the event or object at T, and the succession of cross-sections at different times shows how the event or object moves through space over time.

The 'worm' of a demonstration. One end is at Hyde Park and 1 p.m., and the other at Trafalgar Square and 3 p.m. (Katy Papineau)

Still, despite these similarities, we think of events and objects very differently. We think of events as being made up of *stages*. A football match has a first half and a second half, and if you've only seen the first half, you haven't seen the whole match yet. But this doesn't apply to objects. We don't feel, just because your audience with the Pope only lasted a few minutes, that you didn't meet the whole Pope, but only a small part of him.

As philosophers put it, persisting objects are *wholly present* at any time when they exist. With events, by contrast, only a stage, or *temporal part* occurs at any given time. The whole event is the sum of those temporal parts, from the beginning of the event to its end.

Think of the 'spacetime worms'. A temporal cross-section of a political demonstration's 'worm' doesn't represent the whole demonstration – it's just a freeze-frame representing one moment-ary stage in the demonstration. But a temporal cross-section of a persisting object's 'worm' represents the whole object. At the risk of confusing things, imagine a *spacetime* worm of an *earth*worm moving across a garden from a tree to a flowerbed. This portrays a succession of earthworms at different points in time, not a succes-sion of earthworm stages, whatever those would look like.

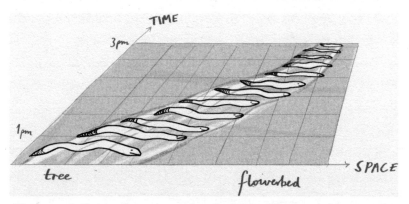

The 'worm' of an earthworm crossing the garden. This 'worm' (but not the earthworm) stretches from the tree and 1 p.m. to the flowerbed and 3 p.m.
(Katy Papineau)

Some philosophers think that these differences between persisting objects and events involve deep metaphysical facts about being and time. I think that's making a meal of it. At bottom, both objects and events simply fill up volumes of spacetime. The difference lies solely in their different internal structures.

What makes objects different from events is their stability. My facial features don't alter much from day to day, nor my bodily shape, nor my gender, nor the languages I speak, nor the way I walk. The same goes for artefacts and inanimate objects. My fishing boat doesn't alter significantly between outings, apart from its capricious motor, and the north London hill I can see from my study is positively moribund.

Events are different. They are in constant flux. You can't read off the later properties of an event from its earlier properties, as you can with objects. The battle may start with the cavalry and infantry in formation, but it will swirl around and lose combatants as it progresses. The storm may begin gently, but gather pace and leave destruction in its course.

This difference means that there is no *point* in breaking persisting objects into temporal parts, as we do with events. Because of their stability, we would gain no advantage in thinking of objects as having event-like temporal stages. There would be no variations for this temporal differentiation to track. Imagine. Here's the Monday David Papineau, and the Tuesday one, and so on – but they are all pretty much the same.

So, in my view, we distinguish parts of reality as persisting objects precisely because we can reliably read off their later properties from their earlier ones. Of course, this doesn't work for all properties. I might wear a blue shirt on Tuesday even though I wore a white one on Monday, and you shouldn't assume I will be sober tomorrow just because I was sober today. But, still, it works fine for facial features, gender, languages spoken, gait and a wealth of other properties, even if not for shirt colour and sobriety. And in general, for any kind of persisting objects, there will be a wide range of properties that they maintain over time.

So what about sports teams? Do they display enough stability over time to be taken seriously as persisting objects? I don't see why not. They typically wear the same kit from game to game, select their sides from the same pool of players, play to a given standard, host home matches at the same ground, belong to a given league, and so on. Once you have played a team once, you will know an awful lot about what to expect the next time.

With professional clubs, there is even more stable information you will glean from an initial encounter. You learn about the stadium, manager, assistant coaches, nicknames, favoured tactics, type of fans, chants, and many other such items. You don't have to check these things every time you watch the team. You can work on the assumption that they will stay the same from one match to the next.

Of course, some of these things will change in the long run. Players move on, managers get sacked, new kits are designed. But that's not the point. The idea that persisting objects are distinguished by the stability of their properties doesn't require that these properties never change, only that they normally remain the same from one encounter to the next. People grow taller and fatter, their features coarsen, they learn and forget languages. But we generally work on the assumption that such changes can be ignored in the short to medium term.

So I say that the Old Talbotians I left in 2005 were the same team that the *Now!* journalists had founded a quarter-century earlier. If you met them one season, they would be roughly the same the next: mostly the same players, of roughly the same strength, with the same opening bowlers and star batsmen, the same laggard who always arrives late, the same fixture list, playing the same teams on the same grounds, the same level of sociability after the game, etc.

Over time, these features gradually altered, with the result that the team at the end differed significantly from its original incarnation. But, precisely because these changes were gradual, you could still rely on this season's Old Talbotians being more or less the same as the side you played last year.

What if a team's features change suddenly? Then things are different. In the decade after the Second World War, the Brooklyn Dodgers were one of the greatest sides in baseball history. They reached the World Series in 1947, 1949, 1952 and 1953, only to be beaten each time by the Yankees of Joe DiMaggio, Mickey Mantle and Yogi Berra. 'Wait 'til next year,' Brooklyn parents would tell their kids. In 1955 next year finally came, and the Dodgers beat the 'Bronx Bombers' in a 4–3 Series to take the title. Even I, with my limited knowledge of baseball, can name the iconic figures: Pee Wee Reese, Roy Campanella, Duke Snider, Jackie Robinson.

Then in 1957 the owner of the Dodgers, Walter O'Malley, moved the team to Los Angeles to make more money. He has never been forgiven. My older Brooklyn friends put him right up there with Hitler and Stalin.

At first, some of the Brooklyn-based fans remained loyal to the players O'Malley took with him. But once those players had moved on, there was little to connect the Californian side with the original. Different stadium, different fans, only half the name. Nowadays, the Los Angeles Dodgers organization still lays claim to the pre-move history, but scarcely anybody else regards them as the same side. The traumatic changes wrought by O'Malley cut the thread of historical continuity.

It's rather the same when teams merge. At a stroke, everything is changed. When my Balmain Tigers were amalgamated with Wests, we suddenly had a bunch of new players, a strip that we didn't recognize, and a new stadium out in Campbelltown for half our home games. A lot of the dispossessed fans supported the new club, for want of anything better, and it has achieved some success, winning the Premiership in 2005, but it's only a shadow of what we had before.

The Old Talbotians eventually met a similar fate. Towards the end of my career we started struggling for players, and so, a year or two after I stood down, we joined forces and fixture lists with a similarly challenged side, Gustavus Adolphus (don't ask). We original Talbotians are still included in the emails from the new composite, now known as the G & Ts, and we follow the fortunes of our surviving ex-teammates with interest. But we don't identify. When we have our annual reunion, in Ye Olde Cock Tavern in Fleet Street, it is strictly Old Talbotians only.

When teams divide, this can also obliterate the original club, but in a different way. Splitting doesn't necessarily involve any sudden imposition of alien features from outside, and both offshoots can be largely continuous with the original. Still, the mere fact of plurality can be enough to cut links with the joint origin.

Israeli football mirrors many features of the larger society. The teams are all identifiably either Jewish or Arab, though most feature players from both groups. The most prominent Arab team is Bnei Sakhnin ('sons of Sakhnin'), currently in the premier division, and based in the northern town of Sakhnin (where, incidentally, I gave a talk in 2014 on the mind–body problem and al-Kindi's 'flying man argument' to the town's outstanding specialist science school).

Bnei Sakhnin's bitter rivals are Beitar Jerusalem, distinguished by their rabid supporters and long-standing policy of never signing Arab players. When Beitar recruited two Muslim footballers from Chechnya in 2013, many fans viewed this as a betrayal of the club's motto 'pure forever', and weren't satisfied by the manager's revealing clarification that 'there is a difference between a European Muslim and an Arab Muslim'. Unsurprisingly, matches between Sakhnin and Beitar often erupt into violence, both on and off the pitch.

Beitar doesn't have a monopoly on Jerusalem soccer, thank goodness. For many years Hapoel Jerusalem were the other professional side in the holy city. 'Hapoel' means 'the worker', and the many sports clubs in Israel with this cognomen originated in the labour movement that flourished before independence. For most of the last century Hapoel were serious rivals to Beitar, but from the 1990s they started sliding down the leagues under the ownership of a pair of fractious businessmen.

In 2007 a section of the fans lost patience and founded a breakaway side, with the joint aims of restoring their collect-ivist ideals and offering real opposition to the noxious Beitar. They've suffered various ups and downs since then, but they are now back with the other Hapoel Jerusalem in Liga Leumit, the second tier of Israeli soccer, under the name Hapoel Katamon Jerusalem (Katamon is the area of Jerusalem where Hapoel originated).*

So, which is the real Hapoel? Both sides can mount a strong case. Hapoel Jerusalem has the more direct line of descent, but Hapoel Katamon claims greater affinity with the club's original vision. Moreover, a significant number of pre-split players have ended up with Katamon, not to mention the preponderance of the fans.

If the two sides have equally good claims, this means that neither can be the original club, which must therefore have ceased to exist. After all, when they play each other in the league this season, it will be a proper match between two different teams, not a club playing itself.

The funny thing is that the disappearance of the original club depends entirely on the duplication of successors, rather

---

* English readers will appreciate the parallels with the way breakaway AFC Wimbledon has risen through the leagues to join their rival parent team MK Dons in the English third tier, League One.

than any discontinuity in inherited features. Suppose that the breakaway club hadn't been founded in 2007, but that Hapoel Jerusalem had developed just as it did in reality, losing some players and shedding some fans in subsequent years. Without the rival side, there wouldn't have been any doubt that this was still the same Hapoel Jerusalem continuing its downward slide.

Or suppose that the owners had formally wound up their Hapoel Jerusalem in 2007, at just the point when the disgruntled fans got organized. Then there would have been no dispute about Katamon's claim to the heritage.

The point is that each club on its own has quite enough continuity with the original to qualify as its continuation. What messes things up is simply the duplication.

This phenomenon isn't peculiar to sporting teams. If the beam-me-upper simply fails to operate, and leaves Captain Kirk on the planet below – well, there he is. And, if it works normally, he's on the *Enterprise*. What causes a problem, though, is when the teleporter duplicates Kirks, for then both have an equal claim to be him. It's the same with ships. The repaired ship and the reassembled ship would each unquestionably be Theseus's ship, if only the other weren't there to contest its claim.

I said earlier that our rationale for discerning persisting objects is that we can read off their later properties from their earlier ones. But we now see that there is more to it than that. We also want to keep distinct objects distinct. From the perspective of anticipating later properties, we might as well lump the two Hapoels together, along with the two Kirks and the two ships. Their common ancestries would provide a perfectly good guide to their many shared features.

Lumping them together, however, would generate any number of tangles in our dealings with the duplicates. Which team gets relegated, when one finishes bottom of the league? Who apologizes, when a Captain Kirk loses his temper? Who pays the bills, when a ship damages its cargo?

Questions like these show why we need to distinguish objects even when they share a common origin and so many of their properties. Despite the similarities between such twins, we still need to keep track of which is which, lest we end up holding one responsible for deeds performed by the other. In effect, the need to keep track of different individuals pulls against the desire to anticipate properties. In the face of duplicates, we have to sacrifice the presumption of stable properties in order to keep count of who did what.

So it is just as well that things don't split often. If they did, we would need to disavow continuities in order to keep distinct offshoots separate, and would lose our ability to read later properties straight off from earlier ones. We should be thankful that duplicate people are largely restricted to science fiction, duplicate ships to philosophical imagination, and duplicate teams to the strange world of Israeli soccer.

Precisely because persisting objects don't normally split up, we can count on them to provide stable reference points for our interactions with reality. We learn about the distinguishing features of different persisting objects when we first meet them, and trust those self-same objects to continue to display those features in future encounters.

It is these continuities that make the world manageable for us. Life would be impossible if we couldn't count on our friends to look the same when we next see them, and our boats to have the same fittings next time we take them out. And, by the same coin, sports fans and players would quickly become confused if their sides didn't remain recognizable from one match to the next. Team sports, just like the rest of life, depend crucially on entities that retain a stable identity over time.

CHAPTER 9

MUTUALISM AND THE ART OF ROAD CYCLE RACING

I came rather late to road cycle racing. Generally, I am not fussy in my sporting interests. Tennis, soccer, rugby, cricket, baseball, golf, basketball, American football, sailing, squash, Australian rugby league . . . the list is long. But I drew the line at cycling. It looked like a tedious trial of strength, and I attributed its fanatical support in Europe to a Latin predilection for machismo over sporting subtlety.

But I couldn't have been more wrong. It was the 2012 Olympics that woke me from my dogmatic slumbers. There was a great deal of interest in the road cycling in Britain because for once the men's team had a real chance of gold. Bradley Wiggins had just become the first Briton to win the Tour de France, and the team also contained legendary sprinter Mark Cavendish and future Tour de France winner Chris Froome.

But in the event, the men's team flopped. I didn't manage to watch the race, but the newspapers afterwards said that the British failed to win gold because the Australians and Germans didn't help us enough – which somehow seemed simultaneously puzzling and unsurprising.

Still, all the brouhaha had piqued my interest, and the next day I caught the second half of the women's road race. As it unwound I became transfixed. With about 40 of the 140 kilometres left to go, a group of four women from different countries broke away from the pack, and promptly proceeded to operate as a team, taking turns at the front to shield the others from the wind.

At first this made no sense to me. I knew that wind resistance is a crucial factor in cycling, and that road racing involves teams who share the load of pushing through it, going to the front in turn in order to let the ones behind 'draft' and conserve their energy. But I was watching four women with no common interest working together. An Englishwoman, a Dutchwoman, an American and a Russian. More like the beginning of a joke than a natural collective. What were they doing collaborating?

But they clearly were, so with the help of the commentators and some cycling friends I started to figure it out. The rationale for breakaways in a road race is to stop the sprinters like Mark Cavendish winning. If the whole pack – the 'peloton' – arrives at the finish in a bunch, then some squat figure with thighs like an elephant will shoot through and grab the gold.

So the taller, more wiry cyclists need to leave the sprinters behind. Plan A for most teams is to shepherd their pet sprinters around the course and release them at the end. But if your sprinter starts lagging, or if you don't have a good one to start with, then plan B is for the wiry types to strike out and leave the sprinters behind.

That's what I was watching. Four skinny ones who were unlikely to win in a mass finish but who had a good chance of a medal if they could keep ahead of the pack. So for the moment they were working together. On their own they would quickly get exhausted, so to stay ahead of the peloton they were taking turns. Each helped the others for a while, shielding them from the wind while they got their breath back.

Philosophers, along with economists and biologists, spend a lot of time worrying about cooperative behaviour. Standard assumptions about economic rationality and biological evolution imply that humans are natural competitors, not collaborators. Still, there on the television was direct proof that even sporting rivals will sometimes work together.

It occurred to me that the cyclists might have something to teach the theorists. It turned out I couldn't have been more right. The deeper I went into the tactics of road cycle racing, the more lessons I discovered for the logic of rational action. As we shall see in the course of this chapter and the next, cycle racing provides an unparalleled resource for anybody who wants to understand the interplay of individual and collective motives in human life.

Let us start with the traditional 'puzzle of altruism'. Why do people, and many animals, do things that benefit others more than themselves? Why do they pay their share, wait their turn, and generally do their bit? This can seem illogical: if everybody else is going to be public-spirited, I'll be better off quietly stealing a march; and if the others aren't going to be public-spirited, I'll be wasting my time being nice. So, either way, what's in it for me to be unselfish? ('But suppose every-one felt that way,' Yossarian is asked in Joseph Heller's *Catch 22*. 'Then,' said Yossarian, 'I'd certainly be a damned fool to feel any other way, wouldn't I?')

This puzzle about altruism is often illustrated by 'the pris-oner's dilemma'. Imagine Alan and Bill have been picked up by the police after a burglary. The cops aren't sure they have the right men, so they put them in separate cells and offer them both the same deal. 'If you turn state's witness, and the other guy refuses to cooperate, we'll put him away for twenty years, and you can go home right now. But you'd better hope that he doesn't also confess, as then we won't need your evidence, and we'll lock you both up for five years. And in the unlikely event that you both manage to keep quiet, we'll keep grilling you for a year, but then, damn it, we'll have to let you both go.'

We can summarize this with a 'pay-off matrix'. The rows represent Alan's two choices, the columns represent Bill's, and the two numbers in each box signify the years that Alan and Bill will respectively spend in the clink for each pair of choices.

		BILL	
		Confess	Keep Quiet
ALAN	Confess	5, 5	0,20
	Keep Quiet	20,0	1,1

It's a nasty set-up. If Alan is looking after number one, he'll reason as follows: 'Perhaps Bill will confess. If so, I'd better confess too, as I don't want to be the mug who gets twenty years while he gets off scot free. On the other hand, maybe he won't confess. But then it will also suit me to confess, as I can avoid a year's unpleasantness and go straight home to my ever-loving family.' Either way Alan's self-interest argues for confessing. And if Bill is like Alan, he will reason just the same. So, two selfish burglars will both confess – with the result that they will get five years each, when they could have both gone home after one year, if only they had kept their mouths shut.

This is why theorists are puzzled by public-spirited behaviour. Even in cases where everyone can see that it would be best to pull together, the logic of rational choice pushes us apart. There seems no reason not to 'free ride' without a ticket and leaving it to others to pay the fares that will keep the trains running. But then everybody does the same, and the train company goes out of business, and we are all worse off.

In real life, of course, there are normally extra constraints to stop this from happening. The ticket inspector enforces the rule that passengers must have a ticket, and fines anyone caught without one. Alternatively, enough travellers have 'internalized' the norm about tickets, and simply feel that it would be morally wrong not to pay. (When C. E. M. Joad, the national celebrity and inventor of 'gamesmanship' from Chapter 6, was found without a ticket on the London–Exeter train, the public reaction wasn't just that he was a fool for being caught. Far worse, in most people's eyes, he was also exposed as a moral knave for cheating the railway company.)

Still, in many cases there must be a simpler explanation for cooperation than the pressure of official or moral sanctions.

Think of the Olympic cyclists. They're not subject to any norms requiring them to support a joint enterprise. If anything, it's the opposite. They're supposed to be competing, not collaborating.

A crucial factor here is the small number of cyclists. Here's a comparable case. Suppose that there are half a dozen of us in our office. Our planned Christmas outing needs at least four to chip in, otherwise it's off. Contributions are made privately, to spare the less well-off embarrassment. I know I'll enjoy it a lot, and I can afford it, so I cough up. Nothing puzzling there. But note that my behaviour is already a kind of altruism, in that I alone bear the cost of my contribution, but all will share the benefit of the outing if it now goes ahead.

The key factor in my decision is that my contribution might easily tip the balance. In a big office with hundreds of people, there's no real chance that my failing to pay up will kibosh the outing, and so no economic motive for me to chip in. But when the numbers are smaller, it is all too likely that my money will matter.

Small-scale cooperation like this is common. People pick up litter in their own street, they organize stalls at the school fair, they take their turn driving for the car pool. The familiar economists' question is – why do they exert themselves in this way, if they can see that their contribution will be pointless? But in small-scale cases like these, the question is often misplaced. When it comes to street litter, school fairs, car pools and office outings, their individual contribution may be far from pointless, but the crucial difference between success and failure.

And this was just the kind of set-up I was watching in the women's road race. Each rider had an interest in doing her time at the front, even though this hurt her and helped the others, because, if she didn't, it would kibosh the whole break-away. It takes a lot out of you doing a spell at the front. You use about 50 per cent more energy that those you are pulling along. If a slacker left it to the other three in the group to take turns, then those doing the work would tire more quickly, the breakaway would lose momentum, and the bunch behind would reel them all in.

A better model for small-scale cooperation is the 'stag hunt', not the prisoner's dilemma. Here Alan and Bill are hunters, not burglars, and their choices are whether to hunt a stag (worth five days of food each) or a rabbit (just one day's food). There are plenty of stags around, but catching them is a two-man job, while a single man can always bag a cottontail. So, if Alan leaves home with his stag-catching gear, but Bill opts for a sure rabbit, then Alan will end up empty-handed.

		BILL	
		Stag	Rabbit
ALAN	Stag	5,5	0,1
	Rabbit	1,0	1,1

Now the reasoning comes out differently. It's no longer true that Alan is better off chasing a rabbit, *whatever* Bill does. True, it will suit him to chase a rabbit if Bill chases one, as hunting for a stag on his own will ensure he ends up empty-handed. But, on the other hand, if Bill does leave home ready to hunt a stag, then it will be very much in Alan's interests to do likewise. So, provided that Alan thinks there's a reasonable chance of Bill setting out to hunt for stag, it will be rational for him to follow suit. And since Bill can figure things out similarly, they're likely both to end up happily feasting on venison.

Note how opting to hunt stag means that Alan is putting himself out, foregoing his sure rabbit, and making a choice that benefits Bill as much as himself. The same applies when I go out of my way to pick up litter in my street, or organize a school fair stall, or contribute to the staff outing. I make an effort, and others benefit. Still, the reason I'm so helping the others is clear enough. I too will suffer, if my non-cooperation means a rabbit rather than a stag, or an ugly streetscape, or a dud fair, or no outing.

You might wonder whether these cases should count as real altruism. After all, everybody involved is serving their own interests. While they may be benefiting their colleagues even more, they aren't going so far as to choose an option that positively work against their own welfare.

Theorists distinguish between 'weak' and 'strong' altruism. Weak altruism is when your colleagues also reap the benefits of a choice that benefits you. What is good for you is also good for the group. Strong altruism is when your choices positively leave you worse off.

To avoid confusion, I shall use the term 'mutualism' for weak altruism from now on. Weak altruists are like a mutual benefit society. They pull together because it is in their individual interests to do so. The cyclists and the stag hunters aren't being strongly altruistic. While their contributions help the others, they also help themselves. By chipping in you make it more likely that the breakaway will succeed, or that a stag will be caught, things that are very much in your personal interests.

With strong altruism, by contrast, there is no personal pay-off. I help a little old lady across the road. I give money to Oxfam. These actions help the old lady and developing countries, but bring me no obvious gain.

Mutualism may be enough for stag hunts, but we need strong altruism to get out of the prisoner's dilemma. Enlightened self-interest can do the trick in stag hunts, precisely because each hunter's self-interest is best served if they both cooperate. But in the prisoner's dilemma, each prisoner's self-interest is best served by non-cooperation, *whatever* the other does.

Because of this, the prisoner's dilemma is only solvable if Alan and Bill are good enough friends to care about what happens to the other, even if it costs them something themselves. If they are both prepared to forego immediate release, because that would cost their mate twenty years inside, they should manage to end up with only a year in jail each. And, more generally, strong altruism will lead people to support social enterprises even when it would be cheaper for them not to.

Some cynical people doubt whether anybody is ever altruistic. (We can drop the 'strong' now, since we're using 'mutualism' for the weak version.) In the end, the cynics insist, everybody is looking out for number one. Aren't our actions inevitably guided by our own desires? So doesn't it follow that our choices will inevitably be designed to further our own interests?

No. While altruism does face serious challenges, it can't be ruled out that quickly. Of course, everybody's actions are triggered by their own desires, rather than anybody's else's. That's not the issue. The interesting question is what their desires are *aimed* at. Most people will no doubt have some desires for their own health and welfare. But that's consistent with also desiring good things for others. Nothing in logic rules out desires that are aimed at benefiting other people. And a desire that is so aimed at someone else's benefit, without any associated pay-off for the agent, will be a genuinely altruistic desire all right.

Still, even if altruism can't be ruled out by logic, perhaps it is ruled out by psychology. Am I really sure that I am motivated by the welfare of the little old lady, or the starving millions in Africa? Perhaps my real aim is to win approval for myself, or maybe to enjoy the warm glow I experience when I see how I have benefited others.

But this cynical scepticism about altruism is hard to maintain. What about the terminally ill mother who makes arrangements for her children after she is dead? Or the soldier who throws himself on a hand grenade to save his comrades? They can scarcely be aiming for the warm satisfaction of seeing others benefit, given that they won't be around to observe the results of their actions.

Perhaps the cynics can appeal to the warm glow that arrives once you know you've done the right thing, even if you never see the pay-off. Still, by this stage the cynicism is starting to look forced. What's wrong with the idea that the mother simply wants to benefit her children, or the soldier his comrades? Why keep seeking some self-serving meaning for what look like straightforwardly altruistic choices?

Well, if the cynics were simply mean-spirited misanthropes, then they probably wouldn't be worth taking seriously. However, they can also bolster their cynicism with a serious theoretical argument. This appeals to biological evolution. Natural selection favours animals that favour themselves. This raises real questions about the idea of evolved beings favouring others at their own expense.

We need to go a bit more slowly here. Natural selection is about genes. So far we have been talking about desires. They're not the same thing. Our desires are influenced by our environments and our culture, as well as by our genes. So, it would be too quick to rule out altruistic desires simply on the grounds that natural selection works against altruistic genes. Perhaps it is our cultural training that induces us to be altruistic, even if our genes don't.

Still, the evolutionary argument can't be dismissed that easily. Our desires aren't completely independent of our genes. Apart from anything else, our tendency to acquire desires from our cultural surroundings is itself a product of natural selection. So, if altruistic feelings were an evolutionary no-no, we might expect our biological nature somehow to veto them.

Some of you might be wondering why natural selection should be supposed to be in tension with altruism in the first place. Doesn't biological evolution favour things that are for the good of the *species*? And won't cooperation among animals help to preserve the species? From this perspective, you'd think that altruism among animals would be the biological norm.

For better or worse, evolution doesn't work like that. When I was a twelve-year-old, I hugely enjoyed the nature film, Disney's *White Wilderness* (1958). In one famous scene, we saw a swathe of Norwegian lemmings purportedly responding to an overpopulation crisis by throwing themselves off an Arctic cliff. According to the sonorous voice-over, this was to ensure that the remaining lemmings would have enough resources to flourish and preserve the species.

Even at a young age, I found this puzzling. (Let's put to one side that they were brown lemmings from Canada, not Norwegian ones, and that they didn't jump, but were pushed by the Disney camera crew.) Suppose that there are two kinds of lemmings, those with an innate urge to jump over cliffs when it gets crowded, and those who hang back and enjoy life once the others have gone. Now, which sort would you expect to predominate after a few population crises? Lemmingkind as a whole might well do better when there are self-sacrificers around, but that doesn't alter the fact that the selfish ones will leave more descendants, simply because their altruistic cousins have so helpfully eliminated themselves from the scene.

The lemmings show why natural selection generally works against altruism. Biological evolution doesn't favour characteristics that are good for the species, but those that help individual animals to have more children than their conspecifics. If you favour others in the species at your own expense, you're simply helping them to get ahead in the breeding competition.

Still, whatever biological theory says, it certainly looks as if there is plenty of altruism in the animal world. Meerkats act as sentinels, literally sticking their necks out to watch for predators; vampire bats share harvested blood with comrades who have come home hungry; worker bees disembowel themselves when they sting intruders to their hive.

Over the past fifty years, evolutionary biologists have pondered this conundrum long and hard. The consensus nowadays is that we shouldn't be too quick to rule out biological altruism. The Disney scriptwriters might have got into a muddle about lemmings. But, under special conditions, it is perfectly possible for altruistic genes to evolve.

The key requirement is that the benefits of altruism should tend to fall on other altruists. Then the upshot of altruistic behaviour will be that other altruists will prosper and have more children, and as a result altruistic genes will spread through the population.

Think of the prisoner's dilemma again. Altruistic pairs of prisoners will do better than selfish pairs, both getting out after a year, rather than festering inside for five. Of course, a selfish prisoner paired with an altruist will do even better, going straight home after ratting on his partner. Still, the fact remains that, if altruists tend to be paired with other altruists, they will spend less time in jail on average than the self-servers. And, by the same coin, altruistic genes will spread faster than selfish ones, provided only that altruists tend to hang out with other altruists.

A number of different circumstances can ensure that altruists cluster together. For a start, most animals live in extended family groups. So, if there are genes that foster altruistic behaviour, they will tend to run in families, with the result that altruists will benefit from the presence of their altruistic kin. But kinship is not essential. Certain kinds of geographical segregation can have the same effect. Or perhaps altruists simply tend to seek each other out. One way or another, there seems plenty of scope for biological altruism to evolve.

In the end biology offers no support to cynical doubts about altruistic motives. Evolution leaves plenty of room for animals that benefit others at their own expense. Once we view human psychology in this light, there's no good reason not to take apparent acts of charity and self-sacrifice at face value.

Road cycle racing is a case in point once more. It arguably offers frequent displays of genuine altruism, in addition to its episodes of self-serving mutualism. Consider the organized teams, as opposed to the temporary alliances within mutually cooperating breakaways. The *domestiques*, as the French bluntly term the lesser team members, slave away shepherding their team leader around the course. Their aim is to increase their leader's chance of a medal, but in doing so they sacrifice any hope of winning prizes themselves. (Curiously, despite the essential role of teams, road cycle races don't normally have any team prizes, only individual ones. The domestiques gain no formal recognition when their leader crosses the line first.)

A cynic might retort that there is nothing noble about the

domestiques. A motley of other motives can explain their subservience, apart from a selfless desire for the team leader to win the gold. For a start, there is money. At the higher levels of road cycling, the working members of the team are paid, and well paid at that. And we can add in such incentives as the desire to enhance your cycling reputation, and perhaps to gain a future chance as a team leader.

But this doesn't explain all the cases. Underneath the Tour de France and the other prestige events lies a huge pyramid of amateur road races. Even at the lowest levels, the cyclists voluntarily form themselves into teams. I quote from the website startbikeracing.com: 'Team riders decide among themselves which has the best chance of winning. The rest of the team will devote itself to promoting its leader's chances, taking turns into the wind for him or her ... and so on.' At the lower levels, there's no money involved, and few competitors are concerned with any kind of cycling career. They really don't seem to be after anything except victory for their leader.

I don't want to go overboard on the cooperative aspects of road cycling. After all, these are *races*. The whole point of the exercise is competition. Who will reach the finish line first? Still, you won't understand cycle racing until you appreciate the complex dance of altruistic, mutualistic and selfish motives that are in play in a road race.

Let's go back to breakaways. As in the 2012 women's Olympic race, the logic of mutual support pushes the riders to share the load equally. But at the same time this cooperation is under constant threat from the individual aspirations of the competitors.

Each rider would prefer to conserve energy in order to maintain an edge over the others as the finish line approaches. So they'll be inclined to hang back a bit and let the others do more work. But they can't be too obvious about this, since the others won't want to pull them along only to be left behind at the end. If they think that's what's going to happen, they'll give the breakaway up as a bad job.

This kind of thinking might seem to imply that a breakaway will only keep rolling if all its members are equally good finishers. After all, why would you put in all that effort if you know that one of the others is sure to beat you in the finale? However, now another level of calculation enters the picture. The stronger finishers will tolerate the weaker ones making less of a contribution to the breakaway. This might level the playing field for the final dash, but the good finishers still need the others' help to keep the breakaway going. So the stronger ones will try to gauge it right, and let the others retain a bit more energy, but not so much as to let them succeed in the final sprint.

The weaker ones will also be making similar calculations. And then there is the question of when to stop cooperating and strike out for the finish. As the line draws nearer, the danger of being overhauled by the peloton diminishes, and the need to conserve energy comes to the fore. It's a complicated game that calls for delicate judgement on all sides.*

---

* For an insider's view of how this all works, I recommend Tim Krabbé's novel *The Rider* – a transfixing narrative entirely devoted to a 140-kilometre amateur race through the mountains of Provence.

Of course, all these fine-grained tactics are premised on the assumption that the breakaway will stay ahead of the peloton, with its complement of squat sprinters itching for a mass finish. In truth, however, successful breakaways are very much the exception rather than the rule. One of the strangest things about cycle racing is that the peloton can nearly always catch a breakaway. According to Chapatte's Law, named after Robert Chapatte, the doyen of French cycling journalists, the peloton needs only 10 kilometres to eat up a lead of one minute.

This might seem puzzling. We're talking about speeds of around 50 kilometres per hour, so Chapatte's Law means that the peloton can go about 10 per cent faster than a breakaway. If I didn't know better, I wouldn't have believed that an unwieldy mass of 100-plus cyclists, packed together on narrow roads, could so easily outrace a well-organized and determined breakaway. The peloton does have the advantage of a large pool from which to draw temporary front-runners, and so spread the energy drain more thinly. But still, why would any member of the peloton choose to tire themselves out at the front, ceding the advantage to those who hang back?

The answer lies with altruism and mutualism once more. The basic reason the peloton can go faster is that the domestiques are ready to sacrifice themselves. If a team has no one in the breakaway up ahead, then it needs to do what it can to reel them in. So some of its members will altruistically devote themselves to bridging the gap, even if they exhaust themselves in the process.

Still, one team normally won't want to do this on its own. There's no point in expending all your domestiques too early, as then you won't have any left to shepherd your sprinter through the rest of the race. A single team won't want to use up more than two or three catching the breakaway. But now mutualism comes to the aid of the party, this time at the team level. A number of the teams in the pack will often have a common interest in catching the breakaway, so they will each sacrifice a few members to the cause, pooling resources to sustain the drive.

This too can be a matter for fine judgement. The teams in the peloton must now make the same calculations as the individuals in a successful breakaway. If one team has an outstanding sprinter, then the weaker teams won't be so keen to tire themselves out; the strongest team will need to tolerate this to some extent, since it needs help in catching the breakaway; and so on. (It was on this tactical reef, as I understand it, that the British Olympic hopes foundered in 2012. Because Mark Cavendish was the stand-out sprinter, there was scarcely any incentive for the Australian and German teams to help Britain, and so the breakaway got away.)

A few years ago, I wouldn't have dreamed that cycle racing was so interesting – and I have only scratched the surface so far. It becomes even more intricate when we note that the division between domestiques and leaders can be vague and fluid, and that riders in multi-stage tour races often need to choose between pursuing various different stage and overall prizes.

With all this in play, it is often hard for riders to know which way to jump when a breakaway is launched. Should they join it, or let it go, or try to sabotage it? When a rider sits at the back of a breakaway, should they tolerate this, or aim to drop the shirker, or abandon the breakaway as a bad job?

Some riders are better at these computations than others. Lance Armstrong was apparently preeminent in this field, but lesser lights are prone to blunder under the pressure of the moment. Nowadays, in the big professional races, the team managers instruct their riders on radios. It strikes me that it would be more fun without them.

In any case, cycling offers an unparalleled resource for students of human cooperation. Mutualism, altruism, allowances for those with lesser resources, choices of when to go it alone – it's all there. Don't be put off by the macho facade. If you want to understand the many ways in which humans manage to work together, you'll do well to become a road cycling fan.

CHAPTER 10

GAME THEORY AND
TEAM REASONING

In the last chapter, I talked about the altruism of road cycling 'domestiques' who sacrifice themselves for their team leader, like worker bees slaving for their queen. The idea was that they are motivated by a desire for their leader to win first prize, rather than by any promise of benefit to themselves.

As we saw, this doesn't necessarily apply at all levels of cycle racing. Professional riders are often well paid for their pains, not to mention their ambitions to rise up the hierarchy of working cyclists. Still, neither of these factors applies at the lower amateur levels. There really doesn't seem to be anything in it for the amateur drudges, apart from their altruistic aspirations for their leader's victory.

Whenever I put this idea to my cycling friends, however, they invariably disagree. Oh no, they say. The domestiques aren't being altruistic. They don't care about their leader. They want their *team* to win, and are simply pursuing this personal desire.

At first, I suspected that my cycling friends were making the old mistake of ruling out altruism from the start, on the spurious grounds that everybody always acts on their own desires. So I explained to them that, while that's of course true, it doesn't decide the more interesting question of what people's desires are *aimed* at. And, I continued, since the domestiques' desires really are aimed at someone else's benefit, namely their leader's victory, rather than any reward for themselves, they should be counted as genuinely altruistic.

But my friends were insistent. No, they assured me, they understood the idea of altruistic desires all right. The trouble was that I didn't understand the motivation of cycling team members. The cyclists don't want their *individual* leader to benefit. They want their *team* to win.

On reflection, I realized that my friends had a point. I was thinking too much like an economist. I was assuming that teams are nothing more than collections of individuals. I had bought into Margaret Thatcher's vision of the world: 'There is no such thing as society. There are individual men and women and families.'

Teams give the lie to this individualistic vision. As we saw a couple of chapters back, they are funny things, which transcend their individual members, whatever Margaret Thatcher and the economists may think. A team can survive the loss of any individual player, indeed the loss of all its players. (Think of those long-suffering Red Sox fans, and all the years they prayed for a World Series win. If they'd been committed to a bunch of individuals rather than a team, they would never have had their prayers answered, since the athletes they originally supported had long moved on.)

So I started thinking harder about the significance of teams for theories of motivation and decision-making. I realized it isn't easy to accommodate them in the way philosophers and economists think about choices. Indeed, the more I thought about the subject, the more it struck me that teams make deep difficulties for conventional theories of decision-making.

The insistence of my cycling friends was just the start of it. They certainly had a good point. Cyclists who care about their *team* are hard to place on the conventional selfish–altruistic spectrum. Precisely because the object of their concern transcends any set of individuals, they don't fit into the normal definitions used by economists.

Behind this issue of defining altruism, however, there also lies a deeper truth. As well as being possible objects of concern for decision-makers, teams can also be decision-makers themselves. This kind of 'team-reasoning' challenges the whole structure of conventional decision theory, not just its definitions. The economists don't like it at all. But the sporting examples make an irresistible case for recognizing teams as agents that can make decisions in their own right.

Let us start with the initial definitional point about 'altruism'. This arises because the Thatcherism implicit in economic theories of decision-making leaves no room for agents to care about anything but individual people. Whether agents are selfish, aiming to help themselves, or altruistic, aiming to help others, they are always concerned about individuals. As economists see it, there's no question of caring for teams as such. After all, there are no teams, only individuals.

But what then are we to say about the domestiques who devote themselves to a team victory? Their goal is a living testimony to the way teams transcend their members. They want their team to win, not the leader to gain the winner's medal. The leader's prize just happens to be the symbol that cycling uses to mark which team has won. It is nothing but a historical quirk, my cycling friends assure me, that the prizes are given to individuals and not to teams. In truth, road cycling is as much a team sport as rugby or basketball.

Sometimes cyclists seem to take this logic to extremes. The road cycling races in the Olympic or Commonwealth Games, for example, have gold, silver and bronze for the first three over the finish line, and no official recognition for teams at all. In this respect, it's like the 1,500 metres, rather than the water-polo tournament.

So, if you didn't know better, you'd think that's what the athletes wanted. One of the medals. Gold if you can get it, but failing that silver or bronze. But you'd be mistaken. The members of each country's team devote all their efforts to getting their leader first across the line, happy to share the glory of a team victory, even at the cost of a medal.

I watched a striking example of this in the Commonwealth Games women's road race in 2014. One of the England riders, Emma Pooley, broke away from the leading bunch with some 30 kilometres left to go. The idea was to make the opposition chase her, so they'd be out of puff when the England leader Liz Armistead made her bid for gold. And so it went. But what puzzled me, in my ignorance, was why Armistead didn't help Pooley when she passed her with 7 kilometres left and they were a minute ahead of the rest. Armistead was safe for the gold, and could have made sure that the now-tiring Pooley won the silver by forming a temporary alliance of two and helping her push through the wind.

I was tweeting my puzzlement at the time. Richard Williams, former chief sports writer of the *Guardian*, and himself a keen cyclist, posted a reply: 'Now that would be, as they say these days, a big ask. The team rides for the leader: the leader's responsibility is to win.' This struck me as oddly harsh, given that Games medals were at stake. But it makes good sense once you realize that, from the riders' point of view, all that matters are the teams, not their individual members. (Happily, Pooley did hang on for the silver – but no thanks to her teammate.)

Our current concern is with the definition of altruism. Does wanting your *team* to win count as altruistic? The normal definitions of altruism are stymied by this question, precisely because they take it for granted that the objects of desires are always individual people. If you are aiming to benefit yourself, then you are selfish, and if you are aiming to benefit someone else, then you are altruistic. This doesn't say anything about where you stand if you're aiming to benefit a team.

I'm not entirely sure what we should say here. On the one hand, there is something selfish about team aspirations. To the extent that you identify with the team, you yourself will share in its success. But, by the same coin, since others are equally involved, you are aiming at their success too, and so to that extent you are thinking altruistically.

I don't think it matters too much which way we go. If the normal economists' distinction between selfish and altruistic desires fails to deal with all the cases, that's scarcely our problem. It just shows that people care about more things than are dreamt of in economic theory. Perhaps we should stretch the definition of 'altruism' to cover team aspirations. Alternatively, we could introduce a third category of 'collectivist' desires to cover the extra cases. As I said, it doesn't really matter. In the end, we can stipulate as we choose. (In the rest of this chapter, I'll take 'altruism' to cover ambitions for teams.)

So, one consequence of the reality of teams is that they put pressure on standard definitions of altruism. Perhaps that doesn't seem worth writing home about. But teams also matter to decision-making in a second and far more interesting way. Once you are part of a team, you can address your problems differently. You are no longer limited to asking 'What shall I do?' Now you can ask 'What shall *we* do?'

In line with their Thatcherite vision of the social world, orthodox theories of rational choice think of team choices as the sum of individual choices. Each member of the team separately selects the action that promises the most of what they want (that 'maximizes their expected utility', as the economists put it). The strategy adopted by the whole team is then the sum of these individual choices.

However, there is no compelling reason for us to think of group decisions in this individualist way. Humans naturally form themselves into families, foraging parties, friends on a night out . . . and sports teams. And when they do, they tend to think as a group. They select that joint strategy that promises to maximize benefit to the group, and then they all play their allotted parts.

It makes a big difference. Consider the set-up known in the game-theory literature as the 'Footballers' Problem'. Arsenal's Jack Wilshere has the ball in midfield and can slide it to Olivier Giroud down either the left or right channel. Giroud's run and Wilshere's pass must be simultaneous. Both know the defender on the left is significantly weaker. What should they do?

Go *left*, of course. But surprisingly the branch of orthodox thinking that deals with coordinated actions – game theory – fails to deliver this result. This is because it starts with the choices of each agent, and the best choice for each agent depends on what the other does, and what the other does is supposed to be predicted by game theory ... so orthodoxy runs into sand, and fails to select *left* as the uniquely rational option.

But now suppose the players are thinking as a team. They have four joint options. Pass right, run left; pass left, run right; pass right, run right; pass left, run left. What should *we* do? It's a no-brainer – the last option is clearly best.

This is just one example of how *team reasoning* can find solutions that individual game theory cannot reach. Perhaps it is worth going a bit slower here. To better understand why individual thinking breaks down in such cases, it will be help-ful to introduce the notion of a 'Nash equilibrium' (named after the Princeton mathematician and Nobel laureate John Nash, whose troubled life was portrayed by Russell Crowe in the film *A Beautiful Mind*). The basic reason that team reason-ing often trumps individual thinking is that many problems of coordination lack a unique 'Nash equilibrium'.

Let me explain. Theorists normally divide problems of rational choice into 'decision theory' on the one hand and 'game theory' on the other.

Decision theory covers cases where only one person is doing the thinking. I'm wondering whether to go to the beach or to the movies. I'll enjoy the beach more, but only if it doesn't rain. Let's imagine we can measure my pleasure: 10 for the beach on a sunny day, 0 for a rainy day at the beach, 5 for the movies either way.

	Sun	Rain
Beach	10	0
Movies	5	5

According to decision theory, rationality requires me to 'maximize expected utility' – that is, to choose the action whose average pay-off across sun and rain, weighted by their respective probabilities, is the greatest – which in our case will be the beach if, and only if, the probability of sun is over 50 per cent.*

Game theory comes in when a number of people make choices simultaneously, and the pay-offs for each depend, not on natural events like the weather, but on the choices of the others. Take the Footballers' Problem again, and suppose that the matrix below represents how Wilshere's pay-offs depend

---

* If B stands for Beach, M for Movies, S for Sun, and R for Rain, then:
ExpUtility(B) = (10 x Pr(S)) + (0 x Pr(R)) = 10 x Pr(S).
ExpUtility(M) = (5 x Pr(S)) + (5 x Pr(R)) = 5.
So ExpUtility(B) > ExpUtility(M) if and only if Pr(S) > 5/10.

on Giroud's choices. (It's useless passing right if Giroud goes left, or vice versa; it's not too bad if you pass right and he goes right; but it's clearly best if you pass left and he goes left.)

		GIROUD	
		Left	Right
WILSHERE	Left	4	0
	Right	0	1

Now, in principle Wilshere could adopt the approach of decision theory, and ask himself how likely it is that Giroud will go right or left respectively, and use this probability to figure out his best bet. If he does this, Wilshere will find that it will pay him to pass left as long as the chance of Giroud going right is less than 80 per cent, but that right becomes the best bet once it's more than 80 per cent probable Giroud will go right.[*]

But surely Wilshere can do better than that. After all, Giroud is an intelligent fellow, too, not a weather system. So, shouldn't a theory of rational choice predict what Giroud's going to do, too, and not just leave Wilshere with probabilistic guesses?

This is the challenge taken up by game theory. It considers

---

[*]If L is Left and R Right, and the subscripts show who is going which way, then:

$\text{ExpUtility}(L_{\text{Wilshere}}) = (4 \times \text{Pr}(L)_{\text{Giroud}}) + (0 \times \text{Pr}(R_{\text{Giroud}})) = 4 \times \text{Pr}(L_{\text{Giroud}})$.

$\text{ExpUtility}(R_{\text{Wilshere}}) = (0 \times \text{Pr}(L_{\text{Giroud}})) + (1 \times \text{Pr}(R_{\text{Giroud}})) = \text{Pr}(R_{\text{Giroud}})$.

So $\text{ExpUtility}(L_{\text{Wilshere}}) > \text{ExpUtility}(R_{\text{Wilshere}})$ if and only if

$4 \times \text{Pr}(L_{\text{Giroud}}) > P(R_{\text{Giroud}})$

that is, if and only if $\text{Pr}(R_{\text{Giroud}}) < 4/5$.

the pay-offs for both players at the same time, and on this basis tries to deduce what both will do.

		GIROUD	
		Left	Right
WILSHERE	Left	4,4	0,0
	Right	0,0	1,1

But now we see the problem. It's best for them both to go left *if* the other also goes left. But at the same time, it's *also* best for them both to go right *if* the other goes right. So this game has two 'Nash equilibria' – where a Nash equilibrium is defined as a pair of options such that both players are doing the best they can, given what the other is doing. According to individual game theory, both these equilibria are rational solutions to the Footballers' Problem.

This is precisely the kind of case where team reasoning performs better than game theory. We don't want Wilshere and Giroud each individually worrying about what the other will do. They will only get in a tangle. We want them to think of themselves as a unit, and to consider which of their joint options is best.

	Left, Left	4
Wilshere-*and*-Giroud	Left, Right	0
	Right, Left	0
	Right, Right	1

Now everybody, including Wilshere and Giroud, can see that the best joint option is for them both to go left. It's the obvious decision, as soon as they stop thinking of themselves as autonomous agents making separate choices, and see themselves as a team, committed to playing their parts in the team's best strategy.

It is worth emphasizing that team reasoning isn't necessarily a matter of having altruistic aspirations. Wilshere and Giroud mightn't care about each other, or their team. They might be thoroughly sick of Arsène Wenger and north London, and concerned only to show they are good footballers worth a lucrative contract at a new club. They will still do better to reason as a unit. That's what good footballers do.

Think of the examples of mutualism discussed in the last chapter: cyclists in a breakaway, the stag hunt, and so on. In all of these, the actors were only concerned to maximize their own advantage. But it still paid them to cooperate with the others.

In the last chapter I skated over the issue of team reasoning. I emphasized how the cyclists and stag hunters would do best to cooperate, provided the others did so too. But I didn't stop to explain why they should expect the others to cooperate in the first place, beyond some vague suggestion that they would see this as likely.

But why should they see this as likely? This is where team reasoning does its work. If the cyclists and stag hunters are team reasoners, they can simply bypass any worries about probabilities. They only have to ask themselves, 'What should *we* do?', and the answer is obvious.

Sometimes team reasoning and altruistic desires work together to help people find the right answer. As we saw in the last chapter, you need some altruism to get out of the prisoner's dilemma or similar situations. But altruistic desires on their own won't do the whole job. Even if you care about what happens to the other guy, and you know he cares about you too, you still can't be sure of ending up in the best place, if you get caught up in the game-theoretic tangle of asking, 'What's my best strategy, if he does that . . .?' After all, if he is somehow rattled enough to confess, then the best solution all round will be for you to confess too. Once more the key is for you to address the problem as a team. Then you'll have no difficulty both keeping your mouths shut and going home soon.

Economists and other orthodox theorists of rational choice hate the idea of team reasoning. They think it's a cheat. Their Thatcherite vision doesn't leave room for anything except individuals doing their own thing. Even when people seem to be reasoning as a team, they insist, they're in reality each making their own rapid calculations of which individual actions are likely to best satisfy their own desires.

From the economists' individualist perspective, if Wilshere and Giroud both automatically go left, that must be because they are both sure of what the other will do, and as a result know that they will individually maximize their expected utility by going left, too.

But this puts the cart before the horse. No doubt they are both sure about what the other will do. But where did that come from? As we've seen, nothing in the orthodox theory of rational choice dictates that they should both choose left. In truth, the only reason Wilshere and Giroud know what the other will do is that they both take it for granted from the start that the other is a team reasoner.

The economists are missing the point. Of course, it's true that what a team does depends on what all its individual members do. But we are talking about the psychological reasoning that gives rise to their actions in the first place, and there is absolutely nothing in logic or psychology to stop the members of a team all simply asking themselves, 'What's the best joint strategy for us to adopt?' – and then all playing their parts when they have figured out the answer. If the economists have a theory that says that the players in my football team can't possibly be doing this – well, they know where they can stick their theory.

Perhaps the economists are in the grip of some half-baked evolutionary thought that natural selection favours organisms that outcompete their peers in the race for survival. Well, it's not always as simple as that, as the last chapter showed. And, even if it were, that still wouldn't be an argument against team reasoning. Given that the best way to further your own interests is often to think as a team, it would be odd if evolution hadn't made it natural to do so.

None of this means that humans always think as team members. There are cases and cases. Some situations call for teams reasoning, others for us to think as individuals. Think of a breakaway composed of cyclists from different teams. At first the priority is to keep ahead of the peloton, and this calls for the cyclists to think as a unit. But, as the finish nears, the imperatives quickly alter, and it becomes natural to start thinking as individuals instead.

Many sports bring out this kind of interplay between team and individual endeavour. One of the things I used to love about cricket was this possibility of switching between these different perspectives. The best days were when your team won and you played well too. But even if your team lost you might still get runs or wickets yourself. Then there were games where a team victory made up for your individual failure. And even in the worst case, when individual failure was compounded by team loss, you could at least console yourself with the thought that the rest of your side didn't do much better.

Nearly all team sports involve this combination of team and individual aspirations. You want your side to win, but also to play well yourself. Cricket and baseball stand out because their scoring systems automatically calibrate the relative contributions of the players. But they are by no means the only sports where you can take some pride in playing well in a losing team.

As a rule, individual and team imperatives pull together. What's good for you is good for the team. But sometimes the two conflict. We need you to man-mark their midfield playmaker and forget the showy stuff. Your cricket side wants runs quickly even though that puts you at risk of getting out. As a group, competitive athletes are surprisingly ready to put their team's needs above their own. Selfish teammates are very much the exception.

I can't help digressing for a moment. When I first started playing for my cricket team, the Old Talbotians, we didn't care about winning. The idea was to have a pleasant day out, with everybody getting a chance to bat or bowl. We lost a lot of matches and the team started struggling for players. Who wants to play for a losing side?

Then Phil Webster, for many years the political editor of the *Times*, elected himself captain and ran things differently. He too made sure that everybody got to bat or bowl – but only as long as this didn't damage our chances of winning. On one occasion, we were defending a low total against old rivals and the first change leaked seven runs in his first over. Phil promptly whipped him off and went back to the two opening bowlers for the rest of the forty overs. We won that match and a lot more besides. Phil was a peerless captain. Adding the desire for team victory to our individual aspirations made it all much more fun.

It works much better when players care about the team as well as themselves. But that's not always enough, as the prisoner's dilemma showed. Even if you have altruistic desires, you aren't guaranteed to find the best solution unless you also reason as a team and so avoid second-guessing your teammates. And this can be a fragile business. Sides can lose the ability to think as a team.

The danger is that the players will stop counting on each other. After all, asking 'What shall *we* do?' only makes sense if we can all be sure that everyone will play their part once we have decided on the optimal strategy. If this assumption is undermined, for whatever reason, then the power of team reasoning is lost.

This is what happens when teams disintegrate or choke. We can all fill in our own examples. Take Manchester United in the seasons after Alex Ferguson's retirement, or the England rugby team in recent World Cups. It's not that these sides weren't bothered about winning. Far from it – they were desperate for success. It's rather that they lost confidence in their ability to coordinate their actions. They started worrying about the others' choices, and ended up in the plight of the poor game theorist, thinking that if he does that, then I'd better do this, but if he . . . and then no one is sure what to do.

Perhaps, as so often, sport points to a wider moral. In coming chapters, we will look at the ways in which humans form themselves into nations, federations and other social groups. The healthy functioning of these entities requires that their members care about each other, that they are altruistically motivated to foster the welfare of their fellow citizens as well as their own.

As we have seen, though, this concern for the common good isn't necessarily enough on its own. Optimal outcomes also depend on our ability to reason as a team – and this in turn requires us to trust everyone to play their part once a decision is reached.

In complex modern societies, this trust can be a fragile flame. Divergent histories and loyalties can corrode our confidence in each other, and reduce us to the level of a sports team that has forgotten how to pull together. It is in no one's interest for us to lose our faith in each other. Once gone, this kind of trust is not easily regained.

PART IV

TRIBES

CHAPTER 11

CIVIL SOCIETY AND SPORTING ELIGIBILITY

In 2001, when Lionel Messi was thirteen years old, Futbol Club Barcelona brought him over from Argentina on a starting salary of €600,000 per annum. How good can a thirteen-year-old be, you might wonder. But Barcelona knew what they were doing. In the years since, Messi has matured into arguably the finest footballer of all time, and at the time of writing he is still under contract to Barcelona. Nowadays it would cost any other club upwards of €200 million to take him off Barça's hands.

The pressure to scour the world for promising youngsters has intensified in recent years, thanks to the European authorities' attempts to make the big soccer clubs more representative of their countries. Their regulations now require at least eight 'home-grown' players among the twenty-five on first team rosters. This was a silly idea to start with – who really cares how many Spanish players are playing for Barcelona? – but in any case it has backfired.

This is because European Union law currently prohibits any employer, like Barcelona, from favouring Spanish employees over, say, French ones. So, in an attempt to get around this, the European football rules don't equate 'home-grown' with nationality, but with being 'locally trained'. To qualify under this heading for Barcelona, you must have been registered with a Spanish club for three seasons between the ages of fifteen and twenty-one. The hope was that, in the natural course of events, most of these 'local' players would be Spanish.

But you can imagine what has happened. The clubs have realized that, if they want top foreign players, they need to catch them young, or at least young enough to satisfy the 'home-grown' rule. So there has been a marked surge in the number of youngsters being imported from other countries by the big clubs since the new rules came in.

One curious result has been uncertainty about which national teams these talented kids will end up playing for. Take Messi, for a start. He has lived in Spain since he was thirteen, and he now has Spanish as well as Argentinian citizenship. He could easily have followed in the footsteps of his great Argentinian predecessor, Alfredo Di Stéfano, heart of the all-conquering 1950s Real Madrid side, who became a fixture in the Spanish national team once he was naturalized.

As it happens, Messi has remained loyal to Argentina on the international stage. In other cases, however, it is a genuinely open question which country will benefit from some prodigy's talent.

Consider Adnan Januzaj, who has been on Manchester United's books since shortly after his sixteenth birthday. Januzaj's parents are ethnic Albanians who fled Kosovo in 1992 to avoid the Yugoslav army draft. Adnan was born in

Belgium three years later, and moved to Manchester to join United's youth programme in 2011.

Once Januzaj broke into United's first team two years later, his talents generated much debate about which national team he would end up playing for. Kosovo doesn't have a side – not yet anyway – but Turkey, Albania, Serbia, Croatia, Belgium and England were all mentioned as possibilities.

The idea that Januzaj might in due course qualify for England prompted some interesting reactions. Jack Wilshere, the very home-grown Arsenal midfielder, was particularly forthright: 'The only people who should play for England are English people,' he insisted, when quizzed about Januzaj by the press.

I'm a great admirer of Wilshere's onfield skills, but his attitude strikes me as indefensible. As someone whose maternal grandparents were born German Jews, and whose formative years were spent in apartheid South Africa, I am naturally sympathetic to those who seek to forge a new life in a new country. But even those who don't share my cosmopolitan sentiments should think twice before siding with Wilshere's little-Englandism.

The crucial issue here is citizenship. By and large, national sporting eligibility in the modern world depends on citizenship. And citizenship in turn depends on residence. Nearly all countries allow those who have been legally resident for some fixed period to become 'naturalized' citizens. In Britain, the required period is five years, which would make Januzaj eligible for citizenship at any point past his twenty-first birthday, assuming he is still with Manchester United or another English club.

Somewhat less familiarly, most countries make residence necessary for citizenship, as well as sufficient. Use it or lose it. A family that takes up residence outside its original country for too many generations will find that its descendants stop being citizens.

True, most countries allow a bit of wiggle room. Children born abroad are normally granted their parents' citizenship. But this is basically a device to avoid mothers having to scurry back to their homeland to give birth. The basic principle is still that citizenship is for residents. That's why scarcely any countries allow expatriates to transmit their home citizenship down generations indefinitely.

The rule in Britain used to be that you were all right as long as you had a grandparent who was actually born in Britain. Nowadays it's rather less permissive. You need your father or mother to be British citizens in their own right, and not just courtesy of their parents' citizenship. The United States is even keener on residence. Children born abroad to one American parent don't automatically acquire citizenship unless that parent has lived in the States for five years, two of which must have been after the age of fourteen.

Curiously, France is one of the few modern countries that allow expatriate families to keep their citizenship indefinitely. In its view, it doesn't matter if you've all lived in Tashkent since the seventeenth century. If you are French, then your children are French, until the end of time. (But don't assume that in practice you can get accredited as French just because you have a set of French great-grandparents. The bureaucratic barriers are formidable.)

Actually, this isn't the oddest feature of the French attitude to non-resident citizens. They also allow expatriates who have never set foot in France to vote in parliamentary elections. You might think that there would be an obvious problem – which constituency do these exiles vote in? But the French are ahead of you. They have divided the rest of the world into eleven special constituencies, precisely to enable non-resident citizens to vote for their own deputies. There's someone in the Assemblée nationale who represents the French voters of South America. Amazing. Good luck to them.

Anyway, whatever their rationale for these strange arrangements, the French are outliers. As I said, in most other modern countries residence is both necessary and sufficient for citizenship, give or take a bit, and ancestry doesn't really come into it.

It might seem surprising that residence counts for so much and parentage for so little. As a political policy, you wouldn't expect this openness to new citizens to command widespread support. By and large, sympathy for far-flung 'kith and kin' wins far more votes than enfranchisement of immigrants. It was ever thus and, if anything, anti-cosmopolitan sentiments have been growing in recent decades.

Moreover, chauvinism isn't the only motivation for wanting to restrict citizenship to those with a shared background. You don't have to be Enoch Powell or Donald Trump to recognize that civil society depends on more than common geographical boundaries. A healthy community requires a mutual sense of acceptable public behaviour, of how to settle disputes, of your obligations to neighbours and acquaintances, and so on.

Rising levels of immigration in the modern world have prompted a fierce debate among philosophers about the nature of citizenship. On the one side lie the 'universalists', who focus on the shared rights and obligations of citizens, and emphasize the need for immigrants to assimilate to the customs of their new country. As the universalists see it, equal treatment by the law and public institutions calls for a shared commitment to the traditions of the nation.

In opposition to the universalists, 'differentialists' argue that an insistence on a common culture often serves as a disguised defence of established interests. Respect for so-called national traditions can result in the marginalization of minority groups. According to the differentialists, true equality requires a respect for multicultural diversity, not an imposed cultural uniformity.

There are good points to be made on both sides of this debate. Still, pretty much everybody involved agrees that citizenship needs to follow residence. Only an extreme fringe wants to tie it to ethnic origin. Even those universalists who stress the importance of shared traditions accept that citizenship needs to be available to immigrants.

The reason is obvious enough. After all, movement of people across national boundaries is inevitable in the modern world. Political realignments, refugee crises and, above all, commerce lead inexorably to a build-up of non-citizens inside national boundaries. And the problem is that, if these newcomers are left as non-citizens indefinitely, they are likely to start resenting it and stirring up trouble. They are paying taxes and are subject to the laws of the country. So how come they don't have a vote and access to the full range of opportunities open to citizens? Any immigrant groups who find themselves permanently excluded in this way are likely to be limited in their enthusiasm for their hosts' way of doing things.

The smart solution is to incorporate them, to sign them up to the deal on which all modern democracies rest. We will make you full citizens with all accompanying rights, and in return you will respect our shared way of doing things.

This has long been the modern solution to religious minorities. Dissenters have often found themselves at odds with the official religion of the state. Persecution and insurrection are one way things can develop. But from the seventeenth century onwards, civilized countries have moved in the direction of toleration. Provided you subscribe to our public practices, the nonconformists are told, you can uphold your religion in private and enjoy all the rights of full citizenship.

The xenophobic fringe will say it won't work with immigrants, even if it does the trick with religious minorities. How can a Ghanaian become Italian, or a Vietnamese Australian, or indeed a Kosovan English? Still, history gives the lie to this chauvinism. Maybe you can't lose your ethnicity easily (although that in itself is a complex question, to which I shall return in a couple of chapters). But ethnicity alone is no barrier to gaining a nationality.

The experience of many modern nations over the last century shows that the universalist demand for a shared sense of identity can coexist with a multicultural diversity of communities, each with their own ancestral traditions. My maternal grandparents, who remained loyal to the Orthodox synagogue all their lives, were obsessed with becoming English. (My mother was an encyclopaedia on the niceties of English manners.) Or just think of modern America, where successive waves of immigrants have retained much of their identity as Italians, or Germans, or Jamaicans, while embracing their new citizenship with excitement and pride.

In 1990, the Conservative British politician Norman Tebbit formulated a sporting criterion to decide whether new citizens with foreign backgrounds were sufficiently committed to their adopted country. According to the 'Tebbit test', Britons with an Indian background, say, aren't properly loyal unless they support the English team when it plays cricket against India.

That is chauvinist crap. I am properly British all right. All my grandparents were in Britain by 1900. Still, because my father's job took my family to South Africa during my teenage years, I root for South Africa whenever they play the perennially one-dimensional English rugby union team. I don't see that it follows that I'm somehow wanting as a citizen.

To resist the Tebbit test is not to deny that new citizens of a country are under some obligation to respect its way of doing things. The universalists are right to insist that a healthy community rests on shared ideas about proper public conduct. Immigrants should certainly adjust some of their behaviour to accommodate to their new society. But this doesn't mean that they have to disown their origins. There are many dimensions to identity. You can respect the public customs of your new country while still celebrating your religious holidays, or dressing in a traditional style, or indeed supporting your country of origin on the sports field.

And even the last can be a nuanced matter. While I support South Africa at rugby against England, I am conversely frantic for England to win when the two sides play soccer. Similarly, I would expect that most young Britons of Indian background will back India against England at cricket, but will be firmly behind England when they play soccer. (All right, maybe they would side with India at soccer too, if India ever played England – but I can't say that I have ever noticed an Indian soccer team.)

Still, what about immigrants actually representing their new country on the sports field? Clearly there is no room for divided loyalties at that point. You wouldn't want Adnan Januzaj playing for England against Belgium if his heart was really on the other side.

Such things are by no means beyond the bounds of possibility. The cricketer Kevin Pietersen was born and bred in South Africa, but eligible to play for England because of his British mother. As a young player first forging his career with the KwaZulu-Natal side, he felt he was being held back by the preferential treatment given to players of colour in South Africa.

So he transferred his allegiances to England. He scored a lot of runs for the England test team, but was always a disruptive influence in the dressing room. After a number of tumultuous years, England decided that they were better off without him.

A cricketing memoir by the Australian Ed Cowan includes a telling anecdote. He describes a cricket lunch break when Pietersen, nonplussed by an item on the buffet, asked, 'What the fuck is this?' Cowan explained that any true Englishman would recognize bread-and-butter pudding. Pietersen replied: 'I'm not English, Eddie. I just work here.'

Still, it is not to be assumed that all immigrants will be similarly half-hearted in their commitment to their new countries. Loyalty is particularly to be expected from those who actively choose naturalization, rather than benefiting from some ancestral qualification like Pietersen. It's a pretty reliable indication of commitment to their new country. After all, those eligible for naturalization will usually have gained permanent residence rights already. If they take the extra step of becoming a citizen, swearing allegiance and so on, it's typically because of their emotional identification with their new country.

Of course, there will always be some carpetbaggers who switch nationalities for advantage rather than loyalty. I don't think the media tycoon Rupert Murdoch ditched his original Australian citizenship to become American because of some emotional affinity with the Stars and Stripes. Nor are such mercenary manoeuvres unknown in the sporting world, as we'll shortly see.

Still, if Adnan Januzaj were to become British by naturalization, I don't think that it should be up to the rest of us to decide if his loyalties are in the right place. If he were to say that this is his new country, and he wants to represent it, then I don't see that the rest of us have the right to doubt his word.

Remember the deal on which modern societies rest. You respect our way of doing things, and we will make you full citizens with all accompanying rights. If this deal is to work, it needs to be wholehearted. You'll risk losing the allegiance of the newcomers if they think they are still being treated as second-class citizens. They need to feel that all institutions are open to them – including national sports teams.

That is why I think that Jack Wilshere's attitude is not only mean-spirited but destructive. Once people are living in your country, it does nobody any good to discriminate against them. There is already enough danger of aggrieved minority-group members taking violent action against perceived slights. To insist that they can't become really English, however much they want to, doesn't strike me as a great idea.

Unfortunately, though, it seems as though Adnan Januzaj won't be eligible for England after all, at least not unless some rules are changed. The reason is that nowadays sporting eligibility isn't always a simple matter of nationality. A number of international sporting bodies have become uneasy about the readiness with which some countries hand out citizenship, and so have started adding further requirements to citizenship before you can sign up for a new country.

Perhaps the most notorious instance of country-hopping was the Georgian beach volleyball teams in the 2008 Olympics. Both the men's and the women's pairs were Brazilians who had probably never heard of Georgia until they were recruited and fast-tracked into their new citizenship a few weeks before the Games.

The women didn't get past the group stages, but Renato Gomes and Jorge Terceiro took the Georgian men all the way to the last four, only missing out on a medal when they lost to the real Brazilian team in the bronze-medal match. The Olympic authorities have since tried to block such abuses with extra rules, but the position remains complex, with each Olympic sport having its own eligibility requirements.

English cricket has long faced a similar issue. Here the problem isn't too-easy naturalization, but the large number of colonials, like Kevin Pietersen, who count as citizens because of their British parents. This has resulted in every England side from 2004 to 2015 fielding at least one player born in southern Africa, and often a lot more. Matches against the Proteas came to be a matter of whether our South Africans were better than theirs.

The solution has been to require that even those born British must satisfy a substantial residency condition before they can play for England. Nowadays any British player who hasn't moved to England by the age of eighteen will have to wait a full seven years before they can play for their country. Future Kevin Pietersens will need to think carefully before committing themselves.

It's the same in soccer. A few years ago, FIFA got fed up with the number of Brazilians turning up in other countries' teams, à la Georgian volleyball. So, since 2008, they have decreed that, in addition to citizenship, you must have lived in a country for five years before you can represent it on the football field.

Why is any of this a problem for Adnan Januzaj? If he were to become British on the basis of five years' residence, wouldn't that automatically satisfy the extra FIFA requirement too?

Well, that would work fine if there were a British soccer team – but there isn't. For better or worse, Britain divides itself into four different 'Home Nations' when it comes to soccer. England, Scotland, Wales and Northern Ireland are all recognized by FIFA. This is something of an anomaly, harking back to the long-past time when Britain was the predominant force in world football. But it lives on, and somehow nobody seems particularly keen to change it.

Perhaps simple lack of success will eventually eliminate this surfeit of nations. Though Scotland was once a world force, and Wales is enjoying a resurgence, none of the Home Nations apart from England has made it to the World Cup finals since 1998. Still, as long as the system survives, it adds an extra layer of complexity to national eligibility. Since there is as yet no such thing as Scottish, Welsh, Northern Irish or indeed English citizenship, but only simple British nationality, a special set of rules is needed to decide who gets to play for which Home Nation.

These have evolved over the years, but since 2009 the British football authorities have settled on these requirements: in order to play for one of the Home Nations, you need to have been born in that country, or to have a parent or grandparent born there, or to have been educated there for five years before the age of eighteen.

If you ask me, this wins the prize for mindless chauvinism. It means that you could be a British citizen, required to fight for your country in a war, yet be permanently ineligible for any of its football teams. Even if Adnan Januzaj became British, and lived in Manchester for the rest of his life, he would never be able to play for England. Nor, if you think about it, would anybody who moved here after the age of thirteen.

I'd say that the Home Nations have got it badly wrong. They have put too much weight on descent, and left no room for newcomers to opt in.

But somehow I am not surprised. English football administration has a well-deserved reputation as a sanctuary for moral dinosaurs. When the chief executive of the Premier League acquired a new personal assistant a couple of years ago, he seemed genuinely surprised when she complained about his emails to colleagues mentioning 'big-titted broads', 'female irrationality' and 'cash for gash'. Nor did his employers see any reason to discipline him.

Even the outward-facing press office of the England Football Association seems to live in some long-lost world. Their congratulatory tweet for the returning England women's World Cup semi-finalists in 2015 started with the words 'Our Lionesses go back to being mothers, partners, daughters today'.

A generous view would be that the Home Nations authorities didn't fully think through the consequences of their new eligibility regulations. I fear, however, it is all too likely that they knew exactly what they were doing. Still, whatever their intentions, the result just seems wrong.

Think about what their rules mean. If they had been applied in cricket, for instance, the South African exile Basil D'Oliviera, stalwart of the England side in the 1960s, and a hero of the anti-apartheid movement, would never have played for his adopted country. Nor would Cyrille Regis

MBE, one of the first black Britons to succeed in top-flight soccer, have gained any of his five England caps, because he didn't move here from the Caribbean until he was fifteen.

On the other hand, the Home Nations regulations do nothing to rule out carpetbaggers like Kevin Pietersen who can produce parents or grandparents born in one of the Home Nations, even if they have no other connection with that country. So the Canadian Owen Hargreaves, who gained forty-two soccer caps for England in the early 2000s, courtesy of his English father, would have been eligible all right, even though he had never lived in England at the time he was first selected.

As it happens, these pernicious Home Nations rules do not seem to be widely known. As late as 2013, the England manager Roy Hodgson was talking about the possibility of drafting Januzaj once he had lived in England for five years.

In the event, the issue went away. Januzaj finally opted for Belgium in the run-up to the 2014 World Cup, and has since played for their national team. Perhaps that is where his heart always lay. After all, he did live in Belgium until he was sixteen. But who knows? Maybe the lad fell in love with England once he moved there, and would have chosen them if he could.

I would far prefer Januzaj to have been given the option. The British football eligibility rules strike me as taking attachment to kith and kin to extremes. It is one thing to insist, with the universalists, that new citizens must show genuine loyalty to their new country, both on and off the sports field. But that is no justification for permanently rejecting anybody who spent most of their childhood elsewhere. That is nothing but a slap in the face to all immigrants and refugees, telling them they will never become real citizens, however long they live in the country. It is no recipe for a harmonious society.

I'll leave the last word to the athlete Mo Farah, probably the greatest long-distance runner the world has ever seen. Farah moved to Britain from Mogadishu as an eight-year-old in 1991, speaking very little English. His talent was spotted early on at his school in west London, and he progressed through the ranks of British athletics on his way to his unprecedented collection of World and Olympic medals.

After he won the 10,000 metres in the 2012 London Olympics in front of an ecstatic crowd, a gauche interviewer asked whether he wouldn't rather have been running for Somalia. Farah responded instantly, in his strong cockney accent: 'Not at all, mate, this is my country and this is where I grew up. This is my country and when I put on my Great Britain vest I'm proud. I'm very proud.'

CHAPTER 12

SPORTING NATIONS AND POLITICAL GEOGRAPHY

One of my childhood cricket heroes was 'Goofy' Lawrence, an honest South African fast bowler who played five test matches in the early 1960s, and should have played more. The funny thing, however, is that Goofy wasn't South African at all, but a citizen of what is now Zimbabwe and was then Rhodesia, a quite different country, but which in those days was simply annexed by South Africa for cricketing purposes

When Robert Mugabe's ZANU-PF party won an overwhelming victory in Zimbabwe's first independence election in February 1980, the country's cricketers were perturbed. They asked if this meant they weren't part of South Africa any more and would have to stop playing in its domestic Currie Cup competition.

It was an absurd enquiry. The apartheid South African state was then at the height of its international isolation, not to mention that many of the largely white cricket team had been fighting Mugabe in a bloody civil war for the past few years. Mugabe explained to the cricketers that there was no way that they could carry on as before. But then – showing a proper sense of priorities for a life-long cricket fan – he gave them a special dispensation to play out the last matches of that Currie Cup season.

The historical incorporation of Rhodesia into the South African cricket team isn't an isolated case. There are a surprising number of sporting countries that aren't in the United Nations. Sporting nations and political nations don't always line up together. This mismatch offers a number of insights into the basis of nationhood.

We tend to take political states for granted, assuming that their boundaries were laid down by natural divisions long ago. But in truth many recognized states are arbitrary and relatively recent constructions, shaped by the outcome of diplomatic negotiations, or by the happenstantial location of armies when a truce is declared. Sometimes the arbitrariness of existing states is exposed by sudden realignments, as when the end of the cold war precipitated the reunification of Germany and the dissolution of the former Yugoslavia. But in other cases the potential for political repositioning remains implicit in sporting affiliations. In this chapter, we will look at a range of national teams that demand loyalty to countries that don't appear on the official map of nations, from Hong Kong and the West Indies to Ireland and Wales.

Perhaps these sporting allegiances point the way to a more flexible international order for our increasingly globalized age. Healthy political units need their members to think of themselves as engaged in shared projects. But this needn't demand the familiar division into nation states, with a single governing body wielding legitimate power over any given place on the surface of the earth. There are various other possibilities, including federal structures with nested powers, and even overlapping authorities with differentiated responsibilities. We need only think of how the free trade, monetary, customs and migration unions in contemporary Europe all involve different sets of countries.

National sporting success can do much to unite a fragile nation state, as Nelson Mandela demonstrated when he co-opted the traditionally white Springbok rugby team as part of his rainbow project. By donning a South African rugby jersey and joining the newly named 'Amabokke' in lifting the trophy after their 1995 Johannesburg World Cup victory, he did more to reassure the rugby-loving white Afrikaner settler community about their future than any promises could.

But sporting loyalties can also serve to unify people who don't live within the boundaries of a single official country. Some sporting countries lump different political states together, while others split them up. Perhaps political structures would do well to piggy-back on these unofficial liaisons. The wide variety of sporting unions points to the possibility of less rigid political arrangements than fixed divisions into non-overlapping nation states.

The British Isles consist of two principal islands, Great Britain and Ireland. In the nineteenth-century both were ruled as a single country from London, but after the First World War the Republic of Ireland gained independence. It wasn't given the whole of Ireland, though. The largely Protestant north-east corner of the island was partitioned off, and remained within the renamed United Kingdom of 'Great Britain and Northern Ireland'.

You might have supposed that sporting arrangements would have followed suit, with national teams representing the new sovereign state. But that's not how it worked. Soccer is the only game where the Republic of Ireland has its own national team. In every other sporting discipline, it's as if partition never occurred. 'Ireland' teams live up to their name. They represent the whole island, and draw players from both north and south.

Perhaps this isn't surprising for the Gaelic games of hurling and Gaelic football. These largely Catholic and working-class games have long been associated with Irish nationalism, and so might be expected to repudiate the separate existence of Northern Ireland.

But Irish sporting unity is just as strong in games supported by the Protestant middle classes from the other end of the political spectrum. Most prominently, the Irish rugby union side is a world force. They are regular quarter-finalists in the World Cup, and command fanatical support on both sides of the border. In the same vein, cricket, tennis, field hockey and squash all select proud pan-Irish teams. When it comes to sports, the bitter differences that dominate Irish politics seem to go out of the window.

Ireland isn't the only sporting oddity within the British Isles. Scotland is unsure about whether to stay in the United Kingdom. The nationalists narrowly lost an independence referendum in 2015, and the issue is by no means settled. Still, separation wouldn't make any difference on the sports field. In sporting terms, Scotland is already as independent as could be.

When it comes to soccer, rugby, cricket, and nearly every other sport, Scotland is no more part of the United Kingdom than Peru is. It has its own national teams, and the rivalry with England could not be more intense. The annual Scotland–England soccer match was one of the great sporting fixtures, until it was discontinued in 1989 because of the fans' excesses.

Wales is somewhat less favoured in the sporting autonomy stakes. They have their own rugby and soccer teams all right – indeed these are both currently world forces in a way that Scotland's are not – but when it comes to cricket they are simply absorbed into England, Rhodesia-South-Africa style. The governing body is the 'England and Wales Cricket Board', but the team itself is 'England'.

The distinguished and very Welsh cricketer Robert Croft was once asked what he felt about playing for the old Saxon enemy. He explained that when he played for his county Glamorgan, he thought of himself as representing Wales; but that when he played for England, 'I always looked at it as like playing rugby for the British Lions'.

Actually, in these less hegemonic times, we nowadays take care to refer to the 'British and Irish Lions'. Another oddity. Every four years the rest of the rugby-playing British Isles joins in the atavistic Irish pretence that history never happened. When it comes to selecting touring sides to do battle with the rugby giants of the southern hemisphere, we stand united as one nation. The political incoherence of this construction does nothing to dampen the intensity of the sporting contests.

It isn't only Britain and Ireland that ignore political settlements in the sporting arena. Is Hong Kong a country, or

Taiwan for that matter? The People's Republic of China says no. 'One *country*, two systems,' it insists, affirming its sovereignty over these territories. But then what are Hong Kong and Taiwan doing with their own national teams on every international sporting stage, including the 2008 Summer Olympics in Beijing?

The Spanish football club Athletic Bilbao requires its players to have Basque ancestry or upbringing. I must say that this offends my cosmopolitan sensibilities. It strikes me as racist. I'm surprised that it's allowed under European law. You'd think that it violated anti-discrimination rules, not to mention laws against restraint of trade.

All right, maybe it's my intuitions that need examining. When exactly did football clubs stop being emblems of local pride and turn into commercial bodies subject to competition law? Still, whatever you think about Bilbao's sectarianism, it seems to me that FIFA and Spain would do well to take a leaf out of the British book. Why not give the Basques a proper national team, à la Scotland, and release Athletic Bilbao from the need to represent a nation by a club?

This would no doubt be resisted by opponents of Basque independence. But they shouldn't assume that it would encourage the disintegration of Spain. Perhaps it would actually help to keep Spain united, working to make the Basques happier with devolved power in a federal Spain, as has arguably happened with Wales and Scotland in Britain. In the same spirit, perhaps the Catalans would also like to become separate FIFA members, even while remaining part of Spain.

On the other hand, the Catalans might prefer to go the other way, even if they were to gain the full independence they supported in their 2014 referendum. A number of Catalan footballers played a major role in Spain's World Cup and European Championship victories in 2010 and 2012. Their share in the Spanish team's successes might persuade them to stay federated in football even if they become politically independent. The example of Ireland shows that there is no need to break up a functioning nation just because political boundaries get redrawn.

The most striking example of a sporting country that isn't a real country is the cricketing West Indies. The side has played a central role in cricket history. If you ask an average cricket fan about the West Indies, they will probably tell you that it's a country distributed across a number of islands in the Caribbean.

But in truth it's not a country, and never was. The team draws its members from various modern Caribbean countries that were once British colonies. However, these particular islands were never governed together. Although several attempts were made by the colonial powers to amalgamate them for administrative purposes, such plans were inevitably scuppered by inter-island conflicts of interest.

Even so, there have been combined teams on the cricket field since the 1880s, and in 1928 the 'West Indies' became the fourth 'country' to be granted test-match status. Early twentieth-century West Indian society was dominated by fine distinctions of skin colour, and the first test teams always had a white captain. Nevertheless, from early on the sides drew members from all racial groups. As Edgar Mittelholzer explained in his 1950 Trinidadian novel *A Morning at the Office*, 'Cricket was taken too solemnly ... no one stopped to ask what was his shade of complexion or his position in society; his performance was enough. Was he capable of wiping up the Barbados bowling? Was he capable of mowing down the Barbados wickets?'

At the time of decolonization, there was a short-lived attempt to transfer the cricketing unity into the political arena. A West Indies Federation was formed in 1958, with the intention of creating a federal nation from the former colonies, on the model of Canada or Australia. But by 1962 the Federation had collapsed under the weight of the old island rivalries.

The cricket team, though, was unaffected by the political disintegration and indeed was about to enter its period of greatest strength. The West Indies had always been an exciting side, but historically had a reputation for 'calypso cricket', favouring flamboyant gestures over hard-won victories. However, for two decades from the mid-1970s, under the leadership of Clive Lloyd and Vivian Richards, the side added steel to their flair. With their unprecedented phalanx of fast bowlers, they dominated the test-match scene for two decades.

A federal government might always have been a pipe dream, but at a different political level there is no doubt about the significance of this cricketing success. By now there were no white players in the side, and the symbolism of the ex-slaves thrashing their colonial masters was never far below the surface. For many West Indians, both in the Caribbean and elsewhere, the all-conquering cricketing side of the 1980s was a beacon of black pride.

Today the West Indies team is no longer the force it was. Soccer and basketball have been growing in popularity in the Caribbean, and the contemporary cricket side is struggling at the top level of international cricket. Perhaps their time will come again. In any case, the future will not undo cricket's role in creating a post-colonial identity for Anglophone West Indians.

In sporting terms, the United States of America is the mirror image of the West Indies. It is second to none as a political power on the world stage. But when it comes to international sporting competition, it is almost invisible.

Americans don't really do international sport. A couple of years ago, I invited visitors to my website to help me construct an alphabetical list of families that included two or more international athletes (A for the Amritraj tennis brothers from India, B for the soccer-playing Boatengs . . . see the Appendix at the end of the book). I recommended reciting this alphabet as an excellent cure for insomnia, and called for some help with the trickier letters.

One American commenter suggested M for the footballing Mannings. When I queried their international status, he responded that Eli's Giants had once played a game in London. I had to explain that, to the rest of the sporting world, 'international athlete' has only one meaning – you have to represent your country, not just play for your club in some foreign location.

Perhaps I shouldn't have been surprised by my commenter's blind spot. After all, American sports fans have scarcely any exposure to sporting contests between nations. In gridiron, for a start, there's no real question of a national team, for lack of any plausible opposition. The other major sports – basketball, baseball, ice hockey – are played in other countries, and indeed the USA is a presence in most major international tournaments. But their teams are often denied the services of the top professionals. Their clubs that pay their generous wages generally aren't keen to let them go, and in any case many of the star athletes seem to think they have better things to do with their time. While the US teams dutifully turn up, and sometimes win, no one seems to pay much attention.

Soccer is the one exception. Its recent rise in popularity is starting to give Americans a taste for international challenges. Bleacher Report, the leading USA sport website, has a list of the '50 Biggest International Sports Moments in US History'. Not surprisingly, given the dearth of international competition, fully thirty-eight of these are from the Olympic Games (and most of them, for that matter, feature individual rather than team events). Of the other twelve slots, nine involve soccer matches. Both the men's and the women's USA sides have become significant forces on the world stage, and Americans are learning to follow their fortunes.

Still, even here the enthusiasm is muted. During the 2014 World Cup, I watched the last-sixteen knockout match between the USA and Belgium with American friends. It was a riveting game. The US team, led by the creative drive of captain Michael Bradley, came close, but Belgium pipped them in extra time. My companions were excited all right, but somehow seemed uncomfortable at the same time, as if it were unbecoming to get excited about a contest that their country might lose.

I hope that this interest in soccer marks the beginning of a wider trend. Sometimes I can't help feeling that the world would be better off if America were less isolated in sporting terms. Exceptionalism on the sports field encourages exceptionalism off it. A country that shies away from international sport can be tempted to stop thinking of itself as one nation among others.

One of the great virtues of sporting partisanship is that it is so manifestly ungrounded. As I explained earlier, sports fandom hinges on 'agent-relative values', rather than differences in objective worth. Sports fans commit themselves to their teams and care about their fortunes, but only the most pig-headed of them think of their side as intrinsically more virtuous than the opposition.

This ensures a kind of generosity about sporting results. You might be cast down if your side loses, or elated if they win, but you are unlikely to feel that intrinsic entitlement has been thwarted or rewarded. Sporting contests are essentially even-handed. Both sides can see that the other has an equal right to succeed, and that the appropriate result is victory for the more skilful team.

The same point applies on the international sporting stage. Sometimes competing nations will share a history of political conflict and perceived wrongs. But the sporting context itself washes out past resentments and places the opponents on an even footing. On the sports field, all are created equal, and depend only on their skills.

A country that shuns international sporting contests, like the United States, can lack this natural reminder of the standing of other countries. And this can lend support to the belief that the non-competitor is special among nations. A powerful section of the American right supports the exceptionalist theory that their country is entitled to bypass the rules that apply to other nations, just as they bypass those nations on the sports field. Maybe the rise of soccer in the States will in time put pressure on this exceptionalist thinking. Even if you view the United Nations as a tiresome constraint on your world power, it is hard to take the same attitude to the World Cup.

What about the Ryder Cup? Every second September the golfing nations of Europe take on the might of the United States. The European golf fans become terribly excited by these contests. But once more the Americans seem less keen to engage and viewing figures are low. The interest is muted on the other side of the Atlantic. Only one American victory, the spectacular 1999 comeback in Brookline, features in Bleacher Report's 'International Moments'.

Perhaps this lack of interest is a hangover from the monotonous years before 1979 when the Ryder Cup opposition was limited to Great Britain and Ireland, and the USA won time after time. Or maybe it has as much to do with the reversal of power once the rest of Europe came in – since 1985, when Seve Ballesteros inspired the first American defeat in twenty-eight years, the States has won only five of the sixteen matches. In any case, whatever the precise reason, the Ryder Cup proves no exception to the general American pattern of international sporting disengagement.

Still, even if it is no catalyst for American involvement, the Ryder Cup is arguably of broader political significance in the European context. As I said, the golf fans of Europe don't hesitate to join forces every two years. Perhaps this augurs well for a future federal Europe. In general, you'd expect the regulars in the golf club bar to line up on the Eurosceptic right. If they can be made to unite behind a European golf team, perhaps they will also be ready to support other pan-European projects.

Before we draw any political morals, however, I need to explain some points about golf fandom.

The first thing to understand is that every adult golfer who is not American has only one concern when watching any professional golf tournament – they don't want an American to win. Viewers of European TV golf coverage are regularly shown an 'International Leader Board' listing the scores of all the leading non-Americans. Non-partisans might find this puzzling, but from the viewers' angle it makes perfect sense. The point is to keep track of the prospects of some – any – non-American victory.

It seems that this attitude is shared by the players as well as the fans. The English golfer Paul Casey was asked before the 2004 Ryder Cup to confirm that the teams' rivalry was friendly. His response was, 'No, we properly hate them.' Afterwards he said he was joking, but I'm not sure.

This transatlantic golfing antipathy is mutual. Some years ago, I was at a conference in the former Yugoslavia with two archetypical Midwestern philosophers, George Pappas and Marshall Swain. It was the year that the Masters ended in a play-off between Seve Ballesteros, Greg Norman and the journeyman American Larry Mize. It wasn't easy to get news, but in a bar I found a newspaper with a sports section.

'Shit,' I said to Pappas and Swain, 'Mize chipped in from 140 feet to beat them both.' I assumed they would share my disappointment. But, on the contrary, they were all whoops and high fives. How could anybody be pleased at that? It was like a warthog getting into the garden and killing two peacocks.

But I shouldn't have been surprised. After all, their sentiments were nothing but a mirror image of my own. I can appreciate that Phil Michelson and Bubba Watson are charismatic magicians on the golf course, and may well be delightful companions off it. But I will happily sit up until 3 a.m. to watch a Northern Irish grafter like Graeme McDowell beat them in a major.

What's going on here? I'm pretty sure that it's to do with golf rather than America. I count myself as an Americophile. Many of our family holidays have been spent motel-hopping across the States, and I love working in New York. And I don't feel the same about other sports. For example, I experienced nothing but pleasure when Andre Agassi completed his career grand slam in Paris in 1999, or the USA women's soccer team lifted the World Cup before a 90,000 crowd in the Rose Bowl that same year.

Maybe it's to do with the way that America dominated golf for decades after the Second World War. Or perhaps it stems from the time that Deane Beman, the American PGA commissioner, made it so difficult for Seve Ballesteros and other European stars to compete in US tournaments. And we can't ignore the determined provincialism of the many American golfers who rarely test their skills in the rest of the world. (This attitude has a long history. Sam Snead for one was a notoriously reluctant traveller. He regularly shunned the Open after his single 1946 victory, explaining 'As far as I'm concerned, any time you leave the USA, you're just camping out.')

So, I wouldn't be too quick to assume that the European Ryder Cup fervour is a harbinger of European unity. It seems as likely that the Pringle-sweatered blimps in the members' bars are united by their antipathy to the opposition, rather than their enthusiasm for the European project.

Still, who knows? As we have seen, sporting arrangements often uncover political affinities that cross-cut conventional state boundaries. Some national teams represent countries that no longer exist, while others are potential heralds of political units yet to come. The golf fans certainly seem to view Europe as a natural unity. Perhaps this points to an incipient sense of common political purpose.

At the time of writing, the future of the European project is uncertain. Britain has now voted to leave the Union, and other countries seem likely to follow suit. Europe may well now end up as a loose customs union, rather than the federal state favoured by its more enthusiastic supporters.

In this context, it would be interesting to know if pan-European sides in other sports would get their supporters whooping alongside the Ryder Cup fans. I don't find it too hard to imagine cross-national enthusiasm for a European soccer or rugby side. I wonder whether the hard-pressed supporters of European unity should try to make something of this. They might do better to stop touting the supposed economic and political benefits of union, and start appealing to untapped reservoirs of federal sporting fandom instead.

CHAPTER 13

RACE, ETHNICITY AND JOINING THE CLUB

In 1960, I flew from Durban to Bloemfontein to watch the third rugby test between South Africa and New Zealand. (This wasn't a regular thing – my father's employers had chartered a private plane, and he wangled a seat for me.)

It was something for a twelve-year-old to remember: 55,000 fans in the Free State Stadium, Colin Meads versus Johan Claassen in the line-outs, Don Clarke kicking 80-yard touches through the thin Highveld air. The All Blacks came back from 11–3 down to grab a draw and take the series to a deciding final game.

Except that wasn't the proper All Blacks team. They'd left all their Maoris at home in New Zealand. Of course, we all know that South African teams in those apartheid days were racially exclusive. But what isn't so often remembered is that many other countries – including nice, democratic New Zealand – readily went along with this agenda, even into the 1960s, happy to leave out some of their best players to send racially pure 'white' teams to South Africa.

In general, sporting history scores very badly on race. Many major sports were organized on colour lines throughout much of the twentieth century. In America, professional baseball, football, hockey and basketball were all strictly segregated until after the Second World War. The Olympic Games accepted all-white South African teams until 1960. The West Indies cricket selectors insisted on appointing white captains of limited playing ability until the end of the 1950s.

Thankfully, that's all gone now. Overt racial discrimination is now illegal in most places. Moreover, the intensity of modern sporting competition works against any surreptitious racial favouritism. No coach or selector would keep their job long if they allowed skin colour to trump skill when choosing players.

True, there are some places that haven't heard the news. In parts of southern and eastern Europe, the local fans still think it funny to throw bananas at visiting players of colour. Even so, such behaviour is nowadays widely condemned, and organizations like Kick It Out and FARE (Football Against Racism in Europe) take pains to ensure that perpetrators are identified and punished.

But I wonder if we have travelled as far from the last century as we think. We still tend to think in terms of *races*. We have laws against *racial* discrimination. There are organizations, like Kick It Out and FARE, designed to foster *racial* inclusiveness. I'm not sure that this is the right way to set things up. I worry that the very notion of race may be part of the problem, not the solution.

Most people think of races in terms of 'blood', some kind of inner nature that is responsible for racial characteristics. In their view, races like 'Africans', 'Chinese', 'Caucasians', 'Polynesians' and so on all have a defining essence, passed on from parents to children, and responsible for the allegedly distinctive moral characters, physical features and intellectual abilities of each race.

This kind of thinking is a historical throwback. There is nothing in modern biology to support the idea of race-defining essences. But essentialist ideas of race run deep in our culture, fostered by centuries of spurious justification for the enslavement and exploitation of supposedly 'inferior' races.

A give-away is the 'one-drop rule'. People whose ancestry is 75 per cent European and 25 per cent African are still classified by most people as 'black'. This makes no logical sense. Why aren't they more 'white' than 'black'? But things fall into place if you think of African 'blood' as constitutionally inferior, and so as placing anybody with even a drop in their veins outside the realm of privilege.

To the extent that this kind of thinking is built into the everyday concept of 'race', we will do well to reject the whole idea. There are no inner essences dividing people into a hierarchy of races. We should kick out the very concept of race, along with racism.

Some philosophers object that we will lose something if we eliminate races. Racial thinking is not always bad. For example, groups with different historical origins certainly display different distributions of genes, and recognizing this can be scientifically important, as when we are assessing an individual's risk of some disease, or seeking a bone-marrow match.

Fair enough, but these patterns fall short of anything recognizable as traditional races. There's no doubt that many human traits are influenced by genes, and moreover that the frequency of these genes varies systematically between recognizable population groups. But gene frequencies as such are no basis for dividing the human species into distinct races.

For one thing, migration and intermarriage are constantly reshuffling ancestral genes into new combinations, especially in the contemporary world. And, even apart from that, the average genetic differences between different population groups coexist with large overlaps at the level of individuals (just as an average height difference between Germans and Spaniards doesn't mean that all individual Germans are taller than all Spaniards).

In an ideal world, we wouldn't put people into racial boxes at all, but simply see them all as humans differentiated in myriad ways. Maybe that ideal isn't as unreachable as it sounds. I like to think that modern Britain, along with many other European countries, is starting to abandon the idea of race – and moreover that sport has played a pivotal role in bringing this about.

Britain has the advantage of no long-standing history of local racial discrimination, if for no other reason than lack of opportunity. Before 1950 there were fewer than 20,000 non-whites in the country. However, immigration since then has altered the numbers dramatically, and now there are over 7 million people of colour in the United Kingdom, over 10 per cent of the population.

It can't be said that their arrival has always been welcomed. In his memoir of family and football, *The Last Game*, Jason Cowley describes his grandfather Frank, a retired London bus-driver, and initially an unabashed racist. 'The darkies overran the buses,' he would say. 'They're good at sport because they are used to swinging around in trees.'

Then his football side Millwall signed two black players, and his feelings softened slightly. They were still 'darkies', but they played with pride and commitment, and so became 'our darkies'. Later still, Cowley accompanied his grandfather to a match where an opposing black forward was subject to sustained and vicious racial abuse. On the way home, his grandfather was thoughtful. After a while he said, 'It was tough for that black fella up front this afternoon, wasn't it?' Cowley remembers the words: '*Black fella*. My grandfather had always used the word "darkie".'

Nick Hornby tells a similar story in *Fever Pitch*. He describes his strange sense of pride when the foul stream of obscenities hurled at visiting black players by the Arsenal fans began to leave out the racial epithets. Hornby downplays it – 'It's not much to be grateful for, really, the fact that a man calls another man a cunt but not a black cunt' – but I don't see why. I'd say it's rather a lot to be grateful for.

There are currently well over 1 million people in Britain who identify themselves as 'mixed race'. Some of them are prominent athletes: Theo Walcott, Jessica Ennis-Hill, Lewis Hamilton. When asked, they tend to say that they are mixed-race rather than 'black'. They don't see why some bigoted one-drop rule should make them deny their white parents. More generally, I doubt that there are many Britons left who mindlessly stereotype these figures as 'black', or indeed think very much about the issue at all.

Some would argue that an insistent colour-blindness is in danger of throwing the baby out with the bathwater. They feel that we will lose something valuable if we insist on ignoring the diverse origins of many citizens in modern societies.

There is something to this argument. People grow up with nursery rhymes, ancestral stories, special cuisines and local customs. It is right and natural that communities with a joint origin should want to celebrate their common cultures and pass them on to their children.

It is conventional nowadays to talk about 'ethnicity' rather than 'race'. The point of this terminological shift is precisely to move beyond old-fashioned prejudice, and make space for pride in distinctive traditions grounded in shared histories. I don't want to classify people racially, but I recognize that it is important to many people in my country that they have a Gujarati, or Yoruba, or German Jewish, or Bangladeshi, or Polish background.

Not all philosophers are happy about eliminating the idea of 'race' in favour of the more neutral 'ethnicity'. They feel that this demands a wilful blindness to social reality. Sure, they agree, there is no objective basis for the racial categories imposed by many modern societies. But that doesn't mean that they don't have a huge impact on many people's lives. In many parts of the world, your opportunities depend crucially on your perceived race. These classifications may be social constructions, but they are certainly real to those who suffer discrimination in their name.

I remain uneasy. I agree, of course, that we should recognize and resist racial discrimination whenever it occurs. But this doesn't necessarily mean that we should think of the people who are subject to it as groups with shared identities. In my view, this is already to allow the racists to pollute our thinking.

Ethnicity is one thing, race another. Of course, people who share traditions should be able to preserve and celebrate them. But we shouldn't muddle up ethnicity with any classifications based on skin colour or hair type, even in contexts where there are bigots to whom these things matter.

A crucial difference between ethnicity and race is that one is voluntary but the other is not. I can decide whether or not to count myself as a Gujarati or Pole, in a way that those who deal in racial categories will not allow me to decide if I am black or white. This is why ethnic categories are acceptable, but racial ones are not. They do not limit human potential in the way racial classifications do.

The UK Census in 2011 included an 'ethnic group' question, inviting respondents to say whether they were 'White, Mixed, Asian or Black' or some yet further category. The US Census of 2010 similarly asked – this time under the heading of 'race' – whether respondents were 'White, Black, Native Americans' or something else. (The States didn't have a 'Mixed' option, but allowed more than one box to be ticked.) Of course, these queries were designed with good intentions, not least to help locate and stamp out discrimination. But I don't think they should have been asked. They conceded too much ground to people who think that skin colour (as opposed to shared culture) is important.

After the twenty-one-year-old Tiger Woods won the Masters by twelve shots in 1997, he was invited onto *The*

Oprah Winfrey Show. Asked whether he counted himself as African American, Woods demurred, explaining that his two black great-grandparents were outnumbered by two Chinese, two Thai, a native American and a Dutchman.

Woods was widely criticized in America. Many in the black community felt that his refusal to accept an African-American identity was implicitly racist. Colin Powell, later US Secretary of State, and rather lighter-skinned than Woods, was widely quoted as saying that, 'In America, if you look like me, you're black.'

In my view, Woods's critics were just wrong. Of course, everybody should be concerned about prejudice against African Americans in the United States, and especially so if you are yourself a citizen of that country. But this falls a long way short of saying that you have to accept that identity just because other people give it to you. It would make just as much logical and biological sense to count Woods as Chinese as black. If he doesn't think of himself as black, that's fine by me.

Throughout his long life, Charlie Chaplin was often said to be Jewish. In fact, he was of Anglo-Saxon and Celtic ancestry, and no more Jewish than Margaret Thatcher. Even so, he never denied the attribution publicly. He felt that making a fuss about not being Jewish would only add to the tide of anti-Semitism. He didn't want to suggest that Jewish was something you didn't want to be.

I have always thought Chaplin's stance admirable. More generally, the world would be a better place if people stopped demeaning ethnic groups by emphasizing their distance from them. But this is not to say that you need to embrace whatever classification is imposed on you. It wouldn't have made sense for Chaplin to agree that he was a Jew, just because the Un-American Activities Committee said so. Nor does Tiger Woods have to self-identify as an African American, even if he is stuck with many other Americans thinking of him in this way.

If you ask me, it is only acceptable to think in ethnic terms if we grant people the freedom to opt out. Of course, communities who feel united by history should be allowed, even encouraged, to take pride in their common traditions. But the other side of that coin is that everybody should remain free to shape their own identities.

In general, we don't have any difficulty with this idea. If a Polish family immigrating to the United States chooses to submerge its ethnic origins and adopt a generic white American identity instead, who is likely to object? And most of us will feel the same if some young person wants to slough off their identity as a Northern Irish Protestant, or an Amish, or an orthodox Jew. These moves may of course be resisted by these religiously defined communities themselves, but the majority of impartial observers will side with the right to individual self-determination.

I say that the same principle should apply even to categories like 'African American' or 'British Asian'. It is not for the rest of us to tell anybody what kind of people they are. That's down to them. Skin colour shouldn't come into it.

Perhaps I am pushing at an open door here. The idea that 'self-identification' is central to ethnic classification is familiar enough nowadays. We appreciate that people often want to break free of their historical origins.

But what about the other way around? What about *opting in* to ethnic groups? This isn't so straightforward, but I think the same principle applies. Ethnic groups are only legitimate if they are porous in both directions. You should be able to check in as well as check out.

In 2015, Rachel Dolezal, a serving official in the National Association for the Advancement of Colored People (NAACP), was accused of 'passing' as black. Despite having two parents of unequivocally European ancestry, she had been presenting herself as an African American for some years, and had been active in black community politics.

When the story broke, Dolezal was subject to widespread ridicule. Her claim that she 'self-identified' as black was not taken seriously. But I'm not sure that's right.

True, there were some decidedly dubious aspects to the Dolezal case. For one thing, it seems that much of her initial motivation was to distance herself from her fundamentalist Christian parents. We can sympathize with her, along with the many other young people who grow up thinking they've been born into the wrong family, without agreeing that inventing an African ancestry for yourself is a healthy solution.

Then there are issues of discrimination and redress. Historically, African Americans have been subject to terrible discrimination, and organizations like the NAACP exist precisely in order to rectify past injustices. If you have suffered for the colour of your skin, you might well object when a white person uses deception to claim a share of your recompense.

Still, suppose that Dolezal had been motivated entirely by her admiration for African-American culture and the affinity she felt with its tradition. And imagine (if you can) a time when the historical injustices done to African Americans have become a thing of the past. Even then, I suspect, few people would agree that it makes sense for a white person to declare themselves African American. But I don't see why. If we are still going to have ethnic groups in a just future, then I say people should be able to decide which ones they belong to.

After all, such ethnic ingress often seems straightforward. Take the Polish immigrants who adopt the identity of white Americans. Or me, for that matter. I am English. I sang English nursery rhymes to my children, I speak and write like an Englishman, I am proud of Shakespeare and Bobby Charlton. But my forebears on both sides all came to England within the last three centuries, and they certainly weren't English when they arrived.

Still, perhaps these are easy cases. 'American' and 'English' are classic nations of immigrants, about as cosmopolitan as you can get while still retaining some kind of ethnic identity. All right, let's take a harder one. How about French Canadians? I presume they count as a real ethnic group defined by a desire to celebrate their common ancestry, if anything does.

Even so, it doesn't look that hard to become a French Canadian. Maybe someone who moves to Quebec as an adult isn't going to make it. It's tricky to get the accent right, and it could be argued that you need a network of long-standing personal connections. But the grandchildren of such people would seem to qualify fine, supposing that they identify with French Canada and take pride in its history.

It is only when skin colour intrudes that the boundaries become impenetrable. That's the real reason we find it difficult to countenance Rachel Dolezal as an African American. We think that she lacks the biological essence that is present in all black people, and divides African Americans from the rest, whether they like it or not.

To drive the point home, note that it's only white people who are disqualified in this way. I take it that 'African American' refers to an ethnic group whose history is grounded in the West African people who were forcibly transported to the New World as slaves. Maybe it seems unreasonable for a white woman like Rachel Dolezal to try to sign up to this group. But, if so, how come Barack Obama can join?

Most people have little problem with the idea of President Obama as an African American. But in truth his claim is no better than Dolezal's. None of his ancestors was a transported slave. The darkness of Obama's countenance comes from his father, an East African Kenyan economist who met Obama's mother while he was a student in Hawaii, and owes nothing to the history of slavery.

I fear that, in most people's thinking, 'African American' is still basically an old-style racial category. A necessary requirement is that you have some black African 'blood'. Obama has some, so he can get in, but Dolezal doesn't. Just look at their skins.

I say we are better off without such thinking. To repeat, ethnic histories and traditions are often proper objects of memory and pride. But to keep them free of bad racial ideas, we must allow them to be porous in both directions. If you think that a certain kind of blood is needed to be an African American, but not a French Canadian, then you're thinking in the wrong way.

To say this is not to deny that genetic ancestry can make a difference. Funmbi Omotayo is a British Nigerian comedian. In his act, he explains how his dual affiliations enhance his sporting fandom. When England were knocked out of the soccer World Cup, he switched his support to Nigeria. It was the same in the Olympics. He had two sets of athletes to back.

When it came to the 100 metres men's final, though, he was all for Usain Bolt. 'I told my white friend this before the event, and he got really offended. "Why are you supporting Usain Bolt, Funmbi? He's not British or Nigerian. You're only supporting him because he is *black*." But I was like, "Dude, it's the Olympic 100 metres final – they're *all* black." '

Omotayo is, of course, right. There hasn't been a white man in the 100 metres final since 1980. Nearly all the competitors have had some West African ancestry, benefiting from genes that foster the 'fast twitch' muscles essential for top sprinting.

It's the same in many sports that call for extreme physical types. A disproportionate number of top competitors will descend from ancestral populations that evolved in special environments. Long-distance running is another example. Most champions over the last few decades hail from high-altitude populations in North or East Africa.

Still, we can acknowledge this importance of genetic ancestry without reinstating impermeable racial categories. Of course it is true that different groups have different proportions of sports-relevant genes – Jamaicans versus Poles, say, or people with some West African ancestry versus those without.

But this doesn't mean that these groups possess any special racial essence. They were simply sitting in a good seat when the sporting genes were shuffled. The points made earlier still apply. Most modern humans derive their genes from a mixture of ancestral populations, and even those who don't overlap a great deal in their genetic attributes.

If you are a sports fan, you will do well to identify with groups that have been dealt good genetic hands. But don't make the mistake of thinking that they are winners because of their 'racial' composition. In the end, there aren't any races – just people spread across the many dimensions of human difference.

CHAPTER 14

NATURE, NURTURE AND SPORTING FAMILIES

When the Australian cricket team toured England in 2015, the England side featured three players – Stuart Broad, Jonny Bairstow and David Willey – whose fathers had themselves played for England. Non-aficionados may find this striking, but cricket fans scarcely turned a hair.

After all, the previous couple of years had featured two other England players with international grandfathers (Compton and Tremlett), and we only have to track back a quarter-century to uncover twelve further England selections with test-playing fathers or brothers (Butcher, Cowdrey, Headley, the Hollioakes, Jones, Lloyd, Pattinson, Sidebottom, the Smiths, Stewart).

Nor is the pattern restricted to England. The 2015 Australian team itself had two brothers (Mitchell and Shaun Marsh) whose father had played for Australia. The other cricketing countries are the same. The dynastic names ring through history. The Mohammads and the Khans, the Manjrekars and the Roys, the Hadlees, Headleys, Chappells and Pollocks. And that's just a selection of the families with three or more test players. The ones with two run into the hundreds.

What is going on here? Are these clans all blessed with some special cricketing gene? Or is it that you need the right family background to learn top-level cricketing skills? In pursuing these questions, we shall reach some surprising conclusions that take us deep into the nature–nurture debate and cast light on hereditary success across all walks of life.

Cricket isn't the only sport that runs in families. Motor racing (the Andrettis, Laudas, Pettys, Prosts, Stewarts …) and ice hockey (the Howes, Hulls, Richards, Sutters …) are obvious further examples. 'Mr Hockey' Gordie Howe played through the 1970s in the same teams as his two sons Marty and Mark. Cycling also seems to feature a disproportionate number of family relations.

On the other hand, there are sports where sporting families are thin on the ground. Take soccer, for example. While there are a few prominent football clans – the Charltons and the Ferdinands spring to mind – there is nothing like the rampant familiality found in more dynastic sports. A similar paucity of family connections is found in American football and basketball. With a few notable exceptions – like the gridiron Mannings and the basketballing Currys – these sports don't display frequent hereditary patterns either. Nor does athletics. (To repeat, in 2015 *five* of the twenty-two best cricketers in England and Australia had international cricketing fathers.) This contrast between dynastic and other sports will turn out to hold the key to understanding sporting families.

The nature versus nurture debate is a common topic for sports fans. Two excellent recent books stand on opposite sides of the issue. In *Bounce*, the former table-tennis international Matthew Syed argues that elite sports performers are distinguished not by their genes but by the inordinate amount of practice they put in from a young age. David Epstein's *The Sports Gene* responds with evidence that in many sports the most successful competitors are physically and physiologically quite unusual. (As you'd expect, basketball and running figure prominently in his arguments.)

Both books are enthralling. Neither, however, scores a decisive victory. It's not surprising that the debate is hard to resolve. For a start, it's a mug's game asking whether some sporting ability is 'innate' or 'acquired'. All human characteristics depend on both genetic and environmental influences, and vulgar talk of 'innate' traits only sows confusion, as the philosopher Paul Griffiths has long argued.

Griffiths points out that the everyday notion of an 'innate characteristic' covers a number of different ideas. Does it mean *present at birth*, or *universal in the species*, or *impossible to alter*, or a *result of evolution*, or *due to special genes*? These are all different properties, none of which implies the others. As normally used, the term 'innate' is far too ill-defined for serious debate.

What about defining a more specific quantitative notion of innateness, one that aims to measure what *fraction* of some sporting ability is due to genes? But this idea goes nowhere, too. Trying to divide Stuart Broad's bowling average between his genes and his environment is like asking how much of your bathroom's area depends on its length and how much on its breadth – not a smart question, if you think about it.

The only good way to do genetic sums is to analyse the sources of *variation* in a population. Even if we can't divide Stuart Broad's individual skill into a genetic and environmental component, we can still usefully ask how far the cricketing *differences* among youths in general can be attributed to genetic and environmental *differences* respectively.

The idea is to consider how far the disparities would disappear if everybody had exactly the same genes. The more the reduction, the more we should attribute the original variation to genetic differences. The technical notion of 'genetic heritability' makes this idea precise. It uses the normal statistical measure of variation, and equates the genetic heritability of any trait with the proportion of the total variation that would be lost if everyone were genetically identical.

How can we measure that in practice? The classic technique is to study 'identical twins reared apart'. First, find a set of identical twins (that is, genetic clones) who have been separated at birth and given to different families for adoption. Then see how similar they are with respect to the trait of interest, be it bowling ability, obesity or IQ scores. The more they turn out to be similar, despite their different adoptive environments, the less environmental differences matter, and the more the overall variation in the general population must be due to genetic differences.*

The notion of genetic heritability needs to be handled with care. It doesn't always do what you think. It can tell us as

---

* In fact, it is something of a myth that you need identical twins for such studies – which is just as well given how rare they are. Ordinary siblings reared apart will do fine. Since we know that they share 50 per cent of their genes, and so possess exactly half the genetic variation of the overall population, the extent to which they remain more similar than the overall population when reared apart tells us quite enough to work out the genetic component of the original population variation.

much about a population's environmental and genetic diversity as about the nature of the trait in question. This can lead to odd results, with intuitively environmental traits coming out highly 'heritable', and vice versa.

Consider rickets, the childhood bone disease. This seems environmental, if anything is – it comes from not getting enough vitamin D from either sunlight or diet. But in a population where everybody goes out enough and is adequately fed – think of modern Scandinavia, say – rickets could turn out to be 100 per cent genetically 'heritable', simply because the only sufferers are historic immigrants whose darker skins block the thin northern sun. Or, for an example that goes the other way, take an intuitively innate trait like height, and then imagine a population of genetic near-clones, whose height differences nearly all come from environmental causes – in such a group, height will end up with a genetic 'heritability' close to zero.

Still, there is nothing intrinsically wrong with the notion, as long as we take care to remember what it means – how far are the observable differences in the overall population due to genetic differences? So, what about those sporting abilities that run in families? Genetically heritable or not? If someone is an outstanding cricketer, or ice-hockey player or motor racer, is this more likely to be due to special genes or a special environment? Well, perhaps we should start a project to compare sporting abilities in identical twins reared apart.

But I have a better idea. Let's think about the difference between dynastic and other sports. As I said earlier, sports like cricket are unusual in the extent to which they run in families. Other sports – soccer, basketball, American football – don't display anything like the same family patterns. If we can understand the reasons for this difference, then perhaps that will tell us what is going on.

For simplicity, let's stick to cricket and soccer for a bit. At first sight, the distinctive familiality of cricket might seem to argue that cricket is more genetically heritable than soccer. But that's exactly the wrong conclusion.

Think of it like this. If there is more family resemblance among cricket than soccer players, there are two possible reasons. Either genes are more important in cricket than soccer, or family environments are. And once we focus on this question, the choice seems pretty obvious.

There's no reason to suppose that cricket and soccer differ in their genetic requirements. Neither sport is like basketball, or even rugby, calling for extreme physical types. You just need to be lithe, agile, coordinated, sinewy, strong – pretty much the same list for both sports. On the other hand, when it comes to environments, cricket and soccer are like chalk and cheese.

Pretty much every kid gets plenty of chance to kick a soccer ball around. But cricket skills are by no means easily acquired. It's not just that you need special equipment and facilities. In addition, both batting and bowling are very unnatural, all sideways and no swiping. You need to be taught young – if you haven't been initiated before your teenage years, it's probably too late. On reflection, I'd say that the test-playing clans are just the tip of an iceberg. I'd be surprised to find any serious cricketers without at least one committed club player somewhere in their family background.

If environments matter more in cricket than in soccer, then this makes cricketing skills come out as less genetically heritable than footballing ones. In football, most of the differences come from genetic advantages, just because there aren't many environmental differences – opportunities to kick a round ball are everywhere. But in cricket there would still be a wide range of abilities even if everybody had exactly the same genetic endowment, because only some children get a proper chance to learn the game. In effect, environmental factors are doing a lot more to spread the children out in cricket than they are in football.

So my argument is that cricket runs in families because the genetic heritability of cricket skills is relatively low. At first sight, this might seem almost paradoxical. One thing that you can be sure of is that your genes come from your parents. But environmental help can come from many sources apart from family background, and so is by no means sure to be channelled down family generations. So shouldn't we generally expect strong family resemblances when genes make the difference, rather than environments, notwithstanding the example of cricket?

Matthew Syed starts his book *Bounce* with the story of how one Reading street in the 1980s provided more top British table-tennis players than the rest of the nation combined. As he explains, this wasn't due to some genetic mutation that found its way into the water around there, but simply a combination of an enthusiastic local teacher and a twenty-four-hour practice facility. Local residents benefited from this exceptional environment and many rose to the top. But this had nothing to do with their families. They didn't benefit from table-tennis parents, but from a helpful neighbourhood.

My own alma mater offers a similar example. Over the last century Durban High School has produced twenty-five international cricketers, including Barry Richards and Lance Klusener. In the Lord's test in 1960, five of the South African side were from the school, and in the first two tests against Australia in 1969 there were four. The tradition has continued into the modern post-apartheid world – the 2015–16 series between South Africa and England featured two of the school's old boys, Hashim Amla for the hosts and Nick Compton for the visitors.

As I can testify, the school's cricketing facilities are generous and the coaching exceptional. When I was there, the Under 15As' coach was a former first-class cricketer, but not considered experienced enough to manage the First XI. Given this kind of set-up, a family cricketing background was neither here nor there. Any boy at that school already had a big lead in the cricketing environment stakes.

Non-familial environmental influences like these would seem to support the expectation that family patterns will be more common in those sports where genes dominate, like basketball and running, rather than in those that require helpful environments, like cricket. After all, you don't need a good family to get a helpful environmental hand – a good sporting neighbourhood or school will do just as well.

But in fact that just isn't how it pans out. Cricket isn't an anomaly, but part of a general pattern. Across the board, we find family dynasties in those sports that depend on special environments rather than on special genes.

David Epstein's book *The Sports Gene* stresses the importance of highly genetic physical attributes across a range of sports. In basketball, for example, height and arm length yield a huge advantage. Official statistics suggest that fully 3 per cent of twenty- to forty-year-old US men over 6 feet 10 are active in the NBA. Epstein estimates on this basis that if you meet a 7-footer in the States, there will be as much as a one-in-six chance that he is currently on an NBA roster. But even so there are scarcely any basketball dynasties. Nor do we find many in athletics, or American football, or in other sports where genetically based physical attributes play a crucial role.

Rather the sporting clans seem to be restricted to sports where physical extremes are not called for. As we saw, it's not only cricket. There are similar phalanxes of well-known families in motor racing, ice hockey, cycling and baseball.

So why do things come out back-to-front like this? Why is it the environmental skills, rather than the genetic ones, that are passed down the generations? Well, one reason is no doubt the phenomenon known as genetic 'regression to the mean'. You may have a strong chance of playing in the NBA if you are 7 feet tall – but you will have scarcely any chance of siring a 7-foot-tall son. Remember that half your son's genes will come from his mother – and while she may well be tall, she's unlikely to be as much of an outlier as you are. The point generalizes. The children of a physically exceptional parent are nearly always less exceptional themselves.

So, sporting genes are not tightly coupled across generations. By contrast, access to specialist facilities often is. Note that it's specifically those sports that need particular equipment and training that produce the most family resemblances. If cricket calls for uncommon facilities and expert guidance, this is even more true of the other dynastic sports. Not every child gets a try-out in a racing car at an early age.

Family background isn't always essential for such access, as Matthew Syed's street and my school demonstrate. But these examples are the exception rather than the rule. By and large, the surest way to arrive at a motor-racing track, hockey rink, velodrome or cricket net is to have parents who already frequent these places. It's the tight linking of specialist environments across the generations that accounts for sporting dynasties.

I've been talking about sports, but the lesson is general. In the nineteenth century, Charles Darwin's cousin Francis Galton argued that eminence in a wide variety of fields, from law and politics to science and music, had a genetic basis. His main evidence, presented in chapter after chapter of his monumental study *Hereditary Genius*, was the frequency with which leading figures in all these fields were closely related.

My analysis of sporting dynasties argues that Galton drew exactly the wrong moral. His families of famous politicians and lawyers were evidence in favour of environmental influences, not genetic ones.

This is not to say that Galton was wrong to think that genes are important too. Go back to the comparison of cricket with soccer. I argued that environments don't matter in soccer. But this doesn't mean that genes don't matter in cricket. It's likely that excellence in both soccer and cricket demands superior genes, with the consequence that even in cricket no amount of help and practice will lift those with an average genetic endowment. The difference is rather that to be a top cricketer you need *both* exceptional genes and an exceptional environment, whereas in soccer exceptional environments don't come into it much.

Galton's parade of prominent families is evidence that his fields of eminence are like cricket rather than soccer. If genes were all that mattered, then the relevant similarities between parents and children wouldn't be tight enough, and we wouldn't find top composers and judges popping up generation after generation. So, these family patterns show that such social eminence requires a privileged background, as in cricket, and isn't driven by genes alone, as in soccer. It wasn't the genes he inherited from his dad that enabled George W. Bush to follow him as a US president.

This raises a familiar query. Isn't it unfair if children get ahead because of their privileged background rather than their genetic superiority? I must say that I've always found this an odd question. I've never understood why the gene-environment contrast is supposed to matter here. Of course, it is rotten that some children have deprived backgrounds when others have silver spoons − after all, it's scarcely their own fault − and I am all in favour of measures designed to correct this.

But isn't it just as rotten that some kids are born with dud genes when other have good ones? They haven't done anything to deserve their genetic short straw either. So, I am equally in favour of measures designed to compensate for genetic disadvantages. (I'm not thinking of gene therapy or anything like that − just of devoting extra resources to those who fared badly when the genetic cards were dealt out. This isn't such a crazy idea if you think about it. Nobody objects to extra resources for congenital dyslexics or paraplegics. Maybe we should spread that kind of help around a bit more.)

Still, I realize most people don't see it like that. For some reason, they think that we ought to try to remedy unequal environments all right, but that any steps aimed at eliminating or even compensating for genetic disparities are unnecessary, or even sinister.

Curiously, though, when it comes to sports, most people seem unworried even by unequal environments. We all feel that there's something wrong if young James and Jenny get ahead in law and politics because they have a family background in these professions. But I doubt that many people are similarly troubled by the idea of cricketers and ice-hockey players benefiting similarly. It is interesting to wonder about the basis for this disparity.

Perhaps it's something to do with the different routes by which families can advantage their children in these different arenas. What nobody likes is nepotism. It is rightly viewed as scandalous if James and Jenny get ahead simply because their family connections fast-track them into safe parliamentary seats or prestigious law firms.

On the other hand, many people wouldn't look so askance if the young tyros really were exceptional at their jobs, after hours spent at their elders' knees absorbing arcane secrets of their trades. Maybe the reason we don't object to cricketing families is that we think they fit the second model rather than the first. Stuart Broad's eminence isn't due to favouritism, but to the many childhood hours spent honing his technique with his dad.

But I wonder. The family patterns in cricket and similar sports mean that the children must be getting some environmental help from their family backgrounds. Yet the patterns don't tell us whether the help comes from practice or from partiality. Maybe cricket is just as nepotistic as politics and the law.

In fact, there is plenty of evidence that sporting success can be affected by preferential treatment for privileged groups. Consider the 'relative age effect'. More than 60 per cent of British soccer players in the English Premier League were born in the first half of the school year. Why? Because the coaches and selectors were impressed when these bigger boys stood out in their early age groups. Of course, this age difference itself ceased to matter by adulthood, but the earlier special attention had a lasting effect. The kids who were left out of the team because they were too small never had a chance to catch up.

Similar birthday distributions have been observed across many different sports, including ice hockey, baseball and tennis. Perhaps something like this lies behind family patterns in sport. All right, a young cricketer isn't going to keep his place in the team indefinitely if he never gets any runs or wickets, simply because his father played for England. But he might well be in the team in the first place for just that reason, ahead of other youngsters the selectors don't know much about, or who were quickly dropped after one failure.

Should we care? Does it matter if opportunities in sport are unequally distributed, with specious advantages falling to those with the right birthdays or family names? I think it does. Many people care a great deal about sporting success, and this in itself argues against allocating it on accidents of birth. And even if you think that sporting prizes are in themselves insignificant, they are unquestionably a means to things that do matter.

I'm not thinking only of the money and fame that come with sporting stardom. The association between sport and wider success is far more pervasive. Plenty of studies show that athletically accomplished children have higher self-esteem. One of the best ways to help children along in life is to encourage them on the sports field.

The authorities and scouts in many sports have already started taking steps to counter the relative age effect. They don't want the most talented kids to be overlooked simply because they are elbowed aside by their beefier peers.

Maybe we should watch out for family favouritism in sports, too. I have always felt that sporting families are something to celebrate, a kind of personification of the purity of sporting traditions. But don't forget the children who were kept out of the side by the famous names. Perhaps the real significance of sporting dynasties is that they show sport to be no less corrupt than other walks of life.

In any case, the precise mechanism by which families preserve their prominence is a matter of relative detail. The larger point is that dynasties of excellence depend on nurturing environments rather than outstanding genes.

Galton had things back to front. Exceptional genes are inevitably diluted across generations, and so dynasties are rare in fields where excellence rests on unusual genes alone. By contrast, exceptional environments can be transmitted down the generations, which is why family patterns are common in those sports and professions where helpful environments are crucial. When you see children following in their parents' footsteps, you can be sure it is nurture that is making the difference, not nature.

PART V

VALUES

CHAPTER 15

AMATEUR VALUES AND ULTERIOR MOTIVES

Many sports fans look back to a time when sport was unsullied by the imperatives of the professional era. As they see it, sports are meant for enjoyment, for friendly competition in a spirit of cooperative rivalry. To play for money is to contradict the very basis of sport. Fair play and other sporting values invariably go out of the window once the professionals take over.

What a load of tosh. I won't go so far as to say I reach for my gun whenever I heard the word 'amateur'. But give me a crusade to keep a sport pure in the name of amateur values, and I will show you a hypocritical campaign designed to further some selfish interest.

In 1920 the American rower Jack Kelly entered the Diamond Sculls at Henley. He was the top US sculler that year, but this didn't stop the stewards of the Henley Royal Regatta rejecting his entry on the grounds that he had started his working life as a bricklayer, citing a local rule that denied amateur status to anybody who had ever earned wages as 'an artisan or labourer'.

The decision caused a furore and was widely resented in the States, but Henley stuck to its guns and didn't change its rules for another two decades. (Kelly himself shrugged off the slight, going on to become a three-time Olympic gold medallist, a construction multimillionaire, and father-in-law to Prince Rainier of Monaco.)

You might think that the Henley rules were simple snobbery, but the clause before the one about artisans and labourers reveals a further purpose. This rule said that nobody 'shall be considered an amateur who has been employed in and about boats for money or wages'. Back when the internal combustion engine was in its infancy, there were still plenty of working watermen who could row the socks off the part-time toffs who competed at Henley. The point of the rules wasn't just to keep out the riff-raff, but also to make sure that the college men and the city gents who filled the Henley boats could keep on winning the prizes.

Who remembers Alf Tupper, 'Tough of the Track'? He flourished in the pages of British comics like *Rover* and *Victor* from the 1950s to the 1990s. Every week he would leave his job in the welding shop, get into some scrape on the way to the athletics meeting, arrive in the nick of time, tangle with the stuffed shirts from the Amateur Athletics Association, gobble down his newspaper-wrapped lunch of fish 'n' chips, and then sprint past the posh chaps just before the finishing line.

He was immensely popular, largely because of the frisson engendered by the idea of a cheeky working-class chappie outdoing the snobs at their own game. But, of course, it was all a fantasy. The only way for someone like Alf to gain the time and facilities to compete with the middle classes in their flexitime jobs would be to leave the welding shop and make money from running.

Throughout the twentieth century, many international sporting authorities were determined that this wasn't going to happen. Athletics was in the forefront, closely followed by tennis and rugby union, all desperate to keep their sports safe for the stockbrokers and solicitors who formed their core constituency.

The rules on amateurism were responsible for any number of injustices and absurdities. The great Native American athlete Jim Thorpe was stripped of his 1912 Olympic gold medals in the pentathlon and decathlon because he had spent a couple of summers playing semipro baseball for $25 per game. Many of the finest mid-century tennis players, from Bill Tilden to Rod Laver, could only afford to keep playing by embarking on a touring treadmill of one-night exhibitions. (I saw Laver, Ken Rosewall, Lew Hoad and Pancho Gonzales in a tiny stadium in Durban in the 1960s.) In the 1980s, Bill Beaumont and Fran Cotton, models of rugby-union probity and both now reinstated as stalwarts of the game's administration, were banned from all rugby activities for ten years for receiving royalties from their autobiographies.

Perhaps some of the officials who enforced this farrago sincerely believed in the moral superiority of amateurism. But they shouldn't have. There is no reason to think that professionalism as such is morally corrupting.

True, some aspects of life are undoubtedly tainted by the intrusion of money. Sex and friendship are the most obvious examples. But why include competitive sports in this category? If people want to watch elite athletes, and pay them for displaying their exceptional skills, what has gone wrong? We don't think that painters or musicians are corrupted when they make a living from their art. No more should we of athletes.

No doubt the pressures at the highest levels of sport reduce the attraction of quixotic generosity and increase the temptation to behave badly. And nowadays the highest levels are normally professional. But it would be a fallacy to infer that, to the extent that top athletes do behave badly, it is because they are professional. In other areas of life, we don't expect people to forget their manners just because they are acting in a paid capacity.

Maybe there has been a falling-off in the standards displayed on the sports field in the past few decades. I'm not convinced across the board. It may be hard to deny that top-level soccer is increasingly blighted by nasty habits. On the other hand, tennis players seem far better behaved than forty years ago. One can't imagine Roger Federer or Rafael Nadal indulging in the brattish tantrums of a McEnroe or Connors.

In any case, professionalism per se can't be the reason for soccer's declining standards. After all, soccer has been fully professionalized for over a century. If there has been a deterioration, the cause must lie elsewhere, perhaps in the readiness of the fans and the management to allow the end of victory to justify any unsavoury means.

It is instructive to consider those sports, like golf and cricket, that long observed an institutional division between the gentlemen-amateurs and the professional players, but had them competing alongside each other at the higher levels. In neither sport was there any sense that the professionals couldn't be trusted to behave well in the crunch. If anything, it was the other way around. The dominant image of the dour Scots golf pro, or the sturdy county-cricket player, was of a chap who played hard and knew a few tricks, but was never less than fair.

Historically, ensuring that the part-time middle classes remained competitive wasn't the only motive for enforcing amateurism. When I grew up in South Africa, there were three unmentionable sins, practices that we knew about but only discussed in whispers. First came contraventions of the Immorality Act, sex across the official colour lines, not only exotic but illegal. Then there was 'IDB', Illegal Diamond Buying – the De Beers corporation was fiercely protective of its monopoly, and anybody dabbling in contraband was liable to be spirited away by the De Beers special police in the middle of the night. And finally – and just as taboo – was taking the rugby league shilling, emigrating to play professional rugby in England.

Rugby league is an alternative version of rugby, with thirteen players a side to rugby union's fifteen. Back then it was the professional code, and the amateur rugby union authorities issued automatic life bans to anybody over eighteen who played in a league match. Union was the game of the white South Africans, especially the Afrikaners, and Springbok success on the field was a central element in their national identity.

South Africa was obsessed with resisting the lure of professional rugby. They didn't care a hoot about preserving part-time sport – half the national team had sinecures in the police or army – but they did mind about their best players being struck off for life. It was a national tragedy when the great wing Tom van Vollenhoven, scorer of a hat-trick for the Springboks against the British Lions in 1955, left to earn his living playing English league soon afterwards, and this was compounded a couple of years later when he was followed by another fine Springbok winger, Wilf Rosenberg, 'The Flying Dentist'.

Thankfully, most of these contortions about amateurism have now faded into history. But there is one place they remain. American college sports are as fanatical about the amateur status of their athletes as any of the traditional authorities. The National Collegiate Athletic Association leaves no stone unturned in hunting down violations of their amateur rules.

The motive behind the NCAA obsession with amateurism is not hard to discern. It's not protecting part-timers, nor national pride, but simply preserving a system that makes staggering amounts of money. Led by basketball and football, American college sports generate billions of dollars, precisely because they distinguish themselves from the professional leagues by their amateurism. But by the nature of the case this amateur status then means that all that money must flow to the colleges, coaches and administrators, and not a penny to the athletes themselves.

The NCAA's fetish for enforcing amateurism isn't limited to policing under-the-counter payments by wayward colleges. Some of the restrictions would be risible were it not for the penalties imposed on the athletes. College players have been suspended for accepting free tattoos, or for selling their sports jerseys to help cover holiday expenses. Commentators have not been slow to point out that the colleges themselves are happy to peddle advertising space on players' uniforms to the highest bidders.

It gets worse. In 1974, a running back for Texas Christian University, Kent Waldrep, emerged from a play against Alabama's Crimson Tide paralysed from the neck down. After nine months, TCU stopped paying his hospital bills. Waldrep sued the university, arguing that his football-related financial aid meant he was working as an employee when injured, and so was entitled to normal worker's compensation. But the courts sided with TCU and the NCAA, agreeing with their contention that sports scholarships did not mean that 'student-athletes' were employees.

This ruling was par for the course. The US courts have generally been unsympathetic to challenges to the college sports system. It's a catch-22 for the athletes. Because they aren't employees, they cannot claim the protection of employment and competition law. But without that protection, they have no way of challenging their bogus status as 'student-athletes'.

When a discarded football player at Rice University lost his sports scholarship, he argued that the NCAA was illegally price-fixing by banning colleges from offering multi-year scholarships to new students. The courts responded that competition law didn't apply, since it hadn't been shown that there was a commercial market for the labour of student-athletes.

As it happens, the NCAA has subsequently revised this rule, and colleges are now free to offer multi-year scholarships. But the impetus for this liberalization was pressure from the United States Justice Department, rather than any court recognition of the bargaining rights of college athletes. In the same vein, attempts to organize college athletes into labour unions have repeatedly found themselves denied the backing of labour law, on the grounds that the athletes don't qualify as workers.

Every so often, some respectable university becomes embroiled in an athletics-related grade-fixing scandal. A coach or teaching adjunct is discovered to have been helping students in their tests, or allowing unauthorized retakes, or entering unearned marks. The athletics programme is disciplined, the guilty parties are suspended or sacked, hands are wrung.

To some, this represents a sad dereliction of the universities' academic mission. What are things coming to, when staff at serious universities connive in academic fraud? I see it quite differently. Given the way that colleges collude with the professional leagues in constraining ambitious athletes to spend time at university, I'd say that they have a positive duty to ensure that the athletes get the grades they need. It would be a sad injustice if some future NBA star were denied his destiny simply because of academic limitations.

A couple of years ago, I was telling my English teenage daughter how all American football and basketball players go through university before turning professional. 'But what if they aren't interested in any subjects?' Katy asked. I had to explain that she was thinking the wrong way around. If you want to be a pro football or basketball player in the States, you'd better find some subjects to be interested in.

In practice, the only way to be recruited to a professional team is to be a success at college. Neither football nor basketball has any structure of academies or minor leagues for young athletes who don't attend college. Instead, they simply take the cream of the college crop each year. The system is backed up by age rules that prevent pro teams hiring athletes straight out of school.

It's a cosy set-up. The professional leagues outsource development to the colleges, and in return the colleges get rich from the indentured labour of future stars. Still, it is hard to believe that the system is stable. The billions of dollars at stake and the hypocrisy intrinsic to the system mean that the NCAA's regulations are under constant pressure in the courts. College sports need to evolve or die.

One possibility would be to ban sports scholarships, as is already done at Ivy League colleges. Athletic prowess could still add to the strength of a college application, but athletes would need to fund their college degree the same way as everybody else. Since this would no doubt lead to many top athletes skipping college altogether, the pro football and basketball leagues would be forced to open alternative avenues of recruitment, perhaps taking baseball and ice hockey as models.

But would it work? Dodgy college athletes are not a new problem. I was first introduced to the issue by one of the earliest Marx Brothers films. In *Horse Feathers* (1932), Groucho becomes president of Huxley College and decides to engage a few professional ringers to bolster his football team (though he inadvertently recruits Chico and Harpo, with ensuing chaos). The topic recurs in other old movies. For instance, *Trouble Along the Way* (1953) has a similar theme, except this time the recruiter is John Wayne and the film isn't so funny.

The modern package of sports scholarships and NCAA regulations was introduced in the middle of the last century precisely to end such blatant corruption. By introducing the category of 'student-athletes' and allowing colleges to subsidize them, the NCAA aimed to end the surreptitious introduction of non-academic professionals.

If colleges were now to be prevented from offering official financial support to athletes, there would be a danger of a reversion to underhand practices. The Ivy League colleges don't need their sports teams to bolster their prestige. But plenty of institutions in the Midwest and the south depend on their athletics programmes for their prominence.

In the end, I think that the only viable solution is to make the system honest and pay the student-athletes. Just as in the professional leagues, the players would be able to form a bargaining group and negotiate with the employers. They could have a share of the profits they generated, together with a wage structure, proper insurance against injury and future loss of earnings, and all the other protections that normal workers enjoy.

I am not against college sports. They form a wonderful tradition, and play a central role in many people's lives. It would be a sad loss if they were to disappear.

Still, there is no reason why proper payment for college

athletes should threaten college traditions. In truth, it would do little more than normalize current reality. Few of the kids playing for top teams, especially in basketball and football, would be in their colleges if they hadn't been given monetary incentives in the form of scholarships to join the athletics programmes. So, what would change if they were paid, apart from their gaining a fair share of the money they generate?

Some will say that payment would destroy the purity of amateur athletics, undermine the sporting ethos, and obliterate everything that makes college sports worthwhile. But that's exactly what they said about tennis, rugby and the Olympic Games. Yet when these sports turned professional, the roof didn't fall in at all. The only noticeable result was a universal sigh of relief as the crippling burden of hypocrisy was lifted. College sports would do well to attend to the lesson.

CHAPTER 16

THE COASE THEOREM AND SPORTING CAPITALISM

By the time Andrew Luck graduated in 2012, he had broken all records as Stanford University's quarterback and was the hottest property in American football. His reward was to be indentured to the struggling Indianapolis Colts for four years. The annual NFL draft gives the first pick of the new players to last year's bottom team. The Colts had propped up the league the previous season, and they didn't hesitate to requisition Luck.

To European sensibilities, this system seems bizarre. Imagine if the young Steven Gerrard had been told that he couldn't sign for his beloved Liverpool at the start of his career, but had to serve time with some feeble team at the other end of the country, like Hull, say, or Bournemouth. Not only would this strike most non-Americans as both illegal and immoral — it would be more than human nature could bear.

It is tempting to compare the collectivist regulation of American sport with the capitalist spirit that operates in Europe. Isn't it ironic, commentators sometimes quip, that the world bastion of economic competition has centrally planned sporting institutions, while the more socialist countries of Europe subject their sports to the rigours of the free market?

This easy comparison, however, does little justice to the real sporting differences between America and other countries. The contrasts are deep and significant, but it is no simple matter of American socialism versus European capitalism.

For a start, US spectator sports have always been unapologetically commercial. American professional teams are money-making enterprises. The big teams in Europe stand on top of pyramids built out of amateur sports clubs, and are traditionally governed by the same bodies, such as the Union of European Football Associations (UEFA) or the England and Wales Cricket Board (ECB). But American pro sports teams have always had private owners. Bodies like the National Football League (NFL) and the National Basketball Association (NBA) are associations of these owners, and have no connection with amateur sport. (Indeed, American major sports, with the possible exception of basketball, are just too hard for ordinary people to play in their professional form. In Britain, more than 2 million people play in an organized soccer match every week.)

It is the American owners' associations that impose the draft system, along with further measures like salary caps, revenue sharing, and so forth. The rationale is to maintain a competitive balance between teams, lest the paying public lose interest at too many one-sided matches.

Incidentally, you might wonder why bottom-half teams don't deliberately lose their final games to improve their position in the upcoming draft – why not 'Suck for Luck', as some teams' fans urged towards the end of the 2012 season? Apparently, this isn't a serious issue in the NFL, but in basketball the NBA has taken steps to discourage 'tanking' by distributing draft picks among the lower teams by lottery – so they can't be sure that coming last will help. (The Australian rules football authorities have an even more ingenious solution. They determine draft picks by a complex formula based on a number of factors – and then keep the formula secret, to stop clubs gaming the system.)

Curiously, there is little evidence that the draft and allied devices succeed in enhancing competitive balance. The win–loss statistics have never changed much when the rules have been relaxed to allow greater player freedom. This might look paradoxical, but there is an elegant theoretical explanation. Let us enter the weird and wonderful world of sports economics.

The 1991 Nobel Prize for economics went to Ronald Coase. The idea for which he is best known is the 'Coase theorem'. This is based on an insight first developed in connection to baseball player trades by Simon Rottenberg (in 'The Baseball Players' Labor Market', *Journal of Political Economy*, 1956). Rottenberg's original thesis, which was then generalized by Coase, is that the ownership of legal rights never makes any rational difference to their economic deployment.

An example will make the principle clear. Suppose WindCo wants to build a wind turbine near Jane's house. Jane goes to court, arguing that they have no right to make noise in her space. WindCo responds that it's a free country for normal amounts of noise. It looks like the court will decide whether the turbine goes up, right? No. According to the Coase theorem, the legal ruling won't make any difference to the skyline.

This might seem illogical, but look at it like this. There must be some amount of profit WindCo will make from the turbine – call it $X per annum. And there must also be a sum that signifies how much Jane wants to avoid the noise – $Y per annum. The turbine being built depends only on whether X is bigger than Y, not on what the court says.

Even if the court finds for Jane, the turbine will go up if X is bigger, for then WindCo will buy Jane off and still make a profit. And even if the court finds for WindCo, there won't be a turbine if Y is bigger, for then Jane will be prepared to buy off WindCo. The court can decide who has to buy off whom, but not whether the turbine goes up. (What if Jane is too poor to pay? Concentrate. We're doing economics here. No bleeding hearts. If Jane is poor, the sum Y that she'll be ready to pay to avoid the noise will be smaller, and the turbine more likely to go up. You might think that's a shame, but it doesn't affect the analysis.)

Now let's do it with football players. Suppose that Andrew Luck is worth $Y per annum to the Indianapolis Colts owner, but a larger $X to the owner of a big city team, where he will put more bums on expensive seats. Then it doesn't matter if Luck is initially drafted to the Colts. Economic rationality will direct him to the big city club, who will be ready to offer the Colts more than they themselves can earn from Luck's services. (In fact, at the time of writing Luck is in his fourth season with the Colts and doing very well. I can't help that. We're doing economics here. He may still be with the Colts in practice, but it'll never work in theory ... As it happens, the Indianapolis Colts are a relatively prosperous team – their 2012 wooden spoon was an anomaly – who make good money out of Luck's talents.)

What if we do have a genuinely poor club, and it does sell on its fancy draftees to its richer competitors? Won't this still end up helping competitive balance overall? After all, these sales themselves will be a source of income, which the poor clubs can then use to boost their playing strength.

But we're going around in a circle. The original point was that the owners of poorly supported clubs will make more money by pocketing their draft windfalls than by spending them on high-end players who won't boost gate receipts enough. So, while the draft system may indeed transfer some revenue to the poor clubs – it may even help them to stay in business – it won't have the intended effect of making them stronger on the field.

Why do the top athletes put up with the draft? It's clearly not in their interests to be assigned to the lowliest teams, as opposed to selling themselves to the highest bidders. But as things stand they have no choice. All the owners are party to the draft arrangements. None of them is going to break ranks and hire a player who has been drafted elsewhere.

The only recourse for players who don't like their draft assignments is to become 'holdouts'. They can refuse to play until they are traded to another team. One famous example involved quarterback Eli Manning in 2004. Manning's father Archie, himself a distinguished quarterback, had been drafted by the New Orleans Saints in 1971, and played for them for ten full seasons. Despite Archie's heroic efforts, his Saints were probably the worst team in NFL history. They came to be known as the 'Aints', and their supporters took to hiding their heads in paper bags with eyeholes – 'Aint Bags' – in mock shame at their affiliation.

In 2004 the bottom-ranked San Diego Chargers were expected to choose Eli with their top draft pick. In response, the Manning family announced that Eli would rather sit out the next season than play for San Diego. The ploy worked. In the event, the Chargers did draft Manning, but then promptly traded him to the New York Giants, the club where he subsequently won two Super Bowls and still plies his trade.

From time to time, professional American athletes challenge the owners' associations in the courts, arguing that their exercise of monopoly power violates anti-trust legislation. You might think that these cases would be pushovers. Certainly, the European courts in recent decades have always sided with the players in such actions, striking down maximum wages, 'reserve clause' transfer fees, and any other such restrictions on free bargaining.

The American courts, however, have consistently gone the other way. Since the beginning of the last century, they have taken the view that cartels of commercial team owners are necessary for the supply of professional spectator sports. As they see it, the professional leagues are 'natural monopolies', and they have explicitly excused them from anti-trust regulations.

As a counterbalance, though, the courts have actively supported the players' unions. In the early years of the leagues, the owners were able to exploit their monopoly position to depress the players' pay and conditions. But since the 1950s the players have become organized. The courts have backed them by decreeing that the owners' anti-trust exceptions are conditional on agreements with the players' unions.

This way of doing things has one obvious drawback. The professional sports labour markets have effectively evolved into bilateral monopolies. Each has only one buyer and one seller. This means the two sides have no bargaining counters apart from strikes and lockouts. The players can't sign up with other employers, and the owners can't hire alternative players.

So, every so often there are no sports to watch in America, as the two sides test each other's economic resolve by closing down operations. American sports fans have suffered a sad history of interrupted seasons. Baseball had five strikes and three lockouts between 1972 and 1994, culminating in the cancellation of the 1994 World Series. The NFL lost chunks of the 1982 and 1987 seasons. The National Hockey League cancelled all the 2004–5 season and parts of 1991–2, 1994–5 and 2012–13. Basketball missed half of 1998–9 and two months of 2011–12.

If you want a paradoxical inversion of economic stereotypes, this is where to find it. The older among us will remember the frequent and crippling strikes that differentiated Europe from America in the decades after the Second World War. The main cause was the nationalization of major European industries, and the consequent monopolization of their labour markets, a development that was largely absent from America. Since then, most of those nationalized industries have been reprivatized, and large-scale European strikes are pretty much a thing of the past. It's funny to think of American professional sport as the one place where the post-war European model survives.

Strikes and lockouts aside, the collective bargaining system works pretty well. The two sides tend to settle when their economic rewards are in rough proportion to their economic contributions. The only people who remain short-changed are those who haven't yet made their way through the draft.

The players' unions have been highly effective in ensuring high wages and post-draft-period freedom of movement. But they haven't done much for those entering their professions. The extreme restrictions on trade implicit in the draft system have been left largely intact. The next Andrew Luck will still be assigned to the worst team. Perhaps that's not surprising. After all, the unions answer to players who have already established themselves. They are unlikely to prioritize the interests of those who have yet to enter the profession.

Does this matter much? What about the Coase theorem? Wasn't that supposed to ensure that top players would get moved to top teams, even if initially drafted elsewhere? Well, for all its theoretical interest, it is not clear how far the Coase theorem actually applies in real sports markets.

The problem is that it assumes economic rationality – which in this context means that the owners of professional sports teams are after money and not glory. And, even by the standards of theoretical economics, that's highly unrealistic. It may have been different in the early days, but now a large proportion of US pro teams are rich men's playthings. Of the 122 teams in the major sports leagues, 59 boast owners who appear on the Forbes 2016 list of billionaires.

When property mogul Donald Sterling was forced to sell the LA Clippers after being caught out making racist remarks, it was the recently retired Microsoft chief executive Steve Ballmer who forked out $2 billion to take the team off his hands. These guys aren't going to peddle their draft picks for a few extra bucks. What they want is to rub shoulders with stars on the winners' platform.

What about the fans, whom this whole spectator circus is ultimately supposed to benefit? In the short term, rich sugar daddies can seem to be on their side. Instead of trying to drain every last cent out of their franchises, they will boost their teams' finances and invest in winning. But sugar daddies can be fickle, and relationships can turn sour.

H. Wayne Huizenga is a capitalist's capitalist. Starting with a single garbage truck in 1968, he spent the next three decades building up (and then selling) three successive billion–dollar businesses (Waste Management, Blockbuster Video, AutoNation). He is also a sports enthusiast, who bought the Florida Marlins baseball team in 1993, and backed them all the way to a World Series victory four years later.

But the next winter he fell out with the Miami-Dade County authorities, and in a fit of pique sold off all his victorious players. In 1998 the Marlins won just a third of their games and became the first World Series champions to come bottom of their division the following year. If you are seduced by a rich suitor, you will do well to remember that he is likely to lose interest in you one day.

The best deal for the fans is undoubtedly to own the club themselves. This is common, if not normal, in European soccer leagues. The German Bundesliga requires all clubs to be major-ity owned by their members, and the two Spanish giants, Real Madrid and Barcelona, have similar ownership structures. By contrast, fan ownership is almost unknown in America.

Still, the single exception is instructive. The Green Bay Packers are the most successful team in NFL history. Although the population of their home town is only just over 100,000, they have finished the season as champions a record thirteen times, most recently in 2010. (The Chicago Bears are next with nine.) There is little doubt that this anomalous success owes something to the 360,584 Packers owners spread throughout Wisconsin and the Midwest. No single owner is allowed to hold more than 4 per cent of the shares.

The advantages of fan ownership are obvious. All revenue is directed towards the future good of the team, and there is no danger of a peeved tycoon packing up his toys and going home. Sadly, there seems little hope of fan ownership spread-ing. If anything, the trend is in the other direction. The English Football League used to proscribe dividends for club share-holders, but this rule was dropped when the Premier League was formed in 1992. And the American NFL positively requires that at least 30 per cent of each franchise must be owned by a single individual. (The Green Bay Packers are protected by a special 'grandfather' clause recognizing their historical idiosyncrasy.)

If fan ownership is out, I think I'd rather have profit-maximizers than dilettante billionaires. Maybe the profiteers will sell on their top-heavy talent, in line with the Coase theorem, and keep the small clubs small. But the European soccer leagues suggest that fans are prepared to tolerate a fair amount of competitive imbalance, and in any case there is always relegation – or the American equivalent of franchise relocation – to eliminate teams that really can't cut the mustard. A more important point is that properly hard-headed entrepreneurs will want to do as well as they can for their clubs. After all, from their point of view, their clubs are capital assets. So they have a direct interest in enhancing their value, as opposed to exploiting them as a status symbol.

As often, sport points to a general moral. Communal ownership often works best overall, but short of that we will do better with proper competitive capitalism, not capricious plutocracy. It's better to be ruled by the rational pursuit of profit than jerked around by the whims of the super-rich.

CHAPTER 17

HISTORY, TRADITION AND THE MEANING OF FOOTBALL

Here and Now is a published collection of letters exchanged between the novelists Paul Auster and J. M. Coetzee in the years 2008 to 2011. I am a big fan of both writers and enjoyed the volume (putting aside the parts where they set themselves to solve the world's socio-economic problems).

One of main attractions of the book, from my point of view, was that Auster and Coetzee are both sports fans. Much of the book is devoted to their athletic enthusiasms. At one point, Coetzee raises an interesting question. Why, he asks, do no new sports get invented any more? Nearly every well-known sport had its rules codified in the second half of the nineteenth century. Since then, scarcely any new games have emerged. So what blocks their creation? Coetzee and Auster both offer answers, but neither is particularly convincing.

In keeping with his day job as a professor of literature, Coetzee wonders whether there is a limited number of viable sporting forms. Perhaps there is some deep structure of games that allows only a restricted range of constructions from a universal sporting grammar.

Auster, as one might expect of a North American sports fan, puts it down to the power of big business. In his view, the giant commercial monopolies that run major spectator sports make sure that no upstarts get a look-in.

I think we can do better than that. I'd say that Coetzee's suggestion is belied by the rich variety of sports that can be found in different parts of the world. And one wonders whether Auster realizes how far North America is an outlier in its devotion to business-led professional sports. Pretty much everywhere else, the principal sports rest on a broad base of amateur participants.

I favour a different answer. The problem that faces any new sport is its lack of tradition. History is an essential component of sport. All established sports can tell tales of past heroes and famous victories. This adds to the significance of athletic achievement. It is one thing to be good at hitting a little ball across the countryside with long sticks. It's another to follow in the footsteps of Old and Young Tom Morris, of Ben Hogan and Sam Snead, of Seve Ballesteros and Tom Watson.

That is why it is hard for new sports to become established. They lack a past to add substance to their contests. They aren't able to look back to a record of memorable achievements. It's not the kind of thing you can manufacture on demand.

If you turn on the television on a winter's Saturday morning in Melbourne, Australia, you are likely to see a group of large men engaged in earnest conversation. They are dissecting the afternoon's upcoming 'footy' matches, analysing possible tactics, rating the players, measuring them against past titans like Ted Whitten, Bob Skilton and Ron Barassi.

You would be hard put, given the gravity of their demeanour, to tell that the game of which they speak is little played outside their city. In Melbourne, 'football' means Australian rules football, a very specific variety of the genus, played on a huge oval field with eighteen players a side, featuring tall rangy forwards who leap high to catch the ball and take a 'mark'. The main clubs take their names from Melbourne suburbs, and the annual Grand Final attracts a crowd of 100,000.

However, in Sydney, the nearest big city, and Brisbane, the next one north, 'football' refers to a quite different game. Here it is rugby league, a thirteen-a-side contest that is itself largely peculiar to the east coast of Australia and the north of England. It is not dissimilar to the more widespread rugby union code, but is distinguished by its history of professional players and working-class roots.

In Sydney, Aussie rules is viewed as a quaint southern oddity, and it is the rugby league heroes that obsess the media. In 2014 the league Grand Final between the South Sydney Rabbitohs and the Canterbury Bulldogs filled the huge ANZ Stadium and attracted a TV audience of 4.6 million. The Rabbitohs' victory was a triumph for their owner, film star Russell Crowe, whose backing had taken the struggling inner-city team to their first final victory in forty-three years.

Intellectual commentators often bemoan cultural imperialism. Hollywood films and English-speaking TV are swamping the world, they complain, eliminating local traditions and turning everything into a homogenized cultural soup.

I wonder how many of these intellectual pessimists are sports fans. They might be right about some aspects of mass-market media – though if you ask me they would do well to get out more – but they are certainly wrong about sports. Each region of the world has its own sporting traditions. There is little sign that they are being eliminated by global brands.

If anything, the opposite is true. Attempts to export sports to new markets are typically ineffective. Sports administrators tend to be evangelical about their own codes, funding development programmes and promoting showcase matches in foreign locations. But it's not clear that these initiatives ever make any difference.

The American National Football League plays some of its games in London each year, but I can't say I've ever noticed the locals paying much attention. Similarly, Major League Baseball held the first game of the season in Australia for a while, but now seems to have given this up as a bad job.

In truth, sporting traditions reach too deep to be uprooted by marketing exercises. They are passed on from generation to generation, and command a loyalty that is central to many people's identity. From an early age, youngsters acquire sporting heroes, team affiliations, and an ingrained sense of how their games should be played. These are not things that you can learn from an advertising campaign.

The term 'football' is itself a testament to the diversity of sporting traditions. Melbourne and Sydney are not the only places that attach their own meaning to the word. In much of the world, of course, it stands for the round-ball game formally designated as association football. But in Ireland it is generally understood as meaning Gaelic football, in New Zealand it is traditionally used for rugby union, while in North America it refers to the gridiron version of the game. As a rule, 'soccer' is the term used for the association variant in these places where other forms of football are dominant.

In the early 1990s, I was fond of a UK-Australian co-produced television series called *The Boys from the Bush*. It was set in a Melbourne detective agency and featured Tim Healy as a British expatriate originally from Shepherd's Bush and Chris Haywood as his Australian counterpart from the outback.

The programme had many virtues, not least its strand of deadpan humour. There was plenty of fun along the lines of 'You won't find him in the office – he's gone to the football.' 'No, that can't be right, he said he couldn't stand the game.' Sadly, the series was discontinued after just two seasons, though it has since acquired a cult following. Perhaps not everybody found the football jokes as funny as I did.

The use of 'soccer' to refer to association football is itself a complex cultural phenomenon. When I first started writing about sport, I found it natural to use the term as a stylistic variant for 'football', even in contexts where there was no possibility of confusion with other codes. Rather to my surprise, a number of my British readers challenged me on this, asking why I didn't stick to the normal English term.

At first I supposed that they were objecting to the outmoded class connotations of the word. My father, who was born in 1910, and played the round-ball game at his private school and Oxford college, never referred to it as anything except 'soccer'. The word originated as a corruption of 'association', and it contrasted with the now little-heard 'rugger', for rugby union, in line with the tiresome Oxford practice of forming slang words by adding 'er' on the end.

It turned out, however, that it wasn't the class angle that was bothering my readers at all. Their gripe was rather that I was surrendering to American influence, allowing transatlantic usage to alter my writing style.

Their complaint was quite misconceived. My objectors had things back to front. In truth, it was they who were guilty of succumbing to American influence.

Until a couple of decades ago, 'soccer' was a perfectly normal alternative to 'football' in British English. It was common in everyday speech and journalism, and by no means restricted to people who went to Oxford. Since then, however, the term has fallen out of favour. The reason is the increased interest in association football among North Americans, and their co-option of the term 'soccer' to distinguish it from their native gridiron game. The British have reacted by coming to think of the usage as a foreign imposition, and now make a fetish of avoiding it themselves.

There is something sadly self-defeating about a country abandoning its own customs in the mistaken belief that they are alien imports. It betrays a neurotic lack of confidence about national identity.

The reaction against 'soccer' is by no means an isolated case. Take the alternative '-ise'/'-ize' spellings for the ends of many words. The British now widely suppose that '-ize' is American usage, and insistently shun it in their own writing. But in fact '-ize' was historically the dominant variation in British

English. My massive two-volume 1970 edition of the *Oxford English Dictionary* doesn't even offer 'realise' as an alternative spelling for 'realize'. I wonder how many of those who nowadays studiously avoid '-ize' know that that they are distorting their own language in response to a phantom fear of American influence.

But let me return to sports. Coetzee is right to observe that nearly all mainstream sports settled into their modern forms in the second half of the nineteenth century. The different codes of football are a case in point. In England, the basic division between association and rugby football was decided when the Football Association laid down its rules in 1863 and the Rugby Football Union followed in 1871. The Gaelic Athletic Association codified its form of the game in 1884. Earlier than all of these, Australian rules had already gone its own distinctive way when the Melbourne Football Club fixed on a code of rules in 1859.

Why did all this happen in so short a period? The obvious answer is the railways. The first commercial freight trains started in the 1820s and by the 1850s all industrialized countries had widespread passenger networks. Until then, each area and educational institution, especially the English public schools, enjoyed their own versions of football. But now it became possible for them to travel to play each other, and this created an obvious need for standardized rules.

The evolution of football codes in North America followed a similar path. Up until the 1860s, a variety of games were played in different schools and colleges, loosely divided into 'kicking' variants like soccer and 'running' games like rugby.

Matches were often played on a portmanteau basis, using the home side's rules for a first game and the visitors' for a second. According to legend, it was the Harvard–McGill match-ups in 1874 that decided the future. Harvard were so impressed with the rugby-style variant offered by McGill that they abandoned their own 'Boston rules' and persuaded other colleges to follow suit.

Other modern sports also defined themselves in the second half of the nineteenth century. Some, like golf, boxing and cricket, had histories stretching back into the seventeenth century and beyond, but again it was the railways that prompted their modern competitive forms. The first Open Championship in golf was held in 1860, overarm bowling became standard in cricket from 1864, and boxing's Queensberry rules were drawn up in 1867.

Yet further sports with less well-defined ancestries materialized. Baseball, ice hockey, field hockey, lawn tennis and basketball all became established as flourishing pastimes by the beginning of the twentieth century.

This history casts light on Coetzee's question. It wasn't always impossible to invent new games. Back at the beginning of modern sport, space on the sporting map was still up for grabs. Some sports evolved from earlier proto-versions, but others were deliberately put together on the drawing board. For example, both field hockey and basketball were created *ex nihilo* in the late nineteenth century, explicitly designed (in Teddington, Middlesex and Springfield, Massachusetts, respectively) as safer winter alternatives to injury-threatening football.

Perhaps the most striking example of an invented game is lawn tennis. In the early 1870s, a Major Walter Wingfield designed a racket game that could be played on croquet lawns. He dubbed it *sphairistike*, from the ancient Greek for 'ball-skill', and started marketing equipment sets in 1874. The name didn't catch on, and only a few of Wingfield's sets were sold, but the game itself spread like wildfire. By the end of the decade the All England Lawn Tennis and Croquet Club was holding an annual tournament in Wimbledon.

The railways weren't the only stimulus for the sporting boom. As important was the emergence of a mass white-collar middle class with the time and ambition for genteel leisure pursuits. Historically, sport had been restricted to private schools and universities, plus the huntin', shootin' and fishin' of the landed upper classes. Now tennis and golf clubs were springing up in every middle-class suburb, and anybody with social pretensions was avid to join.

Not everybody regarded this as progress. In the summer of 1914, the *Times* ran an article about the golf craze that was sweeping the country. It provoked a heated series of letters, mainly from the old guard who viewed the new middle-class sports as a sad index of moral laxity. One leading cricketer wrote, 'The day that sees the youth of England given up to lawn tennis and golf in preference to the old manly games, cricket, polo, football, etc. will be of sad omen for the future of the race.'

The snobbery was even more explicit in other contributions. A writer from the Stock Exchange berated one of the few correspondents who had ventured to defend golf: 'He says he would rather teach his son to hit a golf ball than shoot a bird; we all know the end of that boy, and his father will only have himself to blame.' The condescension is only heightened by hindsight – given the date, the fate of the boy in question was more likely to be death in the trenches of Flanders than a life of moral depravity.

Once a sporting code becomes established in a region, it will tend to monopolize resources, and make it difficult for other games to break in. But what decides which sports gain a foothold in the first place? Often it can be a pretty random business. The history of cricket versus baseball in North America is a case in point.

If there's one thing that divides America and the rest of the English-speaking world, it's their attitudes to these two games. It's a crucial component of national identity. No American regards cricket as anything but a joke, while non-Americans dismiss baseball as nothing but vulgar razzmatazz.

To most Americans, cricket means village greens, cream teas, Miss Marple and the vicar, fat old men dropping catches. Once I was playing in Battersea Park in central London – a fairly serious match between old club rivals – and I heard some passing Americans say, 'Gee, look – cricket.' It was as if our match were the changing of the guard at Buckingham Palace, or some other such London quaintness. The tourists seemed to have no idea that it was a serious game like their own sports.

In fairness, most Britishers are the same about baseball. 'Just a glorified game of rounders,' they will say, secure in their total ignorance of the game and its history. I have expatriate friends in the States who will go to desperate lengths to keep up with world cricket, but won't even look at the television if they're in a bar and the final game of the baseball World Series is showing.

To my mind, these attitudes betray a perverse lack of curiosity. Neither group of dogmatists are real sports fans. In truth, both baseball and cricket are wonderful games, fully deserving of the huge support they command in their respective strongholds.

As a member of the rare breed that follows both cricket and baseball, I can testify that both feature phenomenal athletes with unnatural skills. Indeed, many of the skills are very similar – not surprisingly given that both games feature batters striving to dispatch hard leather balls arriving at up to 100 mph past a phalanx of fielders.

The differences, such as they are, mostly arise because running is never forced in cricket, as it is in baseball. A batsman in cricket can parry ball after ball exactly as he intends for hours on end. It's perhaps this aspect that most puzzles Americans. How can it be exciting to watch a stalemate between batsmen and bowlers, perhaps culminating in a tense draw after days of play?

A cricket fan will warm to the perfection of a well-crafted innings that contains not a false stroke. In baseball, by contrast, the batting is impossibly difficult. Even the best batters hit the ball as they want only once every ten pitches or so. Perhaps the sense of satisfaction when they connect outweighs the frustration of repeated failures. I suppose it depends on which game you are born to.

In any case, the development of shorter forms of cricket, like the three-hour T20 version, is bringing the games closer together. In that format, batsmen have to do or die, just as in baseball. Maybe a T20 tournament in the States would catch on. I wouldn't count on it, though.

The fielding differences are the most interesting. When it comes to stopping groundballs and throwing to base, baseball leaves cricket for dead. The arms are much stronger, the throws more accurate, even from off-balance. And then there is the split-second ballet of double and triple plays. Cricket has nothing to compare.

But with catching, it's the other way around. For a start, the gloves in baseball remove most of the excitement from catching lofted shots to the outfield, which is one of the most spectacular aspects of cricket. And then there is the way that barehanded cricketers will pouch hard-hit drives or deflections coming at 100 mph, often from only a few yards away. Again, the baseball gloves take this ferocious cricketing skill out of the game.

I sometimes wonder whether baseball infielders are really helped by their gloves, especially when they bring them across their body to intercept drives on their throwing side. Cricket infielders make any number of outstretched diving catches with their throwing hands that baseball fielders would never get their gloves close to.

It would be interesting to know if anyone has ever checked on this. Do infielders really do better with gloves? I can see that they are a big help to outfielders with fly balls. But it's by no means obvious to me that a barehanded cricketer in the infield wouldn't stop and catch more balls on the ungloved side. Maybe someone should suggest it to Billy Beane.

Curiously, the Americans and the British weren't always divided by their summer games. In the first half of the nineteenth century, cricket was as popular in North America as the rest of the English-speaking world. All the large cities hosted cricket clubs, with Philadelphia and New York leading the way.

What was the first international sporting contest? Surprisingly, the answer is a cricket match between the United States and Canada. Held in New York in 1844, the two-day match attracted over 10,000 spectators. The fans were said to have wagered over $100,000 on the match, and Canada won by twenty-three runs. This pre-dated the first England–Scotland football match by thirty years.

The rise of American baseball was triggered by the Civil War. Baseball had the great advantage of not needing a flat batting surface. Young men away from home needed ready recreation, and baseball was far easier to organize than cricket. By the end of the 1860s, the game was on its way to becoming the national pastime. The all-conquering professional Cincinnati Red Stockings toured the country, defining many features of the modern game.

Cricket limped on in the States. As late as 1908, a Philadelphia team successfully toured the first-class counties of England, and their star bowler John Barton King topped that season's bowling averages. But by then cricket had subsided into a minority upper-class East Coast pastime. In any case, it was always unlikely that, in the modern era of codified sports, the new American nation would subscribe to a game ruled from London.

Sports fans everywhere will tell you that their own games are the best in the world, unparalleled in the skills they demand and the spectacle they offer. Of course, they can't all be right. Not all games are equally well designed, and some are downright limited in their attractions.

But that's not the point. Sporting traditions aren't entries in some kind of meta-competition to find the world's best game. Rather, their real significance is that they add depth to our athletic pursuits.

In truth, baseball fans don't really have much idea whether their game is better than cricket, nor vice versa. What they do know about are the annals of their own games. That's the reason they are loyal to their own codes. It's like being loyal to your country or your family. The games we play aren't arbitrary creations designed to amuse us. They carry with them histories that help define our lives.

CHAPTER 18

SHANKLY, CHOMSKY AND THE NATURE OF SPORT

According to the legendary Liverpool football manager Bill Shankly, 'Football is not a matter of life and death. It's much more important than that.'

It's a good joke, not least because Shankly wasn't aiming to be funny. But it also highlights a real issue. Where does sport stand in the scheme of things?

You don't have to agree with Shankly to believe that sport adds a positive element to many lives. Still, not everyone concedes even this much. Another important thinker, Noam Chomsky, thinks sport is nothing but a capitalist trick. He dismisses it as: 'an area which has no meaning and probably thrives because it has no meaning, as a displacement from the serious problems which one cannot influence'.

If you ask me, Chomsky is talking through his hat. He may know all about the foundations of linguistics – though I have my doubts about that, too – but when it comes to sport I am with Shankly every time. Only someone who is a complete stranger to the joys of athletic achievement could dismiss sport as having 'no meaning'.

Those few philosophers who have written about the value of sport tend to stand somewhere between Chomsky and Shankly. They don't dismiss sport as meaningless, but at the same time they distinguish it from real life. In their view, sport is worthwhile precisely because it gives us a break from more serious pursuits.

I think that these philosophers have it wrong too. Sport is just as serious as the rest of life. Shankly may have been a tad overenthusiastic, but he had the right idea. Sport reaches deep into human nature, and can be as important as anything else.

Over the last couple of decades, *The Grasshopper* (1978) by the late Bernard Suits has acquired a cult status among philosophers who think about sport. It's a quirky dialogue in which the eponymous grasshopper celebrates game-playing as the supreme virtue. Along the way, Suits offers a convincing definition of games (thereby refuting Ludwig Wittgenstein's claim in his *Philosophical Investigations* that the notion can't be defined).

In summary form, Suits analyses games as 'the voluntary attempt to overcome unnecessary obstacles'. His idea is that all games specify some target state – like reaching the final square in snakes and ladders, or getting your golf ball in the hole – and then place arbitrary restrictions on the means allowed – you must go down the snakes but not up, you must propel the ball with your clubs and not carry it down the fairway.

So far so good. Suits's definition elegantly captures what games have in common, whatever Wittgenstein might have said. Suits goes wrong, however, when he suggests that all sports are a subspecies of games. In truth, while some sports are games in his sense – tennis, cricket, soccer – many others are not, precisely because they aren't constituted by arbitrary rules – running, rowing and skiing, for example.

Moreover, in assimilating sports to games, Suits misunderstands what makes them worthwhile. In Suits's view, the value of all games lies in overcoming the arbitrary obstacles they involve. Indeed, he regards this as the ultimate good. Towards the end of his book, he imagines a Utopia in which all practical needs can be met at the touch of a button. In this world, argues Suits, game-playing would become the only valuable activity. Since the pursuit of practical ends would be pointless, the only challenges worth meeting would be those set by games.

Suits concludes that no activity is essentially valuable, apart from playing games. In real life, we must work to provide the necessities of life. However, such work is never valuable in itself but merely as a means to an end. The only intrinsically worthwhile pursuits are the games we would continue to play in Utopia.

I know nothing of Suits's personal life, but it is hard to avoid the impression that his book was written by someone who never knew the joy of hitting a six back over the bowler's head, or of bodysurfing a wave 100 yards up onto the beach, or of hitting a backhand top-spin crosscourt winner. (All right, I confess: while I have hit sixes, and am proud of my bodysurfing, I don't have a top-spin backhand. I don't care. Ivan Lendl won eight grand slams without one.)

As I see it, the value of sporting achievement is nothing to do with arbitrary restrictions, but lies rather in the enjoyment of sheer physical skill. Suits's account trivializes sport. It reduces the grandeur of physical excellence to the giggly thrills associated with children's board games.

In the end, it is hard to see how overcoming arbitrary obstacles can be worthwhile in itself. If something isn't worth doing, it isn't worth doing even when it's made difficult. If that was all there was to sport, we might as well stick to snakes and ladders, and avoid the physical rigours of serious athletic pursuits altogether.

The real worth of sport, I say, lies in the pure exercise of physical abilities. Pride in physical performance is a deep-seated feature of human nature. Humans hone their physical abilities and take delight in exercising them. Perhaps this originally had its roots in the practical needs of hunting, fishing and fighting, but we have come to value physical performance as an end in itself. We devote long hours to improving our physical skills, and seek out opportunities to test them.

The point generalizes beyond physical skills. Suits assumes that the pursuit of practical ends can't have any value in itself. But this ignores the way in which many people find their deepest gratification in tuning a car, or analysing a balance sheet, or solving a philosophy problem. For many of us, the employment of these skills is itself worthwhile, quite apart from any useful results they might produce. We would want to carry on exercising these abilities even in Utopia.

But let us stick to physical skills. If you want a definition of sport, I would say that it is any activity whose primary purpose is the exercise of physical skills. This definition explains why plenty of sports are not games. While some sporting skills only exist within a game – top-spin tennis backhands, for example – many other sports involve nothing but skills that are already found in ordinary life – running, rowing, shooting, lifting, throwing. These ordinary activities turn into sports whenever people start performing them for their own sake and strive for excellence in their exercise.

Doggett's Coat and Badge is the oldest rowing race in the world, dating back to 1715, when the working watermen on the Thames first tried their skills over a course from London Bridge to Chelsea. What could be more natural than for these young men to test themselves against each other? In fact, there seems no limit to the range of everyday activities that can turn into sports in this way. Bronco riding, sheepdog trials, medieval jousting, catfish noodling, trailer-truck reversing, competitive bricklaying . . .

My favourite example is fishing casting. When I was a youngster in Natal, the local surf fishermen vied to see who could cast out furthest beyond the Indian Ocean breakers. Soon some of them decided to skip the fishing and concentrate on the casting – and so ended up holding casting competitions on sports fields with special equipment.

What is the relation between sport and competition? As I see it, there is a natural connection, but it is by no means essential. To want to exercise a *skill* is to want to do something *well*, indeed as well as is feasible. And a natural way to test whether you are doing as well as you can is to measure yourself against other people. It is scarcely surprising that people who take pride in how far they can cast a fishing line will want to see if they can cast further than others.

Still, even if sport lends itself naturally to competition, it does not require it. A rock-climbing team that sets out to conquer some challenging ascent need not be competing with other teams; when I became keen on golf, I was desperate to break 100, and then 90, and then 80, and played many solitary rounds in pursuing these challenges; recreational wind-surfers, skiers and hang-gliders are not out to beat anybody.

In those sports that are competitive, it is of course essential that you play to win. If you aren't competing, you aren't trying. But it would be a mistake to infer that victory is the only thing that matters in competitive sports. For most participants, playing well is just as important as winning. After all, if people got nothing out of matches they lost, it is hard to see why most contests would take place. Among my regular tennis opponents are some I rarely, if ever, beat. But it doesn't occur to me to stop playing them on this account. It is enough that I measure up to my own standards. I don't need to be better than everyone else.

Perhaps competition is crucial to spectator sports, and indeed a large part of the reason why people watch them. But that is a different issue. I am talking about the nature and value of playing sports, not watching them. There may well be a number of further features needed to make a sport worth watching, beyond those that make it worth playing. (Most obviously, it will need to be visually engaging. Many very popular participant sports fall at this first hurdle. Squash and field hockey spring to mind.)

In his attempt to lever all sports into his definition of games as 'voluntary attempts to overcome unnecessary obstacles',

Suits focuses on the rules that become necessary whenever there is competition. Thus, he argues that it's not enough to breast the tape to win the 200 metres sprint – you must stick to the track and not cut across the bend, you must run and not ride a bicycle, and so on.

This is scarcely enough, however, to show that sprinting is defined by 'unnecessary obstacles'. The essence of the sport is simply running as fast as you can. You don't need any rules for that. The rules only come in when people want to measure themselves against each other. Their purpose is not to define some new activity into existence, but simply to enable people to see who can really run the fastest.

In any case, Suits's idea of sports as games has no grip at all when it comes to non-competitive and rule-free activities like recreational windsurfing or hang-gliding. When I was younger, I used to take my windsurfer out every weekend in Essex and have fun zooming around the Blackwater Estuary. I can remember my doctor once asking me whether I did any active sports. 'Tennis, golf, cricket – and I go out windsurfing at weekends,' I said. I doubt that it occurred to my doctor to object that 'Solo windsurfing isn't a *sport*.'

Of course, some sports are also games in Suits's sense. While running and windsurfing don't depend on rules for their existence, tennis, baseball and many other pastimes do. There wouldn't be any such thing as a tennis shot if the rules didn't require you to hit the ball over the net and within the lines. Still, even with sports that are games, their value lies in the physical abilities they involve, and not the obstacles they set. Top-spin crosscourt backhands are good because they are admirably skilful, not because you have to overcomes tennis's arbitrary rules in order to win a point.

Not all games are physical – think of bridge, chess, ludo, Monopoly, baccarat, craps. And those games that aren't physical don't count as sports, for just that reason. But even with non-physical games we need to go beyond Suits to appreciate their value. If a game is worth playing, it is worth playing for some other reason than the obstacles it presents.

Thus, some games are worthwhile because of the mental powers they demand – bridge and chess would be the paradigms. Other games engender excitement, such as children's dice games like snakes and ladders or gambling games like roulette. And in general, contra Suits, any game worth playing offers some further value beyond its arbitrariness.

I have defined a sport as any activity whose primary purpose is the exercise of physical skills. So what about dancing? The stars of ballet and modern dance are certainly distinguished by their exceptional physical skills, and spend much of their lives developing and improving them. So should they then be counted as athletes, on my theory?

Well, some forms of dance are indeed sports. Ice dancing is one of the major disciplines at the Winter Olympics. Rhythmic gymnastics, in which the competitors perform routines accompanied by music, has been part of the Summer Olympics since 1984. Competitive ballroom dancing is nowadays called 'dancesport' by its practitioners, and has been recognized by the International Olympic Committee as an eligible sport, though it languishes low down on the list of pastimes waiting for a spot in the Games.

Even so, I agree that it would be odd to count ballet and modern dance as sports. But these activities are different. While they undoubtedly involve physical skills, the exercise of these skills is not their primary purpose. Balletomanes and other dance enthusiasts look to the dancers to entertain, to interpret the music and to otherwise edify. The physical skills of the dancers are only a small part of what the fans find to admire in the dance.

Down on the lower reaches of the cable channels, you can nowadays follow the competitive barbecuing circuit. This is a big business, especially in the United States, and its followers tout it as a fast-growing 'sport'. But I think that's pushing it. There is an element of physical skill all right, but that's not the main point of the exercise. After all, the judges aren't interested in your skill per se, but solely in how your meat is cooked. Your particular technique for preparing a perfect piece of pork is no concern of theirs.

I'd take the same line with baking, pottery and sewing. All of these feature in popular televised competitions – the annual final of *The Great British Bake Off* regularly attracts over 10 million viewers – and all of them demand high levels of physical skill. But again, it is the product that is judged, not the skill. Similarly with musical performance, which demands physical ability all right, but is appreciated for the sounds produced, not the dexterity behind them.

I go the other way with speed-eating, though. You may have trouble thinking of fat men stuffing their faces for fun as a sport. But, if so, let me tell you about Takeru Kobayashi.

The blue riband of competitive eating is Nathan's Coney Island Hot Dog Eating Contest, held every year on the Fourth of July. In 2001, a slim twenty-three-year-old from Japan stepped onto the stage and revolutionized the sport. The existing record was twenty-five hot dogs in twelve minutes, but Kobayashi ate fifty. By combining rigorous training with inventive techniques, he showed that the limits of fast eating had scarcely been explored. One result has been an upsurge of interest in eating contests. It might not be the most athletic of sports, but I don't see why it has any less claim than other activities whose primary interest is to test the limits of the human body, like weightlifting or free diving.

What about video games? Many young men spend inordinate amounts of time hunched in front of a screen trying to outshoot the virtual competition. Why doesn't that qualify as sport? The whole point of these games is the digital skill, with their levels and time limits designed specifically to elicit higher and higher levels of dexterity. (I know what I'm talking about. I went through a *Tetris* phase a few years ago. You wouldn't believe how good I became. By the time I lost interest, the virtual falling blocks I was manipulating were just a blur.)

Perhaps you haven't heard of eSports. In 2015, a capacity crowd of 20,000 filled Madison Square Garden to watch the top two American teams vie for a spot in the *League of Legends* World Championship. The championship itself attracted 36 million online streaming viewers, and the six-strong eventual winning team shared a prize of $1 million. *League of Legends* and similar games support a large community of professional athletes and coaches. I don't see any reason not to count video gaming as a sport.

My analysis leaves no room for sports that don't involve physical skills. Some games players will object. Both chess and bridge are on the list of 'eligible sports' that the International Olympic Committee periodically considers for inclusion in the Summer Games, along with tug-o-war, waterskiing – and 'dancesport'. Neither has as yet managed to win a place, but their governing bodies are indefatigable in pursuit of the goal.

The status of bridge became a question for the British courts in 2015. Sports in Britain receive large amounts of funding from National Lottery profits. When the Lottery people decided that bridge wasn't a sport, its defenders took legal action. Mr Justice Mostyn in the High Court was sympathetic. In his view, 'You are doing more physical activity playing bridge, with all that dealing and playing cards, than in rifle shooting.'

Nevertheless, with all due respect to Mr Justice Mostyn and the International Olympic Committee, bridge and chess are not sports. They are not tests of physical skill. There may be physical effort involved in playing the cards or moving the pieces, indeed more effort than in a rifle-shooting contest. But that's not what the competitors are trying to be good at.

After all, it would make perfectly good sense for an armless competitor to play bridge or chess by telling someone else how to play the cards or move the pieces. But you aren't competing in a shooting event if you arrange for someone else to shoot on your behalf. Shooting is a sport because it is essentially physical, in a way that bridge and chess are not.

What about chess-boxing? In this hybrid sport, three-minute rounds of chess and boxing alternate, with victory being decided either by a boxing stoppage or a chess victory. The tactical possibilities are intriguing. You don't want too many punches to addle your mind, lest this induce a false move on the board.

The game was invented by a Dutch performance artist, Iepe Rubingh, but has since outgrown its artistic origins, and regular tournaments are now held throughout Europe. Whether it will take off as a mass sport remains to be seen. Still, whatever its fate, I'd say that it qualifies as a sport, in virtue of the boxing element, even if that is diluted by the chess.

Perhaps there is a more general moral here. I say sports are activities whose purpose is to exercise *physical* skills. But I don't intend this to imply that there isn't also a mental side to sport. As I emphasized in Part I, any physical skill needs mental backing. Athletes who do not have their minds right will not perform to the best of their ability. So all sports call for the exercise of mental abilities alongside physical ones. Chess-boxing is just the extreme end of the spectrum, in isolating periods where mental abilities are displayed on their own.

In the end, perhaps we should simply accept that no analysis of sport will fit all the marginal cases. Exactly what is counted as a sport often depends on arbitrary facts of social history, rather than any principled definition.

One of the favourite books in my library is *The Oxford Companion to Sports and Games*, edited by John Arlott and published in 1975. It is a large, old-style compendium, with entries arranged alphabetically, and plenty of detail about the history, rules and prime exponents of pretty much every sport you can think of. (And it is specifically about sports. I'm not sure why 'Games' is in the title – bridge and chess aren't included, let alone ludo or Monopoly.)

The book is comprehensive and emphatically international – two of the longest entries are for pelota and kendo. But there are some curious omissions. There is no entry for darts, nor for snooker. I don't know what to make of this. True, at the time the book was compiled neither of these were the major spectator sports they have since become on world television. But they were scarcely unknown.

In particular, snooker, along with its sister game billiards, already had a proud history. I grew up with tales of past champions. My teenage friends and I were keen players, and spoke with awe of the English brothers Joe and Fred Davis, and their epic mid-twentieth-century battles with the Australians Walter Lindrum and his nephew Horace. It is odd, to say the least, that a compendium that has room for canoe polo and deck quoits should leave out snooker and billiards.

I can only suppose that these games, along with pool and darts, were shunned because of their historical association with smoky drinking dens. As they used to say, proficiency at billiards is the sign of a misspent youth. But their omission was surely a mistake. As millions of television fans know, the top contemporary snooker and darts players display unnatural levels of physical skill. For the editor of *The Oxford Companion*, the undoubted abilities demanded by these games were somehow obscured by the dissoluteness of their surroundings.

The Companion also includes extensive entries on a number of animal pastimes: equestrian sports, greyhound racing, homing-pigeon racing. I agree that these are sports all right. Still, it might not be clear how they tally with my story. Where's the physical skill? With horses, it is true, the riders must be skilful to control their mounts. But what about greyhound and pigeon racing? It doesn't take much skill to bring your animals to the starting line and let them go.

The puzzle disappears, however, if we switch our focus from the human handlers to the racers themselves. It is the skills of the animals that these events are designed to display, not of their owners. The top racing dogs and pigeons are no less exceptional athletes than Usain Bolt. In the 1930s, Mick the Miller became a household name in Britain when he strung up nineteen victories in a row and won the Greyhound Derby twice. Until recently, his stuffed body was on display in the Natural History Museum in London. The author of his entry in *The Oxford Companion* had no doubt about Mick the Miller's outstanding skills, describing him as 'the greatest exponent of trackcraft in the history of the sport'.

Where do sports stand in the overall scheme of things? From my perspective, the value of sports lies in the worth of the physical skills they involve. Hitting a home run or sinking a long putt is virtuous in itself, independently of any further benefit it may bring. Such achievements are rightfully regarded as objects of admiration and pride. Athletic prowess is something to aim for and cherish, along with other features of a good life.

Some will feel that I am here overvaluing the significance of sports. Do I really want to put athletic achievement on a par with the other important things in life, like happiness, knowledge, friendship and artistic achievement? In the end, many will feel, sports are not really serious. Isn't sport essentially playful, leisurely, light-hearted, the opposite of serious endeavour?

According to Suits's account of sports as games, this unseriousness is essential to sports. Suits portrays sports as the antithesis of work. In his view, where work demands necessary effort to meet essential needs, sports set us unnecessary challenges that we take up for the fun of it. By contrast, my own analysis arguably casts no light on the difference between sport and the rest of life. By saying that sporting achievements are valuable in themselves, I seem to be in danger of blurring the difference between playful games and needful work.

My response is to deny the premise. I do not agree that sport has a different kind of worth from other things. Sporting achievement is as basic a value as anything else. Someone who devotes their life to high jumping or baseball is no less serious a person than someone who devotes it to mathematics, say, or the ballet. There is nothing intrinsically dilettante about sports compared with other walks of life.

Sometimes advocates of sporting activity will point to the benefits it brings, in terms of physical well-being, increased self-esteem, relaxation, and so on. These benefits are all no doubt real, but they are incidental to the worth of sport. Exercising physical skills to the best of your ability is valuable in itself, whether or not it brings any further advantages. Along with happiness, friendship and other basic goods, it is one of the things that makes life worth living. Justifying sports in terms of their positive spin-offs is like valuing friendships because they will advance your career.

I can't help quoting from *Chinaman*, Shehan Karunatilaka's wonderfully scurrilous novel about the world of Sri Lankan cricket:

> I have been told by members of my own family that there is no use or value in sports. I only agree with the first part. I may be drunk but I am not stupid. Of course there is little point to sports. But, at the risk of depressing you, let me add two more cents. THERE IS LITTLE POINT TO ANYTHING. In a thousand years, grass will have grown over all our cities.

Note that Karunatilaka is not here agreeing that there is no value in sports ('I only agree with the first part'). His point is rather that sports are no less important than anything else. Of course, if we set the bar of significance too high – surviving the passage of millennia – then sport will fall short. But so too will the other things that matter – family, friends, prosperity, prizes.

If there is something peculiar about sport, perhaps it lies in the point that Karunatilaka does concede to his family – there is no use in sports. It is true that sport doesn't connect up with other aspects of life. Sporting achievements are generally disconnected from personal relationships, social life or political developments. They do not edify or inform, still less explore and transform our perceptions of the world. And by their nature they are ephemeral – unlike other hobbies, they leave no lasting products, not even a garden or a stamp collection.

Because of this, the rest of life normally goes on the same, whoever wins the big matches. In 1982, France had a supremely talented soccer team. Before their World Cup semi-final against West Germany, their captain Michel Platini was asked how he would cope with defeat. 'The sun will still rise tomorrow,' he answered. In the event, the West Germans (the same side that had featured in 'the disgrace of Dijon' a couple of games earlier) won a fabulous game on penalties, after Patrick Battiston was denied a goal by the most notorious foul in football history. The rest of the soccer world joined with France in lamenting this travesty of sporting justice. But Platini was of course right. The French side might have been denied their sporting destiny, but the next day the banks still opened and the trains still ran on time.

Still, even if sport forms a self-enclosed realm, insulated from the rest of life, this does not mean that it lacks intrinsic worth. As we have seen throughout this book, people across the world celebrate sporting achievement as a self-standing virtue. They hone their skills as participants and applaud their champions as spectators. From their perspective, sport is a matter of seriousness and concern, not the flippant holiday from real life that Suits would make it.

Sporting achievements at any level can be the occasion for justified pride. Even amateurs like me can feel a happy glow remembering long-past feats. Given the levels I played at, I would hope that my professional and personal achievements outstrip my minor sporting triumphs. But, even so, my life would have been thinner without them. They count high among the events I am pleased to recall. For serious athletes, sporting success of course signifies more. If I can think back with pride to feats performed in friendly cricket matches, imagine what it must be like to have led your country to victory over its long-standing rivals.

It is tempting to confuse the insulation of sports with a lack of significance. We are too quick to conclude, just because sports don't matter to other things, that they don't matter at all. But this doesn't follow. Success on the sports field might not advance your career or influence the course of world history. But this doesn't mean that it is not important and valuable in its own right. Even if sporting achievements are cut off from the rest of life, they are still worth striving for.

SOPORIFIC APPENDIX

Here is my current alphabetical list of international sporting families – the cure for insomnia mentioned in Chapter 12:

A *Anand and Vijay Amritraj*, India, tennis. ('A's are not easy. The Durban cricketing Amlas and the London footballing Allens only have one full international player each.)

B *Kevin-Prince and Jerome Boateng*, Ghana and Germany, soccer. (Binational sporting families are becoming increasingly common. See the Xhakas and Zebos below.)

C *Martin and Jeff Crowe*, New Zealand, cricket. (Plus their less successful first cousin, Russell.)

D *Jannie and Bismarck du Plessis*, South Africa, rugby union. (Bismarck du Plessis is my all-time favourite name.)

E *Bill and John Edrich*, England, cricket.

F *Les and Rio Ferdinand*, England, soccer.

G *Frank and Eddie Gray*, Scotland, soccer.

H *Walter, Richard, Dale and Barry Hadlee*, New Zealand, cricket. (Just sticking to New Zealand cricket, there are also the Howarths, Harrises, Hornes and Harts.)

I *Paul and Tom Ince*, England, soccer. (OK, Tom isn't a full international yet, but 'I's aren't easy.)

J *Jeff and Simon Jones*, England, cricket.

K *Vitali and Wladimir Klitschko*, Ukraine, boxing.

L *Michael and Brian Laudrup*, Denmark, soccer.

M *Graham and Rod Marsh*, Australia, golf and cricket. (This and the next two families have the distinction of representing their country in different sports.)

N *Phil, Gary and Tracey Neville*, England, soccer and netball. (And Phil also played cricket for England under-15s.)

O *Chris and Alan Old*, England, cricket and rugby union.

P *Graeme, Peter and Shaun Pollock*, South Africa, cricket.

Q *Derek, Craig and Scott Quinnell*, Wales, rugby union.

R *Karl-Heinz and Michael Rummenigge*, Germany, soccer.

S *Robin and Chris Smith*, England, cricket.

T *Glenn, Greg and Brian Turner*, New Zealand, cricket, golf and field hockey respectively. (Brian has also been his country's Poet Laureate. Sometimes I wonder if there are only a couple of dozen families in New Zealand.)

U *Rory and Tony Underwood*, England, rugby union.

V *Billy and Mako Vunipola*, England, rugby union. I used to think the Vinklevoss twins were so spelt, but in fact they are:

W *Cameron and Tyler Winklevoss*, USA, rowing.

X *Taulant and Granit Xhaka*, Albania and Switzerland, soccer.

Y *Nick, Tom and Ben Youngs*, England, rugby union.

Z *Arthur and Simon Zebo*, France and Ireland, athletics and rugby union.

NOTES AND FURTHER READING

Notes to Chapter 1

'*As a fifteen-year-old*': Robin Finn, 'Seles Stuns Graf', *New York Times* (10 June 1990).

'*Everybody has a plan*': Mike Bernadino, 'Mike Tyson Explains One of his Most Famous Quotes', *Sun Sentinel* (9 November 2012).

'*Skillful coping*': Hubert Dreyfus, 'A Phenomenology of Skill Acquisition as the Basis for a Merleau-Pontian Non-Representationalist Cognitive Science' (2002), p. 13, http://socrates.berkeley.edu/~hdreyfus/pdf/Merleau PontySkillCogSci.pdf.

'*To move one's body*': Maurice Merleau-Ponty, *Phenomenology of Perception* (London: Routledge and Kegan Paul, 1962), p. 139.

supports his case: Knoblauch is discussed by Dreyfus and his opponents in Joseph Schear (ed.), *Mind, Reason, and Being-in-the-World: The McDowell–Dreyfus Debate* (London: Routledge, 2013).

Berra gained his nickname: Laura Bradley, 'The Relationship between Yogi Berra and Yogi Bear, Explained', *Slate* (23 September 2015), http://www.slate.com/blogs/browbeat/2015/09/23/yogi_berra_and_yogi_bear_the_relationship_explained.html.

'*My father says*': Andre Agassi, *Open: An Autobiography* (New York: Knopf, 2009) p. 28.

Leadbetter flattened it out: Dale Concannon, 'David Leadbetter Interview', *Golf Today* (2000), http://www.golftoday.co.uk/news/yeartodate/news00/leadbetter.html.

Further Reading for Chapter 1

Dreyfus's version of the Yoga theory is elaborated, alongside sometimes dissenting views from other phenomenologically inclined philosophers, in the collection Joseph Schear (ed.), *Mind, Reason, and Being-in-the-World: The McDowell–Dreyfus Debate* (London: Routledge, 2013).

Sian Beilock defends her theory of 'paralysis by analysis' in *Choke: What the Secrets of the Brain Reveal about Getting It Right When You Have To* (New York: Free Press, 2010).

In addition to Barbara Montero (*Thought in Action*, Oxford: Oxford University Press, 2017), other philosophers who emphasize the role of intellect in skilled action include Ellen Fridland ('Skill Learning and Conceptual Thought', in Bana Bashour and Hans Muller [eds], *Philosophical Naturalism and its Implications* [London: Routledge, 2013]), Jason Stanley (*Know How* [Oxford: Oxford University Press 2011]) and John Sutton ('Batting, Habit and Memory', *Sport in Society*, 10: 5 [2007], pp 763–86; and John Sutton et al., 'Applying Intelligence to the Reflexes', *Journal of the British Society for Phenomenology*, 42: 1 [January 2011], pp. 78–103).

The distinction between skills and their components goes back to Arthur Danto's work on basic actions in the 1960s; see 'Basic Actions', *American Philosophical Quarterly*, 2: 2 (July 1965), pp 141–8.

Notes to Chapter 2

In major league baseball: David Coburn, 'Baseball Physics: Anatomy of a Home Run', *Popular Mechanics* (17 December 2009), http://www.popularmechanics.com/adventure/sports/a4569/4216783.

eyes will jump ahead: Michael Land and Peter McLeod, 'From Eye Movements to Actions: How Batsmen Hit the Ball', *Nature Neuroscience*, 3 (2000), pp 1340–5.

'I don't believe a word': Personal communication from John Sutton, who was present at the Cricket Australia talk.

a series of jerky movements: John Findlay and Robin Walker, 'Human Saccadic Eye Movements', *Scholarpedia*, 7: 7 (2012), p. 5095, http://www.scholarpedia.org/article/Human_saccadic_eye_movements.

two elite international cricketers: David Mann, Wayne Spratford and Bruce

Abernethy 'The Head Tracks and Gaze Predicts: How the World's Best Batters Hit a Ball', *PLOS One*, 8: 3 (13 March 2013), http://journals.plos.org/plosone/article?id=10.1371/journal.pone.0058289.

compared action photographs: Damien Lafont, 'Gaze Control DURING the hitting phase in Tennis: A Preliminary Study', *International Journal of Performance Analysis in Sport*, 8: 1 (February 2008), pp. 85–100.

'Golf instruction books': Peter Dobereiner, *Dobereiner on Golf* (London: Aurum Press, 1998).

'A recent study': David Mann, Bruce Abernethy and Damian Farrow, 'The Resilience of Natural Interceptive Actions to Refractive Blur', *Human Movement Science*, 29: 3 (June 2010), pp. 386–400.

surveys suggest that contemporary players: Daniel Laby et al., 'The Visual Function of Professional Baseball Players', *American Journal of Ophthalmology*, 122: 4 (October 1996), pp. 476–85.

In a typical such test: Sean Müller, Bruce Abernethy and Damian Farrow, 'How Do World-Class Cricket Batsmen Anticipate a Bowler's Intention?', *Quarterly Journal of Experimental Psychology*, 59: 12 (2006), pp. 2161–86.

Further Reading for Chapter 2

There is as yet no single book devoted to the fascinating work done by sports vision scientists over the past couple of decades, but much useful material can be found in Joseph Baker and Damian Farrow (eds), *The Routledge Handbook of Sports Expertise* (London: Routledge, 2015).

The idea that sport performance often depends on multi-track dispositional 'programs' is developed in my essay, 'In the Zone', in Anthony O'Hear (ed.), *Philosophy and Sport* (Cambridge: Cambridge University Press, 2013).

Notes to Chapter 3

rats, monkeys, crows: Nathaniel P. Daw and John P. O'Doherty, 'Multiple Systems for Value Learning', in Paul W. Glimcher and Ernest Fehr (eds), *Neuroeconomics* (San Diego: Elsevier Academic Press, second edition, 2013).

a topic in psychology devoted to this issue: Mark McDaniel and Gilles Einstein, *Prospective Memory* (Thousand Oaks, CA: Sage, 2007).

'explicit self-monitoring': Beilock, *Choke*, p. 192.

Ravi Bopara was dismissed: Paul Newman, 'Bopara Misses Second Clash with South Africa', *Daily Mail* (29 July 2012).

Further Reading for Chapter 3

Michael Bratman argues for the distinctive role of intentions in shaping human action in *Intention, Plans, and Practical Reason* (Cambridge, MA: Harvard University Press, 1987).

Richard Holton builds interestingly on Bratman's work in *Willing, Wanting, Waiting* (Oxford: Oxford University Press, 2011), focusing on factors that undermine the execution of intentions.

Some of this chapter draws on my paper 'Choking and the Yips', which was published in 2015 in *Unreflective Action and the Choking Effect*, a special issue of *Phenomenology and the Cognitive Sciences*. This issue contains nine other philosophical articles on the psychological barriers to sporting success.

Notes to Chapter 4

anti-corruption investigators: Emmet Malone 'FAI's €5m FIFA Payment not Apparent in Published Accounts', *Irish Times* (4 June 2015).

The Kiwi prime minister: Andrew Alderson, 'Thirty-Five Years are Enough: Time to Get Over the Underarm', *New Zealand Herald* (31 January 2016).

fair play across different sports: Simon Barnes, *The Meaning of Sport* (London: Short Books, 2006), p. 58.

When the saintly Northern Irishman: Patrick Kidd, 'Willie John McBride: 1974 Lions Got Our Retaliation in First', *The Times* (19 June 2009).

Take the 'Bountygate' scandal: Jesse Reed, 'Reviewing the Complete Timeline of NFL Saints Bountygate Scandal', *Bleacher Report* (11 December 2012), http://bleacherreport.com/articles/1441646-reviewing-the-complete-timeline-of-nfl-saints-bountygate-scandal.

A not dissimilar episode: Press Association, 'RFU Extend Harlequins' "Bloodgate" Bans', *Independent* (18 August 2009).

As Thomas Hobbes observed: Thomas Hobbes, *Leviathan* (London: Andrew Crooke, 1651), ch. XIII.

Further Reading for Chapter 4

The thesis that you can't win a game by cheating is upheld by Bernard Suits in *The Grasshopper: Games, Life and Utopia* (Peterborough, ON: Broadview Press, 1978).

Fred D'Agostino goes some way towards recognizing how acceptable sporting practice can diverge from the formal rules in 'The Ethos of Games', *Journal of the Philosophy of Sport*, 8: 1 (1981), pp. 7–18.

Michael Ridge offers a thorough analysis of what it takes to be playing a game in 'Cheating and Trifling', forthcoming, https://www.humanities. utoronto.ca/uploaded_files/content/1630/file/Ridge_Cheating_and_ Trifling_draft_2.pdf.

A good place to start on political obligation is with the *Stanford Encyclopedia of Philosophy* (2014) entry by Richard Dagger and David Lefkowitz, http://plato.stanford.edu/entries/political-obligation.

For one of the few attempts to separate the legitimacy of the state from an obligation to obey the law, see David Copp, 'The Idea of a Legitimate State', *Philosophy and Public Affairs*, 28: 1 (January 1999), pp. 3–45.

Joseph Raz's *The Authority of Law* (Oxford: Oxford University Press, 1979) argues that there is no general moral obligation to obey the law because it is the law.

Notes to Chapter 5

When the eminent Oxford philosopher: Philippa Foot, 'Morality as a System of Hypothetical Imperatives', *Philosophical Review*, 81: 3 (July 1972), pp. 305–16; Judith Martin and Gunther Stent, 'I Think; Therefore I Thank: A Philosophy of Etiquette', *American Scholar*, 59: 2 (1990), pp. 237–54.

the Portuguese defender Pepe: Graham Poll, 'Pepe Was Rightly Shown Red Card But Müller Should've Been Booked', *Daily Mail* (16 June 2014).

a supreme practitioner of this art: Chris Haft, 'Frame Job: Posey an Artist at Coaxing Strikes', *MLB.com* (23 February 2015), http://m.mlb.com/ news/article/110191348/san-francisco-giants-catcher-buster-posey-skilled-at-framing-pitches.

when batsmen 'walked': David Mutton, 'A Short History of Walking', *CricketWeb.net* (30 July 2013), http://www.cricketweb.net/a-short-history-of-walking.

Further Reading for Chapter 5

Elliot Turiel's original research on the moral-conventional distinction is presented in his *The Development of Social Knowledge: Morality and Convention* (Cambridge: Cambridge University Press, 1983). For a survey of subsequent work in this tradition, see Judith Smetana, 'Social Domain Theory: Consistencies and Variations in Children's Moral and Social Judgements', in Melanie Killen and Judith Smetana (eds), *Handbook of Moral Development* (New York: Erlbaum, 2006).

For moral particularism, see the *Stanford Encyclopedia of Philosophy* (2013) entry by Jonathan Dancy, http://plato.stanford.edu/entries/moral-particularism.

Notes to Chapter 6

Thus spoke the Australian: Mike Hytner, 'Kokkinakis Banged Your Girlfriend', *Guardian* (13 August 2015).

The 1947 US Open: Snead's and Worsham's final putts can be seen on film: https://www.youtube.com/watch?v=OR0EpU_UJ50.

As Jack Bannister saw it: Mike Atherton, 'Shane Warne: The Mighty Craftsman', *Wisden Cricketers' Almanack* (London: Wisden, 2007), http://www.mikeatherton.co.uk/2007/the-mighty-craftsman.

'In those days I used to play': Stephen Potter, *The Theory and Practice of Gamesmanship, or the Art of Winning Games Without Actually Cheating* (London: Rupert Hart-Davis, 1947), p. 11.

the 2015 Solheim Cup: Derek Lawrenson, 'Water Hazard on the Course: Female Stars from Both Sides in Tears', *Daily Mail* (20 September 2015).

As Mel Reid: 'Melissa Reid Critical of Suzann Pettersen's Solheim Cup Decision', *Sky Sports News* (22 September 2015), http://www.skysports.com/golf/news/12176/10000606/melissa-reid-feels-suzann-pettersen-did-the-wrong-thing.

the 'C. Joad' whom Potter: 'C. E. M. Joad', *Humanist Heritage* (2010), http://humanistheritage.org.uk/articles/c-e-m-joad.

public humiliation and dismissal: 'Dr. Joad Fined', *The Times* (13 April 1948).

'stamping their taste': Zachary Leader, *The Life of Kingsley Amis* (New York: Pantheon, 2007), p. 697.

'It is a standing insult': Iain Wilton, *C. B. Fry: The King of Sport* (London: Metro Books, 2003), ch. 7.

a well-known story: D. J. Taylor, *The Corinthian Spirit: The Decline of Amateur Values in Sport* (London: Yellow Jersey Press, 2006), ch. 5.

introduced the 'switch-hit': Andy Bull, 'The MCC Endorses Pietersen's Switch-Hitting', *Guardian* (17 June 2008).

The joint statement: 'Explanation of Decision to Adopt Rule 14-1B of the Rule of Golf', *Royal and Ancient* (21 May 2013), http://www.randa. org/~/media/Files/Anchoring/AnchoringExplanation.ashx

guardians of gridiron football: Ben Volin, 'Patriot's Receiver-Eligibility Tactic Could Catch On', *Boston Globe* (13 January 2015).

the women's badminton doubles: Peter Walker and Haroon Siddique, 'Eight Olympic Badminton Players Disqualified for "Throwing Games"', *Guardian* (1 August 2012).

'disgrace of Dijon': Paul Doyle, 'The Day in 1982 when the World Wept for Algeria', *Guardian* (13 June 2010).

1994 soccer Caribbean Cup: Guido, 'Barbados vs Grenada '94: The Most Bizarre Match Ever' (with video), *Bleacher Report* (29 October 2008), http://bleacherreport.com/articles/74831-barbados-vs-grenada-in-94-the-most-bizarre-match-ever.

Further Reading for Chapter 6

The full title of Stephen Potter's classic is *The Theory and Practice of Gamesmanship, or the Art of Winning Games without Actually Cheating* (London: Rupert Hart-Davis 1947).

Gamesmanship does not generally receive a good press from theorists of sport. For an interesting negative assessment see Leslie Howe, 'Gamesmanship', *Journal of the Philosophy of Sport*, 31: 2 (2004), pp. 212–25. A more sympathetic analysis can be found in Robert Simon, Cesar Torres and Peter Hager, *Fair Play: The Ethics of Sport* (Boulder, CO: Westview, 2014; the fourth edition of a book originally written by Simon alone and published by Westview in 1991 as *Fair Play: Sports, Values and Society*).

Notes to Chapter 7

Imagine a woman: The plate of mud example is adapted from G. E. M. Anscombe, *Intention* (Oxford: Basil Blackwell, 1957), p. 70.

The Kansas City Royals: Billy Witz, 'Royals Rally Past Mets for First World Series Title since 1985', *New York Times* (2 November 2015).

Further Reading for Chapter 7

Thomas Nagel's *The Possibility of Altruism* (Princeton, NJ: Princeton University Press, 1970) is a classic treatment of the nature of value and the possibility of agent-relative values.

Bernard Williams's *Utilitarianism: For and Against* (with J. J. C. Smart, Cambridge: Cambridge University Press, 1973) emphasizes the importance of our projects for bringing meaning and value to our lives.

Mark Schroeder's 'Value Theory', *Stanford Encyclopedia of Philosophy* (2012), http://plato.stanford.edu/entries/value-theory, provides a detailed introduction to the philosophical literature on value theory, including the teleology/deontology issue and agent-relative values.

Notes to Chapter 8

the journalists at Now! *magazine:* Geoffrey Wansell, *Tycoon* (New York: Atheneum, 1987); Wansell played for the Old Talbotians in the early years.

The ancient Greeks started it: The origin of the puzzle about Theseus's ship is obscure. It first appears in writing in Plutarch's *Life of Theseus* from *c.* 75 CE.

the Brooklyn Dodgers: Joseph M. Sheehan, 'They Took Our Hearts Too', *New York Times* (28 May 1957).

They can divide into two: Shaul Adar, 'New Jerusalem', *When Saturday Comes* (October 2007), http://www.wsc.co.uk/the-archive/103-Politics/406-new-jersualem.

Further Reading for Chapter 8

Three *Stanford Encylopedia of Philosophy* entries cover the identity of people over time and the more general issue of the nature of persisting objects: 'Identity over Time' by André Gallois (2011), http://plato.stanford.edu/entries/identity-time.

'Personal Identity' by Eric Olson (2015), http://plato.stanford.edu/entries/identity-personal/

'Temporal Parts' by Katharine Hawley (2015), http://plato.stanford.edu/entries/temporal-parts.

Stephen Mumford discusses the identity of sporting teams in Chapter 13 of his *Watching Sport* (London: Routledge, 2011).

Notes to Chapter 9

sprinters like Mark Cavendish: Brendan Gallagher, 'Mark Cavendish Misses Out on Olympic Glory', *Daily Telegraph* (28 July 2012).

a group of four women: Brendan Gallagher, 'Lizzie Armistead Claims Great Britain's First Medal with Silver in Women's Road Race', *Daily Telegraph* (29 July 2012).

'But suppose everyone': Joseph Heller, *Catch 22* (New York: Simon and Schuster, 1961), p. 409.

'the prisoner's dilemma': Steven Kuhn, 'Prisoner's Dilemma', *Stanford Encyclopedia of Philosophy* (2014), http://plato.stanford.edu/entries/prisoner-dilemma.

better model for small-scale: 'The Stag Hunt and the PD', section 8, in Kuhn, 'Prisoner's Dilemma'.

the nature film: Henry Nicholls, '*White Wilderness* and the Truth About Norwegian Lemmings', BBC (21 November 2014), http://www.bbc.co.uk/earth/story/20141122-the-truth-about-lemmings.

too quick to rule out biological altruism: Samir Okasha, 'Biological Altruism', *Stanford Encyclopedia of Philosophy* (2013), http://plato.stanford.edu/entries/altruism-biological, Section 3.2 differentiates weak v. strong altruism.

Even at the lowest levels: 'Road Racing Skills', *StartBikeRacing.com* (undated), http://www.startbikeracing.com/index.php/road-racing/strategy-skills/14-road-skills.

Further Reading for Chapter 9

Elliott Sober and David Sloan Wilson's *Unto Others: The Evolution and Psychology of Selfish Behaviour* (Cambridge, MA: Harvard University Press, 1999) is a classic treatment of both altruistic desires and altruistic genes.

Samir Okasha's 'Biological Atruism', *Stanford Encyclopedia of Philosophy* (2013), http://plato.stanford.edu/entries/altruism-biological, is a good introduction to the natural selection of altruistic genes. The same author's *Evolution and the Levels of Selection* (Oxford: Oxford University Press, 2006) covers some of the same ground in more detail.

Tim Krabbé's novel *The Rider* (London: Bloomsbury, 2002) offers many insights into the tactical issues that arise in a 140-kilometre cycle road race.

Notes to Chapter 10

'no such thing as society': Douglas Keay, 'Interview with Margaret Thatcher', *Woman's Own* (31 October 1987). A transcript of the interview with further comments is on the Margaret Thatcher Foundation website: http://www.margaretthatcher.org/document/106689.

made her bid for gold: Scott Hobro, 'Armistead Takes Women's Road Race Gold', *British Cycling* (3 August 2014), https://www.britishcycling.org.uk/commonwealthgames/article/20140803-commonwealthgames-Glasgow-2014-Commonwealth-Games-cycling-road-race-0.

the 'footballers' problem': the 'Footballers' Problem' is introduced in Michael Bacharach, *Beyond Individual Choice* (Princeton, NJ: Princeton University Press, 2006), p. 37.

Further Reading for Chapter 10

Modern game theory was originally developed by John von Neumann and Oskar Morgenstern in their *Theory of Games and Economic Behavior* (Princeton, NJ: Princeton University Press, 1944). For a friendly contemporary introduction, see Ken Binmore, *Game Theory: A Very Short*

Introduction (Oxford: Oxford University Press, 2007), and for a more advanced treatment, see Ken Binmore, *Playing for Real* (Oxford: Oxford University Press, 2007).

The idea of team reasoning as an alternative to individual game theory is due to the Oxford economist Michael Bacharach. His monograph *Beyond Individual Choice*, edited by Natalie Gold and Robert Sugden (Princeton, NJ: Princeton University Press, 2006), was published posthumously.

Notes to Chapter 11

when Lionel Messi was thirteen: Richard Fitzpatrick, 'Capturing the Atomic Flea', *Bleacher Report* (11 February 2016), http://thelab.bleacherreport. com/capturing-the-atomic-flea.

the European authorities' attempts: 'Protection of Young Players' (rules on 'homegrown players'), *UEFA* (2 January 2014), http://www.uefa.com/ news/newsid=943393.html.

Consider Adnan Januzaj: Matt Lawton and Nick Fagge, 'Inside Adnan Januzaj's World', *Daily Mail* (16 October 2013).

'The only people': Dominic Fifield, 'Jack Wilshere Enters the Januzaj Debate', *Guardian* (8 October 2013).

eleven special constituencies: For a map of French overseas constituencies, go to: http://www.diplomatie.gouv.fr/fr/IMG/pdf/Les_11_circonscriptions_ electorales_pour_l_election_des_deputes_representant_les_Francais_ etablis_hors_de_France.pdf?.

British politician Norman Tebbit: Dan Fisher, 'Split between Britain, US' (interview where Norman Tebbit originally mooted his cricket test), *Los Angeles Times* (19 April 1990).

cricketing memoir: Ed Cowan, *In the Firing Line* (Sydney: University of New South Wales Press, 2011) (the Pietersen story is in the diary entry for 20 November 2010).

Nowadays any British player: Nick Hoult, 'ECB extends qualification period for foreign-born English players', *Daily Telegraph* (30 April 2012).

FIFA got fed up: FIFA tightened its national eligibility regulations in 2008: http://www.fifa.com/mm/document/affederation/administration/ 81/10/29/circularno.1147-eligibilitytoplayforrepresentativeteams_ 55197.pdf.

When the chief executive: David Conn, 'Sympathetic Richard Scudamore Verdict Brings Game into Disrepute', *Guardian* (19 May 2014).

Farah responded instantly: Laura Williamson, 'Mr MOtivator', *Daily Mail* (8 August 2012).

Further Reading for Chapter 11

For an introduction to the philosophical issues surrounding citizenship, see Dominique Leydet's entry on 'Citizenship' in the *Stanford Encyclopedia of Philosophy* (2011), http://plato.stanford.edu/entries/citizenship.

Recent work on the relationship between citizenship and immigration is surveyed by my London colleague Sarah Fine in 'The Ethics of Immigration: Self-determination and the Right to Exclude', *Philosophy Compass*, 8: 3 (March 2013), pp. 254–68.

Notes for Chapter 12

a special dispensation: David Caute, *Under the Skin: The Death of White Rhodesia* (Harmondsworth: Penguin, 1983), p. 437.

'I always looked at it': Sybil Ruscoe, 'England's Welshmen Call for Name Change', *Daily Telegraph* (14 September 2004).

Athletic Bilbao requires: Sam Borden, 'Using Only Local Talent, Athletic Bilbao Goes a Long Way', *New York Times* (5 November 2015).

'Cricket was taken too solemnly': Edgar Mittelholzer, *A Morning at the Office* (London: Hogarth Press, 1950), p. 197.

Bleacher Report: Ross Lipschultz, '50 Biggest International Sports Moments in US History', *Bleacher Report* (25 July 2011), http://bleacherreport.com/articles/776351-50-biggest-international-sports-moments-in-us-history.

'No, we properly': Lawrence Donegan, 'Interview with Paul Casey', *Guardian* (4 April 2005).

Sam Snead for one: David Davies, 'Obituary: Sam Snead', *Guardian* (25 May 2002).

Further Reading for Chapter 12

The relation between culturally defined nations and political states is explored by Nenad Miscevic in his *Stanford Encyclopedia of Philosophy* (2014) entry on 'Nationalism'.

George Orwell wrote negatively about the connection between nationalism and sport in 'The Sporting Spirit', *Shooting an Elephant and Other Essays* (London: Secker & Warburg, 1950). For a collection of contemporary essays, see Dilwyn Porter and Adrian Smith (eds), *Sport and National Identity in the Post-War World* (London: Routledge, 2004).

Simon Lister's *Fire in Babylon* (London: Yellow Jersey, 2015) describes the rise of the 1980s West Indian cricket team and its cultural significance.

Notes for Chapter 13

West Indies cricket selectors: Andy Bull, 'The Forgotten Story of White West Indian Cricketers', *Guardian* (2 February 2009).

'The darkies overran': Jason Cowley, *The Last Game: Love, Death and Football* (London: Simon & Schuster, 2009), p. 106.

'It's not much to be grateful for': Nick Hornby, *Fever Pitch: A Fan's Life* (London: Gollancz, 1992), p. 159.

The UK census in 2011: The census form is available at: http://webarchive. nationalarchives.gov.uk/20160105160709/http://ons.gov.uk/ons/guide-method/census/2011/how-our-census-works/how-we-took-the-2011-census/how-we-collected-the-information/questionnaires--delivery--completion-and-return/index.html.

The US census of 2010: The census form is available at: https://www.census. gov/history/pdf/2010questionnaire.pdf.

twenty-one-year-old Tiger Woods: Michael Fletcher, 'Tiger Woods Says He's Not Just Black', *Seattle Times* (23 April 1997).

Charlie Chaplin was often said: Bernard Josephs, 'Charlie Chaplin a "Secret Jew" Claim in FBI and MI6 Files', *Jewish Chronicle* (7 February 2012).

In 2015, Rachel Dolezal: Richard Pérez-Peña, 'White or Black? Woman's Story Stirs up a Furor', *New York Times* (12 June 2015).

Further Reading for Chapter 13

Sections 2 and 3 of Michael James, 'Race', *Stanford Encylopedia of Philosophy* (2016), http://plato.stanford.edu/entries/race, cover the contemporary debate about the concept of race and its relation to ethnicity.

The arguments of this chapter are much influenced by Kwame Anthony Appiah's 'Race, Culture, Identity: Misunderstood Connections' in Kwame Anthony Appiah and Amy Gutmann, *Color Conscious* (Princeton, NJ: Princeton University Press, 1998). For a defence of the biological reality of human races, see Robin Andreason, 'A New Perspective on the Race Debate', *British Journal for the Philosophy of Science*, 49: 2 (June 1998), pp. 199–225.

Notes for Chapter 14

Griffiths points out: Paul Griffiths, 'What is Innateness?', *Monist*, 85: 1 (2002), pp. 70–85.

notion of 'genetic heritability': Stephen Downes, 'Heritability', *Stanford Encyclopedia of Philosophy* (2015), http://plato.stanford.edu/entries/heredity.

My own alma mater: 'History of Cricket', *Durban High School* (2015), http://www.durbanhighschool.co.za/?page_id=2393.

Epstein estimates on this basis: David Epstein, *The Sports Gene: Talent, Practice and the Truth about Success* (London: Penguin, 2013), pp. 131–2.

'relative age effect': Jochen Musch and Simon Grondin, 'Unequal Competition as an Impediment to Personal Development: A Review of the Relative Age Effect in Sport', *Developmental Review*, 21: 2 (2001), pp. 147–67.

Plenty of studies: Richard Bailey, 'Physical Education and Sport in Schools: A Review of Benefits and Outcomes', *Journal of School Health*, 76: 8 (October 2006), pp. 397–401.

Further Reading for Chapter 14

The sporting cases for nurture and nature respectively are made in Matthew Syed's *Bounce: The Myth of Talent and the Power of Practice* (London: Harper

Collins, 2010) and David Epstein's *The Sports Gene: Talent, Practice and the Truth about Success* (London: Penguin, 2013).

Neven Sesardić analyses genetic heritability and associated controversies in *Making Sense of Heritability* (Cambridge: Cambridge University Press, 2005).

Francis Galton's misguided classic is *Hereditary Genius: An Enquiry into Its Laws and Consequences* (London: Macmillan, 1869).

Notes for Chapter 15

In 1920 the American rower: 'Kelly's Entry for Henley Rejected', *New York Times* (5 June 1920).

'shall be considered an amateur': Eric Halladay, *Rowing in England* (Manchester: Manchester University Press, 1990), p. 81.

Who remembers Alf Tupper: Alf Tupper, Tough of the Track, http://www. toughofthetrack.net.

great Native American athlete: Sally Jenkins, 'Why are Jim Thorpe's Records still not Recognized?', *Smithsonian* (July 2012), http://www.smithsonianmag. com/history/why-are-jim-thorpes-olympic-records-still-not-recognized-130986336.

mid-century tennis players: Robyn Norwood, 'The Circuit Circus', *Los Angeles Times* (24 July 1997).

models of rugby union probity: Sam Wheeler, 'Cotton still Trading in Rugby Sense and Hard Truths', *Yorkshire Post* (21 March 2003).

Then there was 'IDB': Mungo Suggot, 'Making a Killing: Conflict Diamonds are Forever', *International Consortium of Investigative Journalists* (8 November 2002),https://www.icij.org/project/making-killing/conflict-diamonds-are-forever.

National Collegiate Athletic Association: Taylor Branch, *The Cartel: Inside the Rise and Imminent Fall of the NCAA* (San Francisco: Byliner, 2011), ch. 5.

colleges are now free to offer: Thomas Bright, 'NCAA Institutes Multi-Year Scholarships', *De Paul Journal of Sports Law and Contemporary Problems*, 8: 2 (2012).

Further Reading for Chapter 15

D.J.Taylor, *The Corinthian Spirit:The Decline of AmateurValues in Sport* (London: Yellow Jersey Press, 2006), offers a spirited defence of amateur values.

The current arrangements in American college sports are criticized in Taylor Branch, *The Cartel: Inside the Rise and Imminent Fall of the NCAA* (San Francisco: Byliner, 2011).

Notes for Chapter 16

By the time Andrew Luck: Ian Shoesmith, 'Why Andrew Luck is the Best Prospect for 30 Years', *BBC Sport* (26 April 2012), http://www.bbc.co.uk/sport/american-football/17779646.

Australian rules football authorities: Greg Buckle, 'Australian Football League Overhauls Draft Priority Pick System', *Roar* (22 February 2012), http://www.theroar.com.au/2012/02/22/afl-overhauls-draft-priority-pick-system.

'Coase Theorem': Timothy Lee, 'The Coase Theorem is Widely Cited in Economics', *Washington Post* (4 September 2013).

insight first developed: Simon Rottenberg,'The Baseball Players' Labor Market', *Journal of Political Economy*, 64: 3 (June 1956), pp. 242–58.

Chargers were expected to choose: John McClain,'Manning Threatens to Sit Out if Drafted by Chargers', *Houston Chronicle* (23 April 2004).

rich men's playthings: Kurd Badenhausen, 'The World's Richest Sports Team Owners 2016', *Forbes* (1 March 2016).

a capitalist's capitalist: 'H. Wayne Huizenga: The Billionaire Garbageman', *Entrepreneur* (10 October 2008), https://www.entrepreneur.com/article/197648.

The Green Bay Packers: Richard Sandomir,'America's Small-Town Team; Packers Play for Touchdown Not for Profits', *New York Times* (13 January 1996).

Further Reading for Chapter 16

The essays in *The Coase Theorem*, edited by Richard Posner and Francesco Parisi (Cheltenham: Edward Elgar, 2013), explore the significance of the theorem for politics and law.

Soccernomics by Simon Kuper and Stefan Szymanski (London: HarperSport, 2009) covers a range of topics in the economics of soccer.

John Vrooman has written extensively on the economics of American sports. A number of the issues raised in the present chapter are addressed in his 'Theory of the Perfect Game: Competitive Balance in Monopoly Sports Leagues', *Review of Industrial Organization*, 34: 1 (February 2009), pp. 5–44.

Notes for Chapter 17

published collection of letters: Paul Auster and J. M. Coetzee, *Here and Now: Letters 2008–11* (London: Penguin, 2014), p. 65.

The Rabbitohs' victory: Brad Walter, 'South Sydney Rabbitohs Won't Have to Wait Another 43 Years for Next Premiership', *Sydney Morning Herald* (5 October 2014).

their own 'Boston rules': Richard Paisner, 'The History of Harvard Sports', *Harvard Crimson* (13 March 1968).

'The day that sees the youth': B. J. T. Bosanquet, 'Anti-Golf', letter, *The Times* (4 June 1914).

'He says he would rather': Charles Carlos Clarke, 'Nauseous and Unbearable', letter, *The Times* (5 June 1914).

As late as 1908: Raf Noboa y Rivera, 'How Philadelphia Became the Unlikely Epicentre of American Cricket', *Guardian* (28 March 2015).

Further Reading for Chapter 17

John Arlott (ed.), *The Oxford Companion to Sports and Games* (Oxford: Oxford University Press, 1975), has provided me with an invaluable guide to the origins and history of different sporting codes.

A number of the essays in the classic collection *The Invention of Tradition*, edited by Eric Hobsbawn and Terence Ranger (Cambridge: Cambridge University Press, 1983), discuss sports along with other traditions that originated in the nineteenth century.

Notes for Chapter 18

'much more important than that': 'Shankly: The Story of a Soccer Legend', *YouTube*, https://www.youtube.com/watch?v=TPAEpGPA3oE&index=2&list=PLxCPdngYnPL0skXnn82bwRoOauhHVXd34 (life and death quote at 1:22:05).

'area which has no meaning': Noam Chomsky, 'Part 1: Interview', *The Chomsky Reader* (London: Serpent's Tail, 1988), p. 33.

thereby refuting: Ludwig Wittgenstein, *Philosophical Investigations* (Oxford: Basil Blackwell, 1953), sections 66–71.

other way with speed-eating: Tamer El-Ghobashy, 'Takeru Kobayashi Sets New Hot Dog Eating Record', *New York Daily News* (5 July 2001).

a capacity crowd of 20,000: David Segal, 'Behind League of Legends', *New York Times* (10 October 2014).

'You are doing more physical': Caroline Davies, 'High Court Ruling Paves Way for Courts to Decide whether Bridge is a Sport', *Guardian* (27 April 2015).

In this hybrid sport: Greg Bishop, 'In this Sport, Beware of Left Hooks, Jabs and Castling', *New York Times* (7 June 2013).

Further Reading for Chapter 18

Despite my reservations about some of its arguments, I recommend Bernard Suits, *The Grasshopper: Games, Life and Utopia* (Peterborough, ON: Broadview Press, 1978), as a wonderful, eccentric exploration of the variety and nature of games.

The nature of sport is debated by Thomas Hurka and John Tasioulas in 'Games and the Good', *Aristotelian Society: Supplementary Volume*, 80, no. 1 (June 2006), pp. 237–64.

ACKNOWLEDGEMENTS

Many people have helped to bring this book into existence. Let me start by mentioning some old friends with whom I have discussed sporting issues over more years than I care to remember: Andy Hislop, Zach Leader, Jo Shallis, Cathy and Darius Brubeck. My three siblings have exerted a similar long-standing influence on my sporting thoughts: Ric, Sarah and Jacob Papineau.

I have also benefited from the inexhaustible flow of ideas from the regular Saturday morning D'Auria Café post-tennis colloquium held by the members of PHART (Parliament Hill Area Recreational Tennis): Sandy Balfour, Ralph Goodstone, Roy Griffins, Marina Kerdemeledi, Bill McAlister, Nick Norden, Tom Schuller, Mark Sinclair, Anthony Tomei, Howard Tumber, Ardashir Vakil and Paul Williams.

Special thanks are due to my philosophical colleagues in King's College London and the City University of New York. All have been remarkably tolerant of my insistence that sport is philosophically interesting, and some have been generous enough to engage with my often half-baked ideas: in London, Peter Adamson, Bill Brewer, John Callanan, Silvia Camporesi, Sarah Fine, Ellen Fridland, Sacha Golob, David Owens, Matthew

Parrott, John Tasioulas, Mark Textor, Shaul Tor and Robyn Waller; and in New York, Samir Chopra, Michael Devitt, Peter Godfrey-Smith, Barbara Montero, Stephen Neale and David Rosenthal.

When I was first thinking of writing a book combining sport and philosophy, I benefited from advice and encouragement from Juliet Annan, Robbie Cottrell, David Edmonds, Ed Lake, Kenan Malik, Suresh Menon, Peter Momtchiloff, Adrian Sington, Rory Sutherland, John Sutton, Matthew Syed and Nigel Warburton. Bruce Berglund at the excellent website theallrounder.co allowed me to try out thoughts, as did the cricket enthusiasts at Test Match Sofa and its later incarnation Guerilla Cricket: Nigel Henderson, Gary Naylor, Daniel Norcross, Nigel Walker and especially Katie Walker.

Philosophical and non-philosophical friends who have given me ideas for the book include: Mitch Berman, Peter Breen, Tim Crane, John William Devine, Victor Dura Vila, Yuval Eylon, Chris Fagg, Kati Farkas, Tamara Glenny, Chris Henley, Marcela Herdova, Rik Hine, Amir Horowitz, Tom Hurka, Andrew Jarvis, Joanna Kennedy, Uriah Kriegel, Daniel Kostic, Robert Kowalenko, Martin Leeburn, Tim Lewens, Graham Macdonald, Denis MacShane, Antonella Mallozzi, David Mann, Tony Marcel, Marsh Marshall, Owen Marshall, Lucy O'Brien, Tuomas Pernu, Andrew Porter, Diego Rios Pozzi, Ed Schneider, Ed Schwitzer, Nick Shea, Katrina Sifferd, Walter Sinnott-Armstrong, Hannes Smit, Barry C. Smith, David Sosa, David Spurrett, George Starkey-Midha, Laurie Taylor, Michael M. Thomas, Jon Weber, Jamie Whyte, Charles Wild, Jake Wojtowicz, Jo Wolff and Stewart Wood.

Some friends have been kind enough to help weed out

mistakes. Josh Shepherd checked the whole book for un-Americanisms; Totte Harinen vetted the cycling sections; Rishi Modha made sure I understood soccer administration; Natalie Gold inspected me on team reasoning; Boris Ayala did some valuable fact-checking.

Chaim Tannenbaum is owed special thanks for accompanying me to Citi Field and Yankee Stadiums and gently conveying how much there is to know about baseball.

The philosophy of sport community has responded with remarkable generosity to my riding rough-shod over their territory. I have benefited from their invitations and advice, especially from Steffen Borge, Helen Cawood, Alun Hardman, Scott Kretchmar, Mike McNamee, John Russell, Emily Ryall and Angela Schneider.

I can remember other useful comments in seminars, discussions or on my website from: Fritz Allhoff, Alexander Bird, Jon Crowcroft, Jim Brown, Tony Bruce, Taylor Carman, Chris Cook, Trudi Darby, John Doris, Jamie Dow, John Dupré, Philip Ebert, Jonathan Evans, Simon Glendinning, Chris Grimes, Ian Hislop, Miroslav Imbrisevic, Stephen Mumford, Bence Nanay, Robert Northcutt, Samir Okasha, Wally Orchard, Katharine O'Reilly, Eylem Özaltun, Michael Ridge, Don Ross, Declan Smithies, Alistair Sponsel, Galen Strawson, Mauricio Suarez, Joerg Tuske and Robin Luke Varghese.

This book would not exist were it not for my agent Tim Bates, who first suggested the idea and showed me how to carry it through. I am hugely grateful to him and his colleagues at Peters Fraser and Dunlop, especially Laura McNeill, for combining exceptional professionalism with a welcoming friendliness.

I have been very lucky with my two editors, Andreas Campomar at Constable in London, and Lara Heimert at Basic Books in New York. Both have been wonderful sources of enthusiasm, wit and much helpful advice.

The production people on both sides of the Atlantic have been exemplary in their precision and efficiency. From Basic Books, I have benefited from assistance by Alia Massoud, line-editing by Leah Stecher, and copy-editing by Cynthia Buck; I am especially grateful to my project editor, Shena Redmond. At Constable, the production has been looked after by Claire Chesser, and the copy-editing by Howard Watson, who as a bonus proved exceptionally knowledgeable about sport.

I am pleased to acknowledge that versions of some of the material in this book have previously been published: 'Runs in the family, *Aeon* (15 September 2014); 'Foul play', *Philosophers' Magazine* (30 January 2015); 'Code of the "cheaters" ', *Wisden India Almanack* (2016).

Finally, I would like to thank my family, Rose Wild, Katy Papineau – who kindly created the drawings in Chapter 8 – and Louis Papineau. They have responded to my obsessive interest in sport with patience, and to my attempts to write about it with affection and encouragement. Come to think of it, this mirrors their attitude to nearly all my idiosyncrasies. I couldn't wish for a more supportive family. Not a day goes past without my thinking how lucky I am.

Bradwell, Essex, England
5 November 2016

INDEX

Wales 194
Warne, Shane 88–9
Watson, Bubba 202
Watson, Tom 258
Waugh, Mark 33
Wawrinka, Stan 87
Wayne, John 244
Webster, Phil 168
Welsh football team 185
Wenger, Arsène 164
West German football team 102, 287
West Indies 195–7, 206
West Indies Federation 196
West Tigers 121
Whitten, Ted 258
Wiggins, Bradley 135
Willey, David 219
Williams, Richard 158
Williams, Ted 29, 30
Wilshere, Jack 160, 161–6, 175, 183
Wimbledon 53
Wingfield, Major Walter 265

Winter Olympics 278
Wittgenstein, Ludwig 272
Woods, Tiger 211–12, 213
World Cup 102, 200, 217
  1982 102, 287
  2010 61, 67, 195
  2014 80–1, 187, 198
World Series 119, 128
  1994 252
  1997 254
Worsham, Lew 88
Wright, David 119

xenophobia 179

Yankee Stadium 118
yips 46–58, 58
'Yoga' theory of sports psychology 14–17, 19–21, 25–6, 36, 53–5, 58
young talent 173

ZANU-PF 189
Zimbabwe 189